ANTHROPOLOGICAL STUDIES
IN THE EASTERN HIGHLANDS OF NEW GUINEA

James B. Watson, *Editor*

Volume II: Physical Anthropology of the Eastern Highlands
of New Guinea

Anthropological Studies
in the Eastern Highlands of New Guinea

James B. Watson, *Editor*

VOLUMES PUBLISHED:

I.   The Languages of the Eastern Family of the East New Guinea Highland Stock, edited by Howard McKaughan
II.   Physical Anthropology of the Eastern Highlands of New Guinea, by R. A. Littlewood

Physical Anthropology
of the Eastern Highlands
# of New Guinea

By R. A. LITTLEWOOD

With a Foreword by James B. Watson
and Appendixes by John Thomas Barksdale, D.D.S.,
and Russell Conda Boyd II, D.D.S.

UNIVERSITY OF WASHINGTON PRESS
SEATTLE AND LONDON

This book is published with the assistance of a grant from the National Science Foundation.

Library of Congress Cataloging in Publication Data
Littlewood, Robert, 1930-
    Physical anthropology of the eastern highlands of New Guinea.
    (Anthropological studies in the eastern highlands of New Guinea, 2)
    Bibliography: p.
    1. Anthropometry—Papua-New Guinea (Ter.) I. Title.
II. Series.
GN58.P3L5   573'.0995'5   70-117730
ISBN 0-295-95133-8

Foreword

The present volume is the second of a series, "Anthropological Studies in the Eastern Highlands of New Guinea," which will report the results of the interdisciplinary New Guinea Micro-evolution Project. Nine volumes are planned. The present monograph is preceded by a volume of studies in language (McKaughan 1972) and is to be followed by studies in human geography, prehistory, and ethnography. Each volume, in addition to developing technical, descriptive, and analytical matters peculiar to its own topic, is intended to throw light on a set of problems common to the series.

The central theoretical problem of the Micro-evolution Project is change. More specifically it is the diversification of several related peoples of the Eastern Highlands of Australian New Guinea. Four of these are the "study peoples," the principal research concern of the project. On linguistic gounds, the study peoples have all sprung from a putative single source, that is, originated from a single people. Through time, in response to various factors not initially known but in some cases discoverable, they have diversified. Each study people is, though in varying degrees, unmistakably related to its congeners, as is evident in numerous more or less profound similarities. But each people is now also distinct from its congeners in identifiable, sometimes marked, and conceivably significant ways.

The term "micro-evolution" of the project title refers to the details of differentiation or specialization of the study peoples and to the causes or meaning of their specialization, insofar as cause or meaning can be recognized. Micro-evolution here implies a central question of roughly this form: in what ways have these peoples specialized or diversified since their putative common past? In response to what factors? To what extent have they been distinctly shaped, in other words, and what selective processes have shaped them? A logical corollary is the question: To what degree and in what ways have the study peoples remained alike, either through continuity or through parallel development? In these questions lie the issues of exogenous vs. endogenous cause, differential vs. equal impact, and divergence-convergence vs. parallel effect.

The four study peoples are today known, respectively, as Gadsup, Tairora, Auyana, and Awa. Their territories, though each touches at least one of the others, are fairly discrete. Each people speaks a different language and manifests different physical and genetic characteristics. Each follows a way of life distinct in some respects from those of the others. A main purpose of the project has been to assess in detail the character and distinctness of each study people, broadly speaking, in language, race, and culture. An additional purpose has been to assess the habitat of each of the study peoples, recognizing, where possible, environmental factors in their specialization. Through archeology, some control of the temporal dimension has also been sought.

A more expanded statement of the research purposes and methods of the Micro-evolution Project, as well as of the personnel of the research groups, will be found in a paper published in the *Journal of the Polynesian Society* (Watson 1963). Considerable detail concerning individual projects, collective research design, and preliminary findings is also contained in grant applications, nineteen research memoranda (including reports of two research conferences), and several published papers. The monographs of Anthropological Studies in the Eastern Highlands of New Guinea are intended, however, to stand as the principal publications of the Micro-evolution Project. Insofar as possible, they will provide full details of their respective topics, not requiring immediate reference to material published elsewhere. Indeed, the principal collaborators in the project have agreed to present their major findings and conclusions in the monographs of this series rather than in scattered, occasional publications.

The topical monographs are conceived and written to stand on their own in still another sense. The present volume, for example, is a biological assessment of the four study peoples as populations. The anthropometric indices, blood types, and breeding patterns of these four peoples (and others closely related) are described and compared. The degree and character of their biological relationships ("distance") are gauged in view of their differentiation. The light that genetic and adaptive variation can shed will thus be seen. The publication of this volume will surely make the study area one of the best known in New Guinea from the standpoint of population genetics and anthropometry.

A theoretical synthesis is projected as the final volume of the series. Each preceding volume will therefore reflect the larger concerns of the Micro-evolution Project only as far as possible within the terms of its special topic. Given the physical and genetic data alone, it would not be possible to consider, or to give adequate reasons for, all aspects of the specialization of the study peoples. The physical anthropologist could not decide, for example, if the study peoples were more or less differentiated with respect to blood type and body measurement than with respect to linguistic or cultural specialization. Nor, if he knew the answer to that, would he be able to evaluate its significance. He would not be able to tell if the several study peoples show the same order of relative distance in other variables that they display in respect to genetic or morphological indices. Conceivably, each monograph might recapitulate the micro-evolutionary theorizing of its predecessors in a sort of cumulative commentary running throughout the series; but with such a scheme the repetition and successive revisions of theory would surely become burdensome. A final reason for the deliberate focus of the topical volumes is that some readers may be interested primarily in population genetics, for example, or in language, and have but a marginal concern—or none—for the prehistory or the cultural or psychological character of the given populations. A population geneticist will, in fact, find the contents of the present volume developed so as to enhance their value to him as a biologist, whatever his further concerns may be. The best answers to the central questions of the project on the other hand, will arise from a synthesis, in the final volume, of all of the findings of the several topical researchers.

A comprehensive historical treatment of the Micro-evolution Project must also await the final volume of the monograph series. Indeed, the history of the project is still being written. The analysis of data and the writing of monographs continue in several phases of the project—in one case further field work is being undertaken. A brief sketch of the project's early history may nevertheless be appropriate here. A surprising number of individuals have been involved from the initial stages of planning to the present. Beginning in the mid-1950's with a committee of from six to eight members, anthropologists of six West Coast universities (the Universities of British Columbia, Washington, Oregon, the University of California at Berkeley, Stanford, and the University of California at Los Angeles), rather large-scale objectives and broad research aims in New Guinea were considered. The present plan emerged about 1958 as a proposal for a more specific attack on a single area of that vast island by a series of researchers of different specialties sharing the particular theoretical concerns outlined above. Accordingly, the present writer was sent to New Guinea in 1959, with the support of a small grant from the National Science Foundation, to produce a planning and feasibility report and to scout a suitable location for the coordinated study.

In 1962, with continuing support from National Science Foundation, Dr. R. A. Littlewood, associate professor of anthropology and genetics at Washington State University, went to the Kainantu subdistrict of Australian New Guinea as one of the second wave of field researchers for the Micro-evolution Project. (The first wave had included Dr. Howard McKaughan, linguist and editor of Volume I in this series, dealing with the study languages.) Dr. Littlewood spent over a year there, in the company of his wife, Patricia, and their two children. Working in several locations within each of the language areas designated for study, he concentrated upon the same local groups which were being or would be studied in turn by the linguists, the anthropo-geographer, and the ethnographers. Two local groups within each language area were considered the primary foci of attention, though several other populations were also investigated because they seemed strategic to the research. The intention here—as generally throughout the plan of the Micro-evolution Project—was to collect data so that, when Littlewood reached some conclusion about a given local group as a breeding population, that same group could also be characterized, for example, with respect to its dialect status within the larger language area, its rate of intermarriage with other local groups, and so forth.

For some time the physical anthropologist has been aware of confronting "Galton's problem" (or its analogue) in a particularly complex version. He must, to be sure, endeavor to recognize and distinguish endogenous from exogenous factors in the making of a gene pool or the shaping of phenotypic norms and ranges in a local population. But "exogenous factors" are not confined to one main kind or effect. They include the significant input of genes from outside the study area and the exchange of genes among the study populations themselves, thus modifying inheritance. Exogenous factors may also include noninheritable modifications in physical form, resulting from differences of diet, activity, or other environing stresses. Thus, as is well known, the physical form of individuals and populations can vary according to differences other than their genetic make-up. The complex problems that in this light arise in considering phenotypic and genetic trends within the study area are obviously many; and it is with their comprehension that Dr. Littlewood has struggled, we feel, with considerable success.

As a study in population genetics and kindred matters, the present volume needs no special justification, least of all from an outsider to the field. The inclusion of this phase within the larger study, however, may warrant a comment. Dr. Littlewood's work has a two-sided relation to the balance of the Micro-evolution Project. On the one hand taxonomic, it is also, and more especially, concerned with understanding adaptive variation. Measures of interpopulational distance are devised comparable in basic intent with measures of distance, for example, in language and dialect. Certain data were expressly collected, moreover, because of reflecting environmental effects, to give insight into local adaptation within the study area.

In regard to the major question of the Micro-evolution Project, the complexities imposed by the recognition of plasticity and of relatively open breeding systems make the human biology of the study area not merely more difficult but also more interesting. Given closed populations and negligible plasticity, micro-evolution research could presumably focus mainly on chance variation and differences of local selection-adaptation. Differences of gene pool among the study peoples, that is, would reflect mainly chance in the broad sense or selective pressures on the genotype. Phenotypic differences would, in turn, afford a clearer inference of genetic difference. At the same time, however, there would be little opportunity to consider such short-term or local pressures as diet or perhaps terrain which, we know today, produce palpable phenotypic variation while permitting genetic continuity. Were all such variable pressures within the study area to be equalized, to what extent would the several resident populations be reduced in phenotypic range? To what extent, in other words, can genetic differences alone account for the phenotypic differences which Dr. Littlewood describes? Categorical answers are of course not readily within reach, but the questions serve to emphasize that, without the responses which "plasticity" connotes, the investigator would be deprived of a most sensitive additional index of response to variable environmental pressures.

Turning the matter around, one can recognize that either genetic or phenotypic differences may reflect environmental pressures, except insofar as genotype is influenced (exogenously) by extra-breeding or arises by chance. Where genetic differences do not reflect exogenous factors or chance (founder effect, linear effect, drift), moreover, they presumably reflect profound environmental pressures of long standing —profounder and of longer standing, on the whole, than the environmental pressures reflected in phenotypic differences. One can in theory, therefore, take the organism or the population as the index of environment (including, of course, society and culture) and see in its forms and structures which pressures are the more profound, the steadier, the more enduring. Indeed, this broad purpose, with all of its implicit complexity, is one of the principal goals that tie the work of Dr. Littlewood and his immediate Australian and American collaborators to the rest of the Micro-evolution Project.

These magical abstractions serve mainly to suggest how Dr. Littlewood's nonbiologist collaborators view their relationship to his work and his to theirs. They also serve to make the task seem simpler than it is. Nor is it his own purpose, obviously, to expose the reader to a full view of the difficulties—quite the contrary: the more he succeeds in his several intentions, the more will he have concealed these difficulties. It is surely therefore incumbent upon someone to call attention to the nature of the achievement. It involved, of course, the assembling of large quantities of data gathered directly in the field by the analyst and writer, Dr. Littlewood himself. The same hand that stuffed quick-setting dental plaster into nervous mouths, only moments before full of betel, later wielded the pencil and slide-rule and selected the programs wherewith these data were computed. The same mind that planned the project dealt with the practical logistics of the field—how in a roadless country to move an array of camp gear, forms and instruments, solid and fluid laboratory materials, and specimens (some of which required refrigeration and immediate dispatch from remote camp to base, from base to airstrip, and from airstrip to the laboratory in Sydney). The same mind has also had to cope with the statistical expression and representation of variable but intergraded series of physical persons—how to show simultaneously indices of both similarity and difference in a score or more of different directions; how to compare the different directions. Getting sick (Dr. Littlewood contracted hepatitis in the field) is not generally considered achievement, but overcoming such a handicap must be counted a part of his achievement. All of this may well be familiar, no doubt, to any physical anthropologist who has lately considered undertaking in a distant, little developed area the collection of data such as are required for a modern study of population genetics. To them it is perhaps commonplace, or at least they can easily know beforehand what they are getting into. It would perhaps be easy to take it all for granted, even in paying tribute to a man who successfully manages it all. But one should not only note here the larger implication and intention of Dr. Littlewood's contribution to the Micro-evolution Project. Balance demands at least some hint of the actual efforts and trials required in moving, as this book shows he has done, toward the ultimate goal.

JAMES B. WATSON
February, 1971
Seattle

Preface

This monograph is an attempt to throw some light on the human biology of the Highlands of New Guinea both by presenting the data of a physical anthropological survey of the members of the Kainantu (or Eastern) Language Family of the East New Guinea Highland Stock, and by endeavoring to discover the nature and possible causes of physical diversity in this region. Presenting the data answers a need in this part of the world which up to now has only been poorly provided (except for serology). The second goal of the study—the discovery of the kinds and sources of variation—is actually a test of certain modern methods and ideas in the area of human microevolutionary analysis. This was a *post hoc* maneuver, however, since the requirements of the larger study, the University of Washington New Guinea Micro-evolution Project, of which the physical anthropology is but a part, called for an extensive survey and thereby limited the precision necessary for a refined micro-evolutionary analysis.

The larger study involved the activities of ethnographers, linguists, a geographer, an archeologist, and a psychologist in addition to the physical anthropologist. The field phase alone covered a span of nearly five years and aimed at the coordination of all possible lines of investigation which could illuminate the problem of the evolution of a related set of human communities. I have personally found this team effort to be both stimulating and rewarding, and, indeed, many of the inferences drawn in this monograph would have been impossible without it.

Even a relatively straightforward report such as this one requires the direct and indirect efforts of many persons, only a few of whom I can acknowledge individually. My first debt of gratitude is to James B. Watson, the leader of the project, who made the study possible by his initial conception of the idea and his tireless efforts to bring it to fruition over the last ten years. The various members of the larger project—David Cole, Madeleine Leininger, Howard McKaughan, Philip Newman, Karen Pataki, Kerry Pataki, Juanita and Sterling Robbins—provided the friction and affection which held the project together both in the field and around the conference table.

Dr. R. J. Walsh of Sydney not only accomplished the serological analysis but also supplied valuable support, tangible and intangible, for the field phase of the study. Members of the Summer Institute of Linguistics (Ukarumpa), Australian patrol officers, and medical personnel provided transportation, facilities, and guidance in the field. Eugene Giles of Harvard University and Drs. Thomas Bogyo and G. M. Southward of Washington State University guided me in the arcane precincts of the computer, though they must not share the blame for my use of the tools they provided. Drs. John Thomas Barksdale and Russell Conda Boyd, II, and their professors at the School of Orthodontics, University of Washington, enthusiastically carried out the detailed analysis of the dental casts. The data were sorted and prepared for computation by Valerie Carter, Rosemary von Elling, Fred Gaudet, and Blaine Price. Mrs. Ronald Adkins translated my pencil scrawls into finished graphs.

The field phase was funded by the National Science Foundation. Data reduction was carried out with financial assistance from NSF and Initiative 171 Funds of the State of Washington. To my departmental chairman, Dr. Allan Smith, goes my great appreciation for his patience and material support.

Finally, if this monograph were worthy of them, I would dedicate it to my wife, Pat, and to Chris, Erica, and Paula who provided, in the field and out, the essential diversion from my travail.

R. A. LITTLEWOOD

Contents

Illustrations

xix

PLATES

PHYSICAL ANTHROPOLOGY
OF THE EASTERN HIGHLANDS OF NEW GUINEA

1. Introduction

This study will attempt to do two things: (1) describe certain demographic and biological features of the natives belonging to the Eastern (Kainantu) Family of the East New Guinea Highland (linguistic) Stock, and (2) perform a systematic analysis upon the various groupings within this language family in order to reveal biological differences, if any, which exist between them.

It is important to understand at the outset that the study undertaken here was designed as one part of a larger undertaking, the New Guinea Micro-evolution Project. As such, the primary goal of the physical anthropologist was to attempt to establish a biological taxonomy of the peoples studied in an attempt to throw some light on the ethnogenesis of these linguistically related groups. Such a taxonomy would then be compared with the systematics generated by linguistic, ethnographic, and archeological data in the presumption that they would be generally mutually reinforcing, or, where they raised points of contention, would reveal methodological and theoretical questions with respect to one or more of the taxonomic techniques. The central task, however, was to sort the groups out and make some statement about their relative biological distances from one another. Problems of validity of the methods and elucidation of evolutionary process, absorbing as they may be, are tangential to this task and fall into the category of working assumptions rather than hypothetical questions. That is to say, given the demographic setting and the task, reasonable inferences about the operation of nutrition, disease, drift, and the like can be made on the basis of other studies, but the present study was

3

not designed to *demonstrate* the operation of any of these agencies.

In the light of this concern with systematics certain factors such as morbidity and mortality figures, general nutritional status, measurement of children and adolescents for growth data, and many other variables necessary to a complete biological description were either slighted or ignored. On the other hand demographic data leading to an understanding of isolate structure and phenotypic measures and observations which could contribute to the taxonomic analysis were emphasized. In the same vein, in an effort to acquire an adequate sample and minimize variance due to sex or growth factors, the sample was skewed to include mostly males (N = 888; females, N = 172) and only adults were examined.[1] Males were favored for reasons of rapport and because landmarks are easier to establish on their leaner bodies.

THE SETTING

The members of the four language groups which comprise the subject of this study—the Gadsup, Tairora, Auyana, and Awa speakers—live in close proximity within a relatively small area of the Eastern Highlands.[2] A rectangle approximately forty miles long and twenty miles wide with its long axis running southwest to northeast would include them all. Such seemingly short distances are deceptive, however, when the difficulties of terrain, watercourses, and, in pre-contact times, the presence of endemic warfare are taken into account. These and other impediments to movement help to account for the relatively

1. If the adult status of a subject was in doubt, inspection was made for full eruption of third molars. Few subjects appeared to be adolescent. Age estimation was quite difficult, especially for older subjects. I can only state that all determinations were carried out by myself, assuring some measure of comparability. The mean estimated age for the entire anthropometric series was 35.04 years with a standard deviation of 8.42 years and a range of 15 to 65 years.

An F test of the difference in age variance between language groups gave a probability of between .025 and .01. Negative correlations as high as $r = .45$ were found between age and weight, stature, sitting height, and calf circumference. The Awa, who showed the greatest difference from the other groups in these measures, had the lowest correlations. Other measures were not highly correlated with age, and in general the difference in mean age probably is insignificant for the purposes of this study.

In the case of serological sampling children down to the age of eight years were sometimes used.

2. Certain enclaved and peripheral dialect groups were not sampled in the physical anthropology survey. These include Usurufa, Oyana, Kosena, and Agarabi. Two outliers were sampled, Binumarien (linguistically related to Tairora) and Ontenu (related to Gadsup and Oyana), and in the following analyses are sometimes pooled with their parent groups and sometimes treated separately.

high linguistic and, as we shall see, biological diversity within such a small area.

The study area is situated at the northeastern periphery of that system of high valleys which are referred to as the Highlands of New Guinea (Map 1). The eastern and northern boundary of the area is the southern wall of the Markham Valley, a striking, riftlike valley which contains the drainages of two large rivers—the Markham and the Ramu. The former river issues into the Huon Gulf at the town of Lae, the main port of the northeastern part of New Guinea and the terminus of vehicular transportation to the Highlands. While heavy construction items are generally brought by truck over this single road, which is the despair of men and machines, air transport, commercial and missionary, is the principal convenient means of communication with the coast. The road, however, has determined the location of the larger European settlements and with them of the larger commercial airstrips. As such, it has acted as the main acculturative focus for the Highlands. It is from the town of Kainantu and adjacent European settlements in the northern part of the study area that political control, mission activity, medical facilities, cash-cropping, and plantation exploitation have radiated toward the south.

Several different indices of the acculturational gradient are worth remarking. Effective European contacts began in the 1920's with mission activity in Gadsup, followed in the mid-1930's by armed conflict with and subsequent control of the Tairora. In the late 1930's contact was established in Auyana, but the first census there was not carried out until 1953. The *kiap* (government patrol officer) did not come to Awa until 1955 and at the time of this study I was unable to discover a fluent Neo-Melanesian (New Guinea Pidgin) speaker in any of the study villages there. Vehicular feeder roads from Kainantu and Okapa (to the west of the study area) had not penetrated Auyana or Awa by 1962. Village warfare was still being waged sporadically in southern Tairora (not part of the study area) and Awa.

Medical-aid posts become less frequent and more difficult of access as one moves south from Kainantu.[3] An apparent increase in infant

3. The typical medical-aid post is a single native structure manned by a native medical technician who has received rudimentary instruction in first aid and the administration of such medications as penicillin, pills for intestinal parasites, and topical antiseptics. The use of penicillin is sometimes quite extravagant resulting in the administration of shots for presumed or apparent infections (internal and external) as well as general malaise. One man in Auyana regularly took shots for arthritic symptoms when he was about to go on a "walkabout."

A sampling of nasal flora in central Auyana revealed a high rate of penicillin resistant

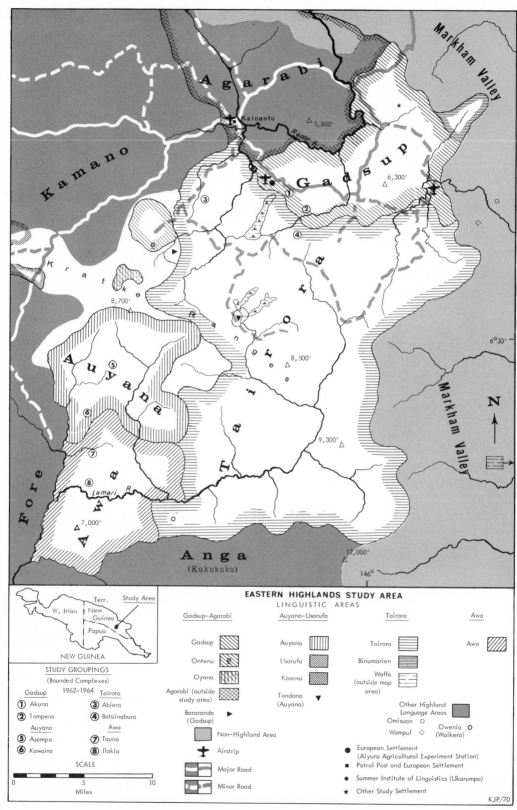

EASTERN HIGHLANDS STUDY AREA

LINGUISTIC AREAS

Gadsup-Agarabi	Auyana-Usarufa	Tairora	Awa
Gadsup	Auyana	Tairora	Awa
Ontenu	Usarufa	Binumarien	
Oyana	Kosena	Waffa (outside map area)	
Agarabi (outside study area)	Tondona (Auyana)		

Bararanda (Gadsup)

Non-Highland Area

Airstrip

Major Road

Minor Road

Other Highland Language Areas

Omisuan ☐   Owenia ○ (Waikera)

Wompul ◇

● European Settlement (Aiyura Agricultural Experiment Station)
■ Patrol Post and European Settlement
◆ Summer Institute of Linguistics (Ukarumpa)
★ Other Study Settlement

STUDY GROUPINGS

(Bounded Complexes)

1962-1964

Gadsup	Tairora
① Akuna	③ Abiera
② Tompena	④ Batainabura

Auyana	Awa
⑤ Asempa	⑦ Tauna
⑥ Kawaina	⑧ Ilakia

SCALE

0   5   10

Miles

NEW GUINEA

W. Irian | Terr. New Guinea | Study Area

Papua

KJP/70

Map 1

mortality figures along a southerly transect may also be a reflection of the decreasing effectiveness of nutritional and medical acculturation.[4]

Southward from Awa lies the region now called Anga, formerly loosely named Kukukuku, a gloss that covers a large and poorly investigated aggregation of groups which Wurm (1961) assigns linguistically to a non-Highland phylum. The circumscription of the study area is completed by the Fore and Kamano linguistic groups to the west. Both languages are judged by Wurm to belong to a language family distinct from that of the Kainantu groups. The Kamano border on the Gadsup and Tairora and have exchanged genes peripherally with them. The Fore, host population for the curious nervous degenerative disease known as *kuru* (Gajdusek and Zigas 1961; Gajdusek, Zigas, and Baker 1961), border both Auyana and Awa and, again, some intermarriage between the two language families is evident in the genealogies.

In summary it will be seen that the study groups are linguistically more closely related to one another than to their surrounding neighbors, implying a more recent point of linguistic divergence. While there is evidence of shuffling among the language groupings within the study area (McKaughan 1964, 1972), no interpenetration of other language families is evident. The location of the study area at the northeastern edge of the Highlands on the other hand has made it a gateway to lowland New Guinea (from Gadsup via the Markham Valley). This is clearly reflected in the acculturative picture and may have been an important factor in pre-contact times, a point to which I shall return in discussing the results of this study.

strains of *Staphylococcus aureus* (Rountree and P. K. Littlewood 1964). The single medical-aid post there has probably been in existence less than a decade. No aid posts were in the Awa territory proper at the time of the study.

4. A rough assessment of family size and mortality figures from the demographic data on measured subjects reveals the following:

Language group	Average number of living children	Average number of dead children
Gadsup	3.29	1.10
Tairora	2.49	1.06
Auyana	2.66	1.19
Awa	2.41	1.74

These figures are taken from a sample of parents of average age 42.2 years (est.), all of them over the age of 35. Although the questions and responses were uniform for all subjects, the mortality figures are probably too low across the sample due to nonreporting of perinatal natural deaths and infanticide. The point of interest is the 25 percent drop in family size and 50 percent increase in mortality figures between Gadsup and Awa as one moves south.

Although the study area is only forty miles long in its longest dimension, dramatic changes in terrain are evident and bear upon the problem of communication and isolation. Starting at the northeastern end of the area, in the Gadsup, the landscape consists of low ridges and mountains (ca. 6,000 feet) with fairly large but rolling valleys (4,000 to 5,000 feet in elevation). Grass and scrub fill the valleys and extend up the gentle flanks of the hills. Some forest remains in patches along watercourses and is extensive along the edge of the Markham scarp, but in the interior and throughout most of northern Tairora the grasslands predominate and timber stands of any size are relegated to the tops of ridges and mountains. This area is part of the upper drainage of the Ramu River which proceeds northward to the Markham Valley and then northwest to the coast.

Passing from Tairora to Auyana one crosses the Kratke Range, descends into the Lamari River drainage (which eventually joins the Purari River and empties into the Gulf of Papua), and encounters a dramatic change in the topography. The ridges are now 6,000 to 7,000 feet moving on up to peaks of 10,000 feet and more in the southern portion of the area. The flanks of these ridges become increasingly steep, descending to narrow rivercourses containing swift streams as low as 3,500 feet in elevation.

While deforestation is not well advanced in Auyana (possibly indicating a relatively late entry into their present location), denudation of the steep canyons and narrow ridges of the Awa region is extensive. The principal cause of deforestation is the continual use of fire for purposes of garden preparation or in hunting small animals in the grass. The *kunai (Imperata cylindrica)* and other hardy grasses flourish under this regime of burning and relatively high rainfall (around one hundred inches annually). In more level terrain burning can be controlled (though this is not often consciously done), but in precipitous regions such as Awa this is out of the question and casual conflagrations carry to the tops of the ridges before expiring on their own.

Settlements tend to be located at the edge of the forest to provide access to fuel, construction materials, game, and virgin soils for gardening. Where this is not possible, as in the large grassland areas of Gadsup and Tairora, small remnant forest groves or the planting of bamboo and casuarina trees partially supply these needs.

The climate of the region is mild and generally clear despite the high annual rainfall. The so-called "wet" and "dry" seasons brought about by the shift in the monsoonal winds are distinguished mainly by more persistent daytime rainfall during the former period. In general one can expect clear days with temperatures in the seventies and eighties (Fahrenheit) falling to around forty degrees at night, with occasional frost at higher elevations. Temperature fluctuations are largest and most rapid in the grassland areas and, therefore, in the settlement zone. Afternoon and evening cloud-cover and the possibility of frost at elevations of 8,000 to 10,000 feet and above sets an upper limit to gardening and habitation in many Highland areas.[5] The lower limit of settlement is established by valley topography and, in some cases, by endemic malaria below the 4,000 foot level.[6]

The People

The Highland native, sometimes referred to as "Papuan," is physically as well as linguistically distinct from his neighbors on the coast. The coastal Melanesian tends to be taller with a more gracile physiognomy than the Highlander. In many measurements and indices the Kainantu populations fall comfortably within the range of Melanesian populations (Swindler 1962), but the more extreme individuals (who are the ones that usually influence most strongly our impression of the "type") tend to shorter stature, longer trunks, lower and longer cranial vaults, heavier browridges, a high frequency of convex noses (the so-called "semitic" nose), and larger dentition, which gives these relatively small people a prognathous appearance (Plates 1-4). Such individuals can be found in many areas on the coast, but the reverse—Melanesian extremes in the Highlands—is rare (but see Plate 2, Subject No. 315 from Eastern Gadsup). This is not surprising since the Melanesians (and some Polynesians) are apparently late entrants to New Guinea, and they have principally penetrated only the coastal zones of the eastern half of the island.

The main subsistence activity is gardening, with sweet potato (*Ipomoea batatas*), yams, taro, bananas, sugar cane, beans, and greens constituting the main crops. Pandanus and other forest products are gathered to supplement the diet. The principal source of an-

5. For a brief but excellent discussion of climate, ecology, and land use in the Highlands of Australian New Guinea the reader is referred to an article by H. C. Brookfield (1964).

6. The Binumarien, who live at the edge of the Markham Valley and who have been driven into that area by warfare in the past, recognize malaria as a great scourge at the lower elevations. Also, a presently uninhabited "pine" forest on the border of Awa and Fore at an elevation of 3,500 feet was cited as a malaria pocket by the medical officer in Kainantu.

Plate 1. Gadsup male from Puntibasa

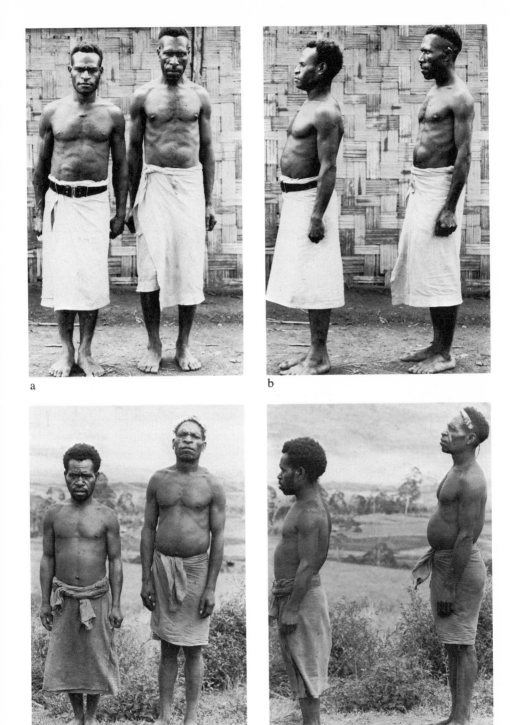

Plate 2. a,b: Front and side views of Gadsup males from Puntibasa. c,d: Front and side views of Tairora males from (left) Baieanabuta and (right) Bairinabuta

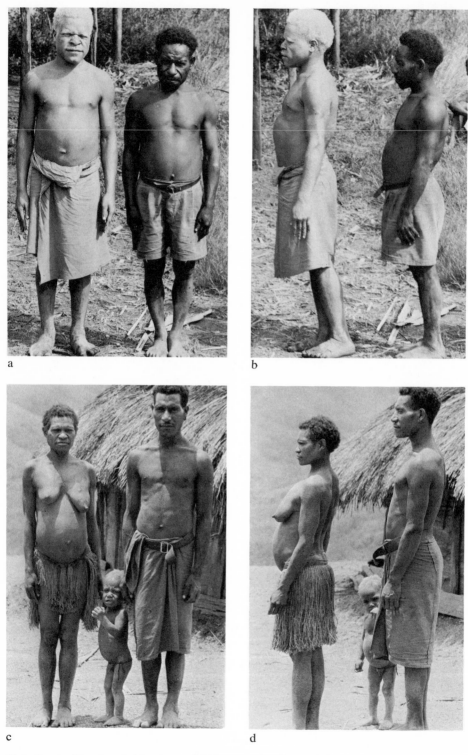

Plate 3. a,b: Front and side views of Tairora males from (left) Babaraai (albino, very light freckles, slight nystagmus, light golden hair) and (right) Baieanabuta. c,d: Front and side views of Auyana family from Asempa

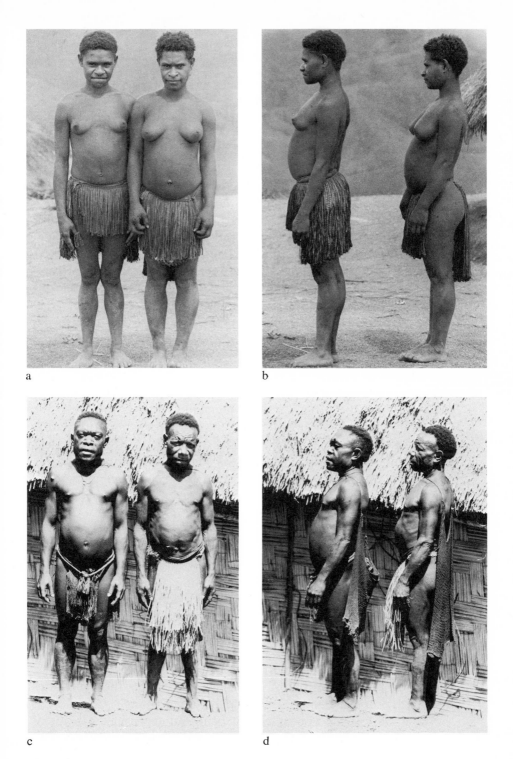

Plate 4. a,b: Front and side views of young Auyana females from (left) Indona and (right) Asempa. c,d: Front and side views of Awa males from Mobuta

imal protein is the pig, domestic and wild. The only other large animals in the area are cassowary and wallaby, but these are difficult to
capture. Birds, rodents, small marsupials, insects, and occasionally
fish from the poorly stocked rivers make up the remainder of the meat
intake. While the diet appears to be low in protein, deficiency symptoms were not observed in the adult population.

The general health of the people in the study area appeared good.
Infant mortality is high (as much as 50 percent before the age of five
years[7]), with the main causes being diarrhoea, dysentery, malnutri-
tion, and upper respiratory disease. Intestinal parasites are common,
as are scabies in the young, and there are also occasional tropical
ulcers. Yaws is practically nonexistent due to large-scale use of penicillin, but evidence of it can be seen in many adults. Leprosy, pockets
of goitre, and malaria are reported in certain parts of the study area.

The high incidence of upper respiratory infection and death from
pneumonia is probably partly attributable to clothing habits and
house design. The technology of making bark-cloth is known
throughout the area, but such garments are rare, the preferred clothing being a simple loincloth for the men and a skirt of grass or bark-
cloth strips for the women. As the temperature drops rapidly in the
evening the people standing about in the open, particularly the children, characteristically cross their arms over their chests, shiver, and
show other signs of chill. The houses tend to be drafty (especially
those built on the European rectangular plan and containing windows) with the sole source of heat a small, smoky fire for which there
is no chimney or smoke-hole in the thatch. The high rate of scleral
pterygia noted among the subjects may also be attributable to this irri-
tating atmosphere.

The traditional houseform is circular with a beehivelike roof of
thatch, walls of bark or woven cane matting, and a floor of dirt or
raised matting. Rectangular houses with windows and raised floors
are frequently seen in the northern groups but relatively rarely in the
southernmost villages. Houses are clustered around compounds within
which communal rock-oven cooking and ceremonial dances take
place. Split-stake fences are often constructed to keep pigs out of the
gardens and sometimes out of the village, but despite these measures
the pigs appear to be quite cosmopolitan in their habits.

Sanitation has the appearance of being rather casual, a point of
constant frustration in medical patrol reports. Body wastes are distrib-

7. Medical Patrol Report, Gimi Subdivision of Okapa Subdistrict, 1966.

uted widely in the bush, streams, and so forth, largely as a response to the fear of sympathetic magic. Personal cleanliness varies, depending often on when the body was last anointed with pig grease or tree oil for cosmetic purposes. The oil then traps dirt and smoke from the fire giving a lacquered appearance to the skin. A bar of soap and some water produce results worth at least three pages in the Munsell skin color book.

SOCIAL STRUCTURE AND HISTORY

I have refrained from using the term "tribe" when referring to the various language groupings in the study area. This is a reflection of the rather loose and complex criteria for social organization which characterize the region (Watson 1965).[8] The names Gadsup, Tairora, Auyana, and Awa refer to territorial groupings of individuals distinguished from one another at the language level. Within each of these territories there may exist two or more dialects. Certain small outlying groups can be related linguistically to the major language groups as dialect variants. The most important of these are Binumarien (Tairora), Kosena-Usurufa (Auyana), and a larger group, Agarabi, which is contiguous with and related to Gadsup, along with Oyana and Ontenu which are relatively widely, separated in space from that parent language (McKaughan 1964, 1972; Wurm 1961).

Within these language domains there is no recognized political hierarchy or cohesiveness although certain aggregates of villages may recognize a common bond of territory, ancestry, or dialect and have been assigned the term "phratry" (Watson 1967). Such alliances tend to be fragile, however, and may crumble before the vagaries of warfare, blood feud, natural disaster, and the attendant refugeeism. The village or hamlet cluster, itself politically acephalous, appears to be the most stable demographic grouping, and, given size enough to include several exogamous groups (sibs, subsibs, or lineages; Watson 1965), it may constitute a functionally endogamous unit. Pataki (personal communication, 1967) has suggested the term "bounded complex" to refer to "the largest aggregate of people with a sense of identity recognizing common access to a continuous territory." Such a definition seems, at first glance, to be unduly vague, but it is appropriate to a situation in which the territory or sense of place may be a more important organizing principle than kinship. The fact that refugees,

8. For a fuller treatment of these matters the reader is referred to the reports of the project ethnographers in subsequent volumes of this series.

adopted children, and other migrants tend to merge their identity with that of the host village, if they remain for any length of time, reinforces such an interpretation.

The fragmented nature of political groupings, the presence of such disruptive factors as endemic warfare in pre-contact times, and the large-scale ecological changes reflected in the deforestation caused by sweet-potato and possibly pre–sweet-potato cultivation (Watson 1964, 1965a,b) all contribute to an historical picture of high mobility. It seems clear from the linguistic evidence that the spatial contiguity of the Kainantu Language Family has persisted for some time,[9] but lexicostatistical and phonostatistical analyses indicate movement within the family which has resulted in a sundering and splintering of previously closely related groups (Map 2). I shall return to this evidence in discussing the results of the biological assay.

While linguistics is a powerful objective tool for revealing the cultural phylogeny of the various language and dialect groups, ethnohistory is of virtually no assistance. Genealogical depth can be traced for three ascending generations at most, and this with considerable difficulty. Beyond this time origin myths and general geographical directions from the "before-time" provide scant historical illumination. The fact that the Awa know little of the Gadsup or even much of the Auyana, their immediate neighbors, argues for strong isolating mechanisms (P. Newman, personal communication, 1966). But, in the light of tenuous native memories, there is no assurance that such a spatial situation has a long history.

In spite of the foregoing I am forced to assume that the distribution of the language groups at contact represents a stable situation with some time depth. Interpretation of the biological evidence will raise some criticism of this assumption, but only further ethnographic and archeological data can hope to put the matter to rest.

THE FIELD SITUATION

A brief comment on the field situation is in order since it bears directly upon the procedures employed and data collected. Since the season 1962-63 in which the physical anthropology assay was carried

9. Glottochronological estimates by Wurm and McKaughan (McKaughan 1964, 1972) of the time of divergence of the various languages range from half a millenium to over two thousand years. Such estimates are open to serious question and McKaughan himself and others have pointed this out. Although it would be most interesting to have an absolute estimate of time depth for these divergences, this study will concern itself only with the estimates of relative separation yielded by lexicostatistics and phonostatistics.

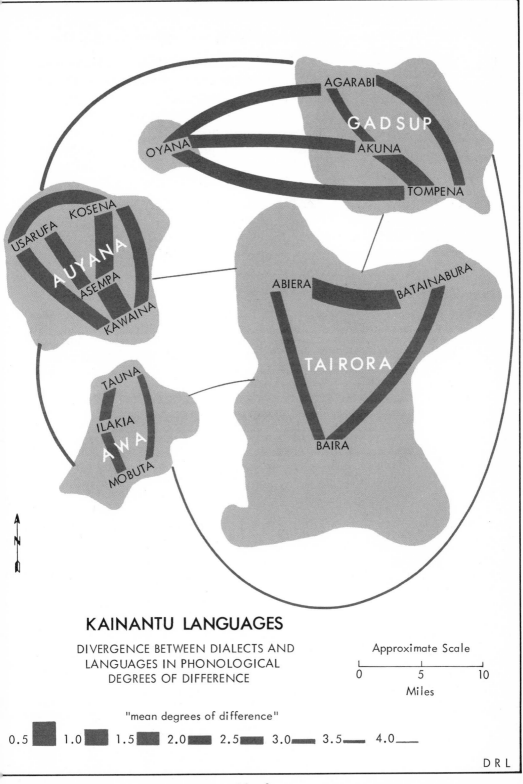

KAINANTU LANGUAGES

DIVERGENCE BETWEEN DIALECTS AND
LANGUAGES IN PHONOLOGICAL
DEGREES OF DIFFERENCE

Approximate Scale

0   5   10

Miles

"mean degrees of difference"

0.5   1.0   1.5   2.0   2.5   3.0   3.5   4.0

D R L

Map 2

out was only the second year of the field phase of the Micro-evolution Project, the situation of the groups to the south of Gadsup was only sketchily known. A field survey of J. B. Watson (1959) and the work of missionary linguists of the Summer Institute of Linguistics (SIL) provided the initial guidance. Certain study villages, two in each language group, had been assigned in the preliminary phases of the project and provided the first dimension of the subsequent sampling strategy. If the language groups were assumed to be the first approximation to the genetically meaningful isolates, it became immediately clear that the eight study villages were inadequate in both number and spatial dispersion for a representative sample. I decided, therefore, to survey as many villages as possible along a transect from Binumarien in the northeast to Mobuta in the southwest, keeping the villages well spaced and obtaining sample sizes roughly proportional to the census numbers in the various language groupings (see Map 3).

Table 1 shows the distribution of the 888 male subjects used in the anthropometric analysis by village-complex and language group. The 172 female subjects were pooled by language group. A great deal of variation in sample size between villages can be observed in the table, particularly in Auyana (see Chap. 2), and this in part reflects the necessarily *ad hoc* methods of acquiring samples. Transportation was by Land Rover where possible, otherwise by foot and native carriers. Initial interest in the esoteric proceedings of an anthropometric survey was high upon entry into a given village, but it quickly waned in ensuing days—especially among male subjects—and by the fourth or fifth day the sample had terminated itself despite informant fees and cajolery. If blood was to be gathered, this had to be done on the last day in order to get it to ice and air-shipment as soon as possible. As a result the serological sample only partially overlaps the anthropometric sample.

The patterns of relationship among sample villages often became visible only after the villages had been surveyed, but, in general, genealogical evidence affirmed their relative independence of one another. Where it was apparent that sample villages were closely related by marriage or had recently split from each other, they were pooled, producing what I have called the "village-complex." As for the sample within the village itself, it most certainly was not "random" but consisted of those individuals who were available and willing. In what manner this method departs from randomness can only be conjectured in a survey as extensive as this one.

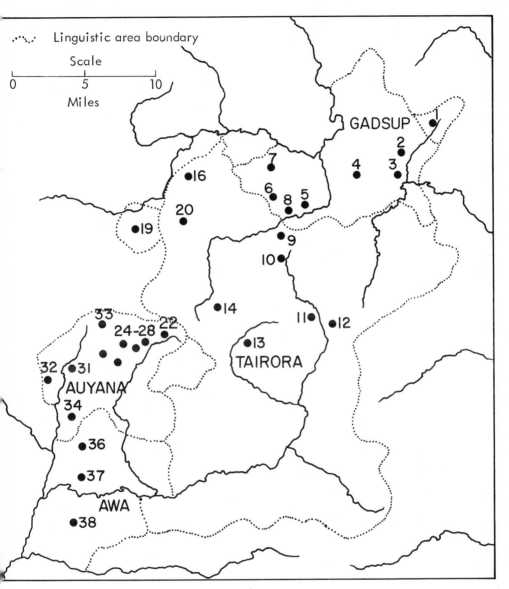

Map 3. Spatial distribution of numbered village-complexes in the sample

TABLE 1

NUMBER OF SUBJECTS USED IN THE ANTHROPOMETRIC ANALYSIS

Language Group	Study Number of Complex	Village-Complex	1961-63 Census Figures*	Number of Male Subjects	Number of Female Subjects
Gadsup			6,399	212	55
	02	Puntibasa		49	
	03	Tompendaka		25	
	05	Inkana		39	
	06	Akuna		45	
	07	Onamuna		27	
	08	Tompena		27	
Tairora			10,245	301	42
	01	Binumarien		14	
	09	Batainabura		36	
	10	Barabuna		30	
	11	Baieanabuta†		40	
	12	Bairinabuta†		28	
	13	Babaraai†		30	
	14	Tondona†		33	
	16	Tonkera‡		62	
	20	Bontaa		28	
Auyana			4,289	260	30
	22	Avia†		33	
	24	Nankona		24	
	25	Ofoimpina		10	
	26	Waifina		11	
	27	Omuna		15	
	28	Asempa†		50	
	31	Arora		34	
	32	Indona		12	
	33	Anokafa		23	
	34	Kawaina (Kawaimpa)		48	
Awa			1,292	90	45
	36	Tauna		28	
	37	Ilakia†		37	
	38	Mobuta		25	
Ontenu (Gadsup)	19	Ontenu	396	25	
Total			22,621	888	172

* These are government census figures for the entire language group and not just the aggregate of the study villages.

† These names have been changed from an earlier publication (Littlewood 1966) to conform to project standards. Village-complex numbers remain the same.

‡ Tonkera includes Abiera and Burauta as a single complex in this study.

Since the primary object of the study was taxonomic it was decided to obtain data for as many hopefully independent biological variables as time and sample size would permit. The following is a list of the various types of observations made:

1. Brief genealogy and vital statistics concerning subject and his immediate family; all subjects.

2. Anthropometric and anthroposcopic observations; 1,100 subjects.

3. Fingerprints (not reported in this study); 1,100 subjects.

4. Full-length photographs, both front and side; 1,100 subjects.

5. Serological samples, 8 ml.; 1,163 subjects.

6. Full-mouth dental casts; 218 subjects.

Most of the data were punched onto data cards and analyzed by the IBM 7090 and 360/67 computers at Washington State University. Figure 15, Appendix I, shows the field data blank with the specific observations made. The reader is referred to Appendix I for a discussion of the particular field techniques used in this study.

The general plan of the following chapters is to establish the village-complex as the minimal unit of comparison, report the data, and attempt to describe the biological differences, and their magnitude, between the study units.

2. The Nature of Isolates

An isolate is a region characterized by reduced information exchange with other such regions. This information can be linguistic, cultural, in the form of matter or energy, or genetic as in the present case. Usually the reduction in the rate of information exchange is not complete and isolates can be viewed as nodes of central tendency in the genetic or diffusional landscape. In some cases these regions are bounded domains with a striking discontinuity in the rate of information exchange characterizing their peripheries—such isolates approach the so-called "island" model (Wright 1931, 1943).

A more difficult situation is that in which no perceptible breaks in information flow patterns exist over long distances and/or large numbers of individuals. A case in point might be large urban and suburban aggregates. Here the observed differences in information content between points widely spaced in the continuous population are in large part attributable to the delay in information flow occasioned by distance alone and may be referred to the "continuous" or "distance" isolation model (Wright 1943).[1]

The importance of defining isolate structure is twofold: (1) meaningful population genetic statements depend upon specification of the nature of the breeding group and its relationship to the sample(s) discussed; and (2) the understanding of the rate and nature of change,

1. Kimura and Weiss (1964) have suggested an intermediate model they call the "steppingstone model," which takes into account the existence of islandlike isolates and the effect of distance within a field of such isolates. Birdsell's concept of "genetic space" (1950) implies the same consideration. Highly refined mathematical models generally fit the human situation only poorly.

genetic and cultural, in some measure involves an appreciation of the conformation and persistence of boundaries to diffusion.

Very few, if any, human populations fall exclusively into one or the other of the polar categories of isolate type, but the island model is often appropriate for groups at the pre-industrial level of technology. Given this premise, it would appear to be a simple matter to discover isolates: one would merely add up or cluster subjects into larger and larger groups until arriving at an aggregate of individuals who mate more frequently among themselves than with other such clusters. However, in a region where the population is spread relatively uniformly over a large area, this method requires intensive sampling and exhaustive genealogical analysis. Such an effort may be appropriate in the case of the data of the ethnographer, but is usually not convenient for the physical anthropologist who is driven to cover large areas by virtue of sampling variation and the search for statistical degrees of freedom (as in the present case).

Also, a serious methodological problem arises in the attempt to define isolates by simple aggregation. Elementary arithmetical and geometrical considerations reveal that any bounded region will show a low rate of out-marriage if that rate is calculated with respect to the number of individuals included within the region (assuming panmixia within the region)—except in the trivial case of exceedingly small isolates (N = 4 or less). This, of course, arises from the fact that there are fewer people in immediate contact with the boundary than are contained in the region itself. The only valid method for determining if a true boundary (a zone of change in the rate of gene flow) exists is to examine the groups or individuals along the putative boundary and establish that they indeed have a higher probability of mating within the region than without. Otherwise the presumed boundary may be simply a statistical artifact.

In the face of such difficulties the more commonly employed method is to look for some type of demographically or behaviorally defined cluster such as a geographic, linguistic, sociopolitical, or kin-based endogamous grouping. The assumption implicit in this procedure is that of panmixia within such groups once they have been shown to be isolated with respect to one another. Such an assumption is always open to further refinement and can produce very misleading results when the operational isolate is made coterminous with some very large group such as a language, a tribe, or an administrative district, as is the custom in many serological reports. Likewise, even small, seemingly homogeneous groups may have emergent subisolate structures which can bias sampling results (L. C. Dunn 1947; Littlewood 1962:102).

Isolate Structure in the Eastern Highlands

On the basis of linguistic diversity alone one would guess that isolate frequency and persistence are high in New Guinea. The great variability in simple genetic traits, such as the blood groups, which defeats attempts to trace any but the broadest clines in Highland New Guinea suggests that isolates are not only numerous, but rather small (Simmons et al. 1961:662; MacIntosh et al. 1958; Giles, Walsh, and Bradley 1966). In the present case, lacking intensive genealogies, the first approximation to the minimal isolate was taken to be the named village or hamlet cluster. This turns out to be a fair assumption for groups in the Eastern Highlands (but villages and hamlet clusters are not a demographic feature in some other parts of the Highlands).[2]

The phrase "minimal isolate" implies that there are other types of isolate boundaries, hierarchically arranged. Dialect and language boundaries appear to be two of these in the study area.[3] Higher levels can easily be surmised such as geographic boundaries within the Highlands, the separation of the Highlands and lowlands, and so on. At the higher levels selection would presumably be the most important differentiating agency while at the lower levels genetic drift may become the predominant force in determining gene frequencies (Morton 1968). Likewise, the tendency of gene flow to level genetic differences between groups becomes attenuated at higher levels and, for monofactorial traits of low selective value, may be overridden by the dispersive effects of drift. I shall return to these considerations in analyzing the results of the study.

A named village or hamlet cluster was taken to be the unit referred

2. See Littlewood (1966:103-4) for a brief discussion of the differences between Eastern and Western Highland settlement patterns and the implications for isolate structure.

3. Livingstone (1963) found a correlation of −.01 for cognate (language) distance and blood group data in eastern Kainantu and Fore regions, concluding that language boundaries are not effective genetic barriers. Two critical comments are in order: the blood group data published by Simmons et al. (1961) lists proveniences by language group and not village or village-complex, and the high drift situation apparent in this region (Giles, Walsh, and Bradley 1966, and this study) combines with the foregoing to frustrate such a conclusion. Livingstone admits to the possibility of drift obscuring the conclusions, and this would indeed appear to be the case. The tendency of serological reports to list results gathered from one or a few isolated communities to represent an entire language group is misleading in the extreme, but unfortunately extensively done.

to in response to the question (Pidgin), "Wanem ples bilong yu?" Place of birth was established by similar questions (see Appendix I) and an attempt was made to verify the location by visual means or discussion. However, the fact that the government was instrumental in awarding place names in the course of census consolidation made the field worker's task more complicated and in some cases defeated refined analysis. For instance, the Auyana data revealed over 150 different place names referring to a range of demographic groupings from house clusters without compounds or sometimes even pig enclosures ("little place") to whole census subdivisions or dialect areas ("big place") and included a fair sprinkling of abandoned living sites. On the other hand the other three language groups reflected very little ambiguity in this regard due to the distinctive physical groupings of named villages, their obvious geographic separation from one another, and greater apparent stability in residence pattern.

Table 2 represents an attempt to estimate both the relative isolation of the various complexes and their relationship to one another and outside linguistic groups. The figures on the diagonal represent the number of individuals used to make up the sample and includes all married persons in the subject generation plus the parents of the subjects. The other figures represent the number of persons who have entered the complex listed at the top of the table from the complex or language at the left. The listing of the study languages at the bottom of the chart indicates a provenience for migrants or mates of that language from complexes other than those included in this study.[4] The complexes used in this study are the result of the pooling, on the basis of intermarriage or migration figures, of more than 280 recorded places of origin for subjects and their parents and spouses. In some cases subjects were lumped into the closest relevant village in order to secure adequate samples. However, wherever this practice appeared to violate the integrity of a bona fide isolate, this was not done and some rather small samples (see Table 1) were the result.

Table 2 reveals some interesting facts. One of these is the high integrity of the language groupings relative to one another (see Table 4). Internal homogeneity of the language groups, however, varies widely,

---

4. The word "in-marriage" will be used to refer to mates coming into a complex or language group from another group. This serves to distinguish such genetic exchange from those of simple relocation ("immigration" here), out-marriage, or intermarriage (which latter includes the idea of exchange of mates in both directions). The word "migration" includes gene transfer by both immigration and in-marriage.

TABLE 2

MATRIX OF IMMIGRATION AND IN-MARRIAGE

Recipient Complexes

Donor Complexes	01	02	03	04	05	06	08	07	09	10	11	12	13	14	16	20	19	22	25	24	26	28	27	33	31	34	32	36	37	38
Binumarien 01	66	11																												
Puntibasa 02	12	251	24	6																										
Tompendaka 03	2	7	150																											
Sasaura 04				212																										
Inkana 05					203	6	3	2																						
Akuna 06		6		1	14	245	9	8																						
Tompena 08					11	11	174	2																						
Onamuna 07							3	115																						
Batainabura 09						1			305	1																				
Barabuna 10									3	109	2																			
Baieanabuta 11									1		216	4	8	3																
Bairinabuta 12											3	117																		
Babaraai 13									1				1254																	
Tondona 14													2	239						1	1									
Tonkera 16															419	9														
Bontaa 20															5	153	1													
Ontenu 19																	195			1										
Avia 22																		282	8	7	7	2						1		
Ofoimpina 25																		7	44	5	5	7	9	1						
Nankona 24																		4		219	9	17	1	1	2					
Waifina 26																		5	29		91	22	9	1		2				
Asempa 28																		9	5	22	17	302	18	10	11		7			
Omuna 27																				1	2	18	75	2	18	4	1	2		
Anokafa 33																		4	1	2	3	15		1104	2	1				
Arora 31																								1	8156					
Kawaina 34																					2	1	2	5	4	378	5	5		
Indona 32																				1		5					38			

TABLE 2 (Continued)

	Oyana	Kamano	Fore	Gadsup	Tairora	Auyana	Awa	Kosena	Tauna	Ilakia	Mobuta
Oyana	17										
Kamano	1	19									
Fore		1	8								
Gadsup	2	2	1	5							
Tairora	2	2		1	3						
Auyana		1	6	2	1	19					
Awa	1		2		1	1	15				
Kosena	2	3		2		8	2	6			
Tauna (36)	10	9	19	2	2	2	3	1	189	6	
Ilakia (37)		1	5	1	3	1	1	19	13	366	
Mobuta (38)	2		2		2	3	8	3	3	194	

Note: The data consist in the pooling of all parents of subjects and all married subjects and their spouses (numbers along the diagonal).

with Auyana showing the greatest internal migration.[5] A glance at Table 3 shows that attempts at pooling Auyana villages to obtain migration rates of less than 50 percent has been successful in only six out of the ten resulting complexes.[6] In order to obtain migration rates comparable to those of the other three language groups it would be necessary to collect the fifteen sample villages (here reduced to ten complexes) into three or at most four large groupings comprising the whole of the Auyana language. That is to say, the average size of an Auyana group having the same gene flow characteristics as a Gadsup cluster of 250-300 persons (census size) would be around 1,000 persons. Such an arrangement comes close to the picture of internal division that the Auyana themselves perceive (Sterling Robbins, personal communication, 1963) and would consist of the following major clusters: Kawaina, Arora-Indona, and the remainder (with the possible exception of Avia-Amaira) falling into a central division with Asempa as its focus.

Table 3 also lists government census figures taken over the period 1961-63. It is apparent that the government figures for several Auyana villages are in reality a generous pooling of otherwise distinct hamlets and villages. A situation as demographically fluid as that of the Auyana, added to the difficulties of terrain, lends itself to such expedients on the part of census patrols. The correspondence between the government's and the author's efforts at lumping cannot be known, but selected ethnographic censuses indicate that agreement between government census units and village-complexes used in this study is very good for Gadsup and Tairora, fair for Awa (newly "unrestricted" areas tend to be incompletely censused at first), and somewhat poorer for Auyana.

While this discrepancy in the case of the Auyana may result in a village census number which is rather too large, it cannot equally be said that the high variability in migration rates is an artifact of census tech-

5. An interesting and informative way of reading the table is to look at the figures at the opposite corners of a "square" the other two corners of which are two villages on the diagonal. This gives the migration figures between these two villages and yields a hint about reciprocity. For example, in central Auyana the exchange between Waifina (26) and Omuna (27) is nine persons from the former to the latter and two persons in the other direction.

6. I hesitate to use the term "gene flow" since that presumes that the genetic effectiveness of the immigrants is known. The term "migration" is less precise and ambiguous since it includes the idea of emigration which is not relevant here (having to do with drift rather than gene flow); but, as my figures have included both immigrants (spouses, both of whom were born elsewhere) and spouses acquired by marriage from outside, it will be used.

nique. It is apparent that relocation and regrouping is responsible for the high in-marriage and immigration rates in several of the villages. On the other hand the extremely low rate of in-marriage for complex number 34, Kawaina, is in part corroborated by the existence of a strong "poison" (magic) boundary between it and the rest of Auyana, a boundary across which cargo carriers would not pass. In addition, the census number for Kawaina already represents a cluster of at least two major village-complexes, Kawaina 2 and Kawaimpa, each of which may be a distinct isolate. The gene flow figure in this case might better be considered a reflection of the possible emergence of a new ethnic entity within the Auyana language group.

In general, the settlement pattern presents a picture of concentrated village clusters in the northern part of the study area which give way to some hamlet and household scattering as one moves south into Auyana, returning to intensive village aggregates in Awa. The explanation for the high village size variability and low isolate stability of the Auyana can only be conjectured, but the impression is that of a people moving rapidly into a confined ecological space. The Auyana are located in what amounts to a broad but very rugged and broken-up valley. Large stands of widely spaced, dead trees give evidence of forest gardens recently worked and passed over in the pressure to expand against the forest margins. One suggestion for this picture is that the Auyana are a group local to the valley for some time past which has begun to feel the pressure of numbers. Another explanation, and both (or neither) may be correct, is that warfare pressures have displaced them from their former range. This suggestion gains some strength from the observation that the Auyana language appears to be more closely related to Awa and Gadsup than to Tairora. There is today no contiguous border between Auyana and Gadsup, an arm of Tairora having interdicted them.

Four of the complexes listed in Tables 2 and 3 require special comment. Binumarien (01) is a Tairora-speaking enclave on the Markham Valley edge of Gadsup. It is a small isolate and the study sample was also small. The people there speak of being forced down into the Markham Valley in the past by warfare only to return as a result of further warfare and the effects of malaria. If the sample is accurate, their present ties are primarily with Puntibasa (02) in Gadsup and not with Tairora proper.

The same cannot be said of Tondona (14), a Tairora isolate at the edge of the Kratke Range which maintains strong ties with Auyana

TABLE 3

CENSUS FIGURES, EFFECTIVE SIZE, AND ESTIMATED MIGRATION RATES FOR THE
STUDY COMPLEXES

Village-Complex	1961-63 Government Census			Approximate Variance Effective Size†	Approximate Estimate of Migration‡
	Total	Adults*			
		Males	Females		
Gadsup					
02 Puntibasa	539	134	133	149	.135
03 Tompendaka	270	73	74	83	.220
04 Sasaura	382	110	96	116	.123
05 Inkana	443	128	109	133	.138
06 Akuna	355	73	99	97	.090
08 Tompena	243	65	59	69	.069
07 Onamuna	346	83	84	94	.113
Tairora					
01 Binumarien	122	32	40	41	.242
09 Batainabura	170	41	57	55	.039
10 Barabuna	314	82	93	98	.001(?)
11 Baieanabuta	237	65	64	72	.023
12 Bairinabuta	227	55	73	72	.085
13 Babaraai	317	85	106	107	.039
14 Tondona	275	76	81	88	.067
16 Tonkera	242	72	78	79§	.064
20 Bontaa	188	55	62	66	.078
Auyana					
22 Avia	409	105	117	125	.117
25 Ofoimpina	353	90	87	99	.432
24 Nankona	246	69	71	79	,338
26 Waifina	258	76	58	81	.593
28 Asempa	361	99	104	114	.358
27 Omuna ‖					.520
33 Anokafa	325	91	85	99	.529
31 Arora	487	115	127	136	.237
34 Kawaina	402	101	101	113	.005(?)
32 Indona	147	37	42	55	.842⌗
Awa					
36 Tauna	129	32	30	35	.132
37 Ilakia	201	48	39	49	.041
38 Mobuta	169	47	50	55	.036
19 Ontenu	396	100	107	116	.169

*Adults in the census were individuals judged by the census officer to be 16 years and over. These figures take into account adults away from the village for reasons of wage labor or as students.

TABLE 3 (Continued)

† After the method of J. F. Crow (1954:543-56). See text for discussion of the corrections used here.

‡ From Table 2. In questionable cases the informants appear to be underreporting and attempts to change the manner of questioning produced no change in results. It can be seen from Table 2 that Kawaina and Barabuna have both contributed several individuals to other complexes, which fact, on the basis of reciprocity expectations, makes their avowed isolation all the more strange.

§ Since the sampling was carried out in three closely approximated villages (Abiera, Burauta, and Tonkera) and the samples subsequently pooled, the figures for Tonkera alone will represent each of the three.

// Included in Asempa figures in census.

This exceptionally high rate reflects three factors: (1) the small sample of subjects, (2) the relative newness of the village site and its peripheral position (near Fore), and (3) the generally fluid situation in Auyana in general.

and has many bilingual members. In terms of migration it appears to be more comfortably placed in Auyana, but geography and physical measurements (Chap. 3) place it firmly in Tairora, a sparsely settled mountain range separating it from the former. Peripheral villages seem to vary greatly in the degree to which they breach linguistic boundaries; an interesting study could be made of this phenomenon and its causes.

Ontenu (19) is one such cosmopolitan enclave. Related linguistically to Gadsup and Oyana but enclaved by Tairora and Kamano groups, the former hostile in times past (Watson 1967), it apparently trades genes with Tairora (minimally), Kamano, Fore, Oyana, central Auyana, and maintains ties with certain villages in western Gadsup. The villages of Tonkera (16) at the edge of Tairora a short distance away from Ontenu, also shows considerable Kamano influx but no tendency to share its other contacts so widely, preferring to maintain a reciprocity with Bontaa (20) in Tairora.

On the basis of a rather small sample from Indona (32) we find a group which has virtually no identity of its own, seemingly a confluence of central Auyanans and the beginning of a vector of Fore migrants which passes through Arora (31) and into central Auyana (Asempa, 28). The extent of Fore incursion into Auyana is surprising, but the fact that *kuru* cases are restricted to the western boundary of the language group may be an indication of the relative recency of that migration (Gajdusek, Zigas, and Baker 1961).

In addition to the census figures in Table 3 an attempt was made to estimate the effective breeding size of the populations in question since this number is genetically more relevant than the census number. Such a number is obtained by applying a set of corrections to the census size. First, we are interested only in that proportion of the population which is actively breeding and must reduce the census number by removing infants, children, and aged individuals. If family size is highly variable (that is, some parents are contributing more genetically than others) this must be entered into the corrections. These two corrections were applied and the results were listed in Table 3. These numbers are undoubtedly still too large and it is worth discussing the reasons why.

In the first place census numbers, especially in Auyana, are probably too high in many instances. Also, family size variance may be higher than observed if adoption—a common practice—is preferred by smaller families thereby reducing observed differences in family size. The effect of preferential mating patterns on inbreeding (Wright's F_{IS}, 1951) could not be assessed from the relatively incomplete genealogies. Unequal parental sex ratio in the form of polygyny or serial monogamy may also be important in further reducing the effective size estimates. However, my data are not extensive enough to reveal how permanent or fecund these matings are. Table 4 gives an idea of the proportion of such marriages.[7] Most of these involve two wives, but fourteen cases involved three wives and there were three cases of four wives in the sample.

TABLE 4

FREQUENCY OF POLYGYNOUS MATINGS

Language Group or Complex	Number of Matings Recorded	Number of Polygynous Matings Recorded	Rate
Gadsup	263	39	.148
Tairora	238	65	.273
Auyana	279	52	.186
Awa	99	10	.101
Binumarien	17	5	.29
Tondona	42	12	.29
Ontenu	32	7	.22

Since random sampling variation (drift) is inversely proportional to the product of effective size and migration rate (Li 1955:337) the accurate evaluation of both these parameters is necessary to the anticipation of drift and the interpretation of variation in the data. However, two other factors have undoubtedly operated in this region to

7. A preliminary report on marriage figures in Gadsup by M. Leininger (personal communication, 1968) indicates a polygyny rate of .41 in the small (160 persons) village cluster of Arona, and a rate of .13 (close to my own estimate) for the larger complex of Akuna.

further reduce the effective population size: the "founder effect," and subsequent rapid population growth. While migrants may often join relatives or friends in other established isolates, it is sometimes the case that a small group of relatives or friends may establish a new isolate. If this phenomenon is followed by a rapid growth of the isolate (not augmented significantly by immigration), the true effective number will be closer to the size of the founder population than to its larger, contemporary size (Wright 1931). If, as some suspect, the introduction of the sweet potato set off a sequence of population fission and expansion (Watson 1965a,b; but see Brookfield and White 1968), then these factors must be taken into account for Highland populations in general.

Periods of high instability in terms of migrations, as seen in the Auyana data, would serve to dampen the effects of drift, and we cannot say on the basis of the evidence at hand that this was not the case for most groups at one time or another in their recent past. In general, however, it can be said that the variance effective numbers listed in this study are a maximum estimate.

Table 5 represents estimates of gene flow between languages, but caution must be urged in interpreting the rates listed. The study did not, of course, include all peripheral villages in each language group, and considerable breaches in linguistic boundaries may have been overlooked. On the other hand it would be inaccurate to assume that all peripheral villages tend to higher rates of extralinguistic migration. The border village-complexes of Tompena (08), Batainabura (09), Bontaa (20), Kawaina (34), and Tauna (36) show relatively little tendency to look outside their language groups for genes.

In conclusion it can be said that demographic clustering and lin-

TABLE 5

GENE FLOW BETWEEN LANGUAGE GROUPS
(Subject and Parent Generations)

| | Source Language | | | | | | | | | | |
	Gad-sup	Tai-rora	Au-yana	Awa	Oyana	Binu-marien	Ton-dona	On-tenu	Ka-mano	Fore	Total
Gadsup	...	.022				.008					.010
Tairora	.001	...	.001						.011	.017	.013
Auyana		.006	...		.018		.002	.006	.001	.017	.049
Awa			.007	...						.005	.012
Binu-marien	.212	.030				...					.242
Tondona		.017	.049				...				.067
Ontenu	.041	.010	.005		.005			...	.097	.010	.168

guistic barriers operate to slow gene flow. A clinal depiction of the hybridization picture would show deceleration in the gene flow rates at the complex, dialect, language, and language family levels. Many factors in the Highlands combine to suggest a high drift situation, not the least of these being small village groupings, founder effects, and periods of putative rapid population expansion.

3. Anthropometry and Anthroposcopy

The selection of the morphological variables used in this study was dependent upon several considerations. The first of these was to obtain a set of measures and observations which would yield discriminating variability between the groups. The second constraint was to include variables which would reflect genetic differences on the one hand and environmental effects on the other. Since both of these criteria could be only poorly assessed at the outset, the third consideration, that of selecting observations which would be comparable to other studies, was undoubtedly the most influential.

With respect to the first criterion, some observations showed so little variation that, especially in the case of anthroposcopic variables, they were dropped in the field—for example, iris color, hair form, and caruncular hair were not judged to show reliably observable variation. In the case of measurements, assessment of their utility had to await the analysis of the data. As can be seen from Figures 1 and 2, several measures taken separately fail to show a significant difference between their within-groups (major language groups in this case) and between-groups variability (F test). In the case of males, where sample sizes were larger, only four measures fail to show significance (P less than .005).[1] For the women, a smaller and probably more heterogeneous sample,[2] fourteen measures fall short of significance.

1. Swindler (1962) in his West Nakanai (New Britain) villages finds very low variance ratios for the same four measurements—bizygomatic, minimum frontal, total facial height, and upper facial height.
2. Women are the principal vectors of gene flow, virilocality being the predominant residence rule.

TABLE 6

MEANS, STANDARD DEVIATIONS, AND COEFFICIENTS OF VARIATION FOR 36 MEASUREMENTS AND INDICES FOR MALES OF THE FOUR MAJOR LANGUAGE GROUPS AND ONTENU

Measurement Number	Variable	Gadsup (N = 212) x̄	Gadsup S.D.	Tairora (N = 301) x̄	Tairora S.D.	Auyana (N = 260) x̄	Auyana S.D.	Awa (N = 90) x̄	Awa S.D.	Ontenu (N = 25) x̄	Ontenu S.D.	Grand Mean	Overall S.D.	Coefficient of Variation $V = \frac{100\,S.D.}{\bar{x}}$
0	Weight	128.7	15.9	130.5	14.4	122.4	13.6	118.9	12.9	122.4	15.1	126.3	15.0	11.87
1	Stature	158.28	6.1	155.97	6.4	153.68	6.1	150.85	5.5	157.48	5.8	155.38	6.1	3.93
2	Trochanteric height	823.0	42.4	798.8	42.3	789.9	38.4	780.8	35.7	823.2	38.0	801.7	40.4	5.03
3	Tibiale height	429.6	25.2	423.5	22.3	420.0	22.3	418.2	17.0	437.1	20.5	424.7	22.4	5.27
4	Sphyrion height	65.1	6.4	66.2	5.6	65.9	5.2	64.6	5.3	66.2	5.0	65.7	5.6	8.56
5	Humeral length	294.9	14.7	295.0	16.1	290.0	13.9	286.7	14.7	297.2	17.8	292.7	15.3	5.22
6	Radial length	252.0	13.4	246.4	15.2	241.7	13.0	237.0	12.0	253.2	12.8	245.6	14.6	5.94
7	Sitting height	802.9	31.0	803.9	32.0	786.3	31.9	769.3	33.0	789.7	29.5	794.6	33.7	4.24
8	Biacromial width	365.0	16.4	364.0	16.6	360.4	15.7	351.6	18.0	359.1	16.1	361.8	16.8	4.64
9	Head height	115.5	7.1	114.1	5.9	111.9	6.3	108.6	7.5	115.0	6.9	113.3	6.8	6.00
10	Hand length	185.2	9.6	183.6	9.6	182.8	8.2	178.0	9.1	184.6	10.0	183.2	9.4	5.13
11	Hand width	97.8	5.3	97.7	7.8	97.3	4.8	93.1	4.9	96.5	4.4	97.1	5.9	6.11
12	Head length	197.0	6.5	197.2	5.7	195.7	6.0	194.1	6.3	196.3	6.2	196.4	6.1	3.10
13	Head breadth	145.6	4.7	145.2	4.5	146.1	4.5	143.2	4.3	146.0	5.0	145.4	4.6	3.16
14	Basal breadth	129.8	4.3	128.3	4.9	130.2	4.6	128.3	5.0	129.9	5.1	129.3	4.8	3.71
15	Minimum frontal	101.8	5.1	101.6	5.1	100.8	4.5	101.3	4.2	101.8	4.5	101.4	4.8	4.73
16	Bizygomatic	140.9	4.9	140.6	5.1	141.0	5.0	141.7	5.2	141.0	4.3	140.9	5.0	3.54
17	Bigonial	103.7	5.6	104.7	5.1	103.7	5.3	102.0	6.1	103.0	4.7	103.9	5.4	5.19
18	Total facial	117.1	6.0	117.5	6.4	116.4	6.4	118.1	6.3	116.8	8.1	117.1	6.3	5.38
19	Upper facial	69.9	5.1	69.0	5.2	69.4	5.1	69.8	4.4	69.2	6.2	69.4	5.1	7.34
20	Mandibular depth	42.1	3.2	40.6	3.5	40.6	3.0	40.9	3.0	41.8	3.4	41.0	3.3	8.04
21	Nasal height	49.8	4.2	50.9	4.5	50.4	4.6	51.4	3.8	51.7	5.6	50.5	4.4	8.71
22	Nasal width	46.6	3.2	48.3	3.7	46.9	3.3	47.1	3.7	47.0	3.6	47.3	3.5	7.39
23	Nasal depth	31.6	2.5	33.3	2.6	33.9	2.6	32.7	2.7	33.5	1.9	33.0	2.7	8.18
24	Palatal diameter	68.2	2.9	68.5	3.7	67.3	3.4	66.9	3.2	68.7	3.3	67.9	3.4	5.00

TABLE 6 (Continued)

25	Dorsal arm skinfold	44.0	9.4	53.0	12.3	45.6	10.4	47.0	8.8	43.6	8.9	47.8	11.3	23.64
26	Subscapular skinfold	106.4	30.7	99.8	22.4	90.3	18.9	87.6	19.2	81.9	16.7	96.8	24.4	25.25
27	Circumference, upper arm	269.2	18.6	264.9	16.9	260.4	17.1	245.5	16.9	255.9	17.2	262.4	18.6	7.08
28	Circumference, calf	333.1	23.9	330.7	21.6	323.8	22.4	311.6	19.7	322.4	26.2	327.1	23.2	7.09
29	Chest girth (xiphoid)	860.8	41.1	845.3	38.2	833.8	36.4	809.1	42.9	831.4	40.7	841.6	41.6	4.94

Indices														
Trunk/stature	50.7	1.4	51.6	1.5	51.2	1.4	51.0	1.4	50.2	1.2	51.2	1.5	2.92
Cephalic index	74.0	2.4	73.7	2.4	74.7	2.7	73.8	2.5	74.4	2.6	74.1	2.5	3.37
Brachial index	85.5	3.1	83.6	3.4	83.4	3.0	82.7	2.7	85.3	2.8	83.9	3.3	3.93
Head height/head length	58.7	3.6	57.9	2.9	57.2	3.2	56.0	3.7	58.6	3.4	57.7	3.3	5.71
Biacromial/sitting height	45.5	1.9	45.3	1.8	45.9	1.8	45.7	2.1	45.5	1.9	45.6	1.9	4.16
Total facial index	82.9	4.2	83.3	4.6	82.4	4.3	83.2	4.5	82.5	5.7	82.9	4.4	5.30
Nasal index	94.3	10.6	95.7	11.7	93.8	10.8	92.1	9.4	91.9	12.4	94.3	11.0	11.66

Note: Weight is in pounds, height in centimeters, all other measurements in millimeters.

One may raise the question at this point as to how much the differences in variance between groups is a function of the increase in reliability of measurement technique with time. It was not possible under field conditions to perform on the same subject the repeated measurements required to determine possible changes in reliability. However, all of the language groups were sampled both early and late in the study, tending to offset reliability trends when the variances are pooled into major language groupings. A comparison of the relative variability (coefficient of variation) of stature among the various complexes revealed no apparent relationship either to the sequence in which villages were sampled or to sample size. The wide range of relative variation observed for this measurement (2.7 to 5.0) reflects most strongly the inherent variability of the trait and the heterogeneity of particular samples. In the case of the present study the latter influence is probably the strongest.

Table 6 presents the values, for the major language groups, of the measurements and indices used in this analysis. The index numbers of the measurements will be used in subsequent tables and figures for the sake of simplicity. Histogram plots of the data revealed approximately normal distributions for all variables except skinfold measures which are skewed toward the higher values, though much less so in the males than in the females.

The most striking feature of the table is the definite cline from Gadsup to Awa in stature and its components. Two other clines with similar direction and slope can be seen in the figures for radial length (6) and the circumferences of the upper arm (27), calf (28), and chest (29). It is not surprising to find strong clines in trochanteric height (2), tibiale height (3), radial length (6), and sitting height (7) since these are all highly correlated with stature (see Appendix II, Table 36). The equally strong clines for head height (9), and the three circumferences (27, 28, 29), appear to be independent of the stature trend although the circumferences are reasonably well correlated among themselves.

Since we are not simply asking how different these populations are, but also in what manner they differ, some attempt must be made to assess the degree to which the observed differences are genetic or environmental in origin. In terms of the former, three agencies could produce genetic differences: natural selection brought about by factors which would, in most cases, be reflected also in environmentally induced (plastic) differences; genetic drift, particularly where dominant genes, "master" genes, or genetically simple traits are not under strong selective influence; and gene flow from outside the area of the language family. We cannot say much about the operation of selection here especially since the first plastic responses to a selective pressure, say for body size or fat and muscle components, cannot be separated from the genetic changes which may be accompanying them.

Though we know this area to be an incipiently high drift situation it is characteristically assumed that metrical features are related to polygenic sources and are thereby relatively resistant to sharp fluctuations in phenotypic frequencies. The presence of a single or a few influential loci in a polygenic set could become candidates for sampling variation in an otherwise complex morphological trait as Birdsell (1950:269) has suggested for total facial height in Australia, but none of the characters here dealt with appear to enjoy the great and seemingly random fluctuations we will encounter with the blood groups. Total facial height, incidentally, shows insignificant variability between the various groups but does become useful in the discriminant analysis.

The effects of gene flow upon the various groupings, complex and language, may be one of the most powerful, short-term factors in either producing or erasing genetic differences. Influences from widely divergent physical types operating at the antipodes of the study area—say Markham Valley influences in Gadsup; Anga (Kukukuku) genes in Awa—could conceivably produce the striking divergences noticed within the Kainantu Language Family. On the other hand gene flow within the language family would operate to reduce genetic variability, especially if it were higher in the recent past than at present. While we cannot eliminate either possibility from our ultimate interpretation, neither can we say anything definitive from the data available.

The other source of observed difference is the effect of environmental variables—nutrition, climate, physiography, disease, altitude, and culture. Two types of environmental influence must be distinguished: factors which operate to produce variation in developed or developing individuals and factors which influence the rate and degree of development itself. The effect of disease and nutrition on development may be reflected in boney tissue as well as soft tissue, whereas the same environmental factors probably have little influence on the skeleton after that system has reached maturation (Hiernaux 1963; Lasker 1946). Stature, for example, while showing a strong genetic component (Osborne and DeGeorge 1959; Hiernaux 1963), can be influenced by environmental change during development as shown in migration studies and the secular trends of increase in height of progeny in many Western countries and Japan. In addition, under conditions of starvation the stature of mature individuals may decrease significantly (Ivanovsky 1923), but this undoubtedly involves no major changes in bony segments comparable to those which can be produced during development.

There is little evidence from the study area concerning nutritional and disease factors which might severely effect development. Taro seems to be more of a staple in the Awa (P. Newman, personal communication, 1966) than in the other groups where sweet potato predominates. In any event this would not explain the smooth cline in stature components over all four language groups, although the abrupt drop in the clines for body circumferences as they enter Awa may be a reflection of a dietary shift (see Table 7). Some evidence for vitamin D and/or calcium deficiency can be seen in the occurrence of "saber shins," a noticeable anterior convexity of the tibia, which occurs in Auyana and Tairora—especially frequent in Batainabura (09). No cases of this condition were noted in Awa, but the possibility of small body size being a satisfactory adjustment to dietary demands cannot be eliminated on the grounds of our present knowledge (Weiner, in Harrison et al. 1964:420).

The steep, exposed soils of the Awa and southern Auyana region plus the occurrence of goitre in that region may also be taken as circumstantial evidence for a mineral imbalance in the diet. But the physiography (cf. Chap. 1) suggests another factor in favor of small size. The taller, neighboring Fore, when asked to carry cargo into the Awa territory, refer to the latter as "the land where the Fore cry." It was an observable fact that Awa carriers moved with dismaying strength and alacrity under heavy loads. This is probably in part a response to conditioning and familiarity, but the advantages of small bodies and short legs cannot be discounted in such difficult terrain where power rather than speed is favored.

While all of these conditions are interesting grist for future mills, it is not possible to resolve these questions with the data of this study. An appreciation of the complexity of both the genetic and environmental agencies at work in the study area prevents an overly sanguine expectation of neat explanations for the observed biological variability. The problem here is to discriminate the groups and to get some sense of the magnitude of the differences between them with the goal of discovering the pattern of their ethnogenesis. If environmental effects are obscuring genetic interpretation, then it is necessary to acquire some sense of the magnitude of influence of the former.

GENETIC AND ENVIRONMENTAL COMPONENTS OF VARIABILITY

Several lines of evidence shed flickers of light on the problem of the relative heritability (i.e., that portion of the population variability in a trait due to heredity) of human morphological traits. None are totally satisfactory and the results of various studies tend to conflict at several points, leaving only broad, general agreements such as the observation of a "relatively greater genetic component of variability . . . for postcranial measurements taken parallel with the long axis of the body" (Osborne and DeGeorge 1959:160). The two basic approaches to the problem involve, on the one hand, studies in which genetic variability is low and environmental differences great (the immigrant studies of Boas 1912, Shapiro and Hulse 1940, Greulich 1958, and the African groups of Hiernaux 1963), and those studies in which the environmental differences are minimized and genotypic differences maximized (twin studies such as those of Newman, Freeman, and Holzinger 1937, and Osborne and DeGeorge 1959, and familial studies such as those of Howells 1953, 1966a).

The derivation of heritability estimates from the comparison of monozygotic (MZ) and dizygotic (DZ) twins is efficient and involves relatively simple statistical methods. The study of Osborne and DeGeorge was selected because it has two advantages for the purposes of the present analysis. It is one of the few twin studies performed exclusively on an adult (eighteen years of age and over) population, and it provides heritability data for twenty-six of the thirty-six measures and indices used in this study. It also provides separate heritability estimates for males and females.[3] The method employed to test heritability is that of comparing the variances within pairs of the monozygotic versus the dizygotic twins. Presuming relative constancy of the environment for each pair, any variability between the members of a pair must derive increasingly from hereditary differences. Traits which have a strong genetic component should vary most in fraternal twins and least in identical twins. The ratio of the variances for a trait,

---

3. Vandenberg (1962) in his summary article on twin study data pools the male and female variances without any apparent justification. The other studies in his summary involve subjects less than eighteen years of age and often yield significant F ratios where Osborne and DeGeorge show no significance. Studies made on different age samples do not appear to be comparable.

TABLE 7

STANDARDIZED ABSOLUTE MEAN DIFFERENCE OF MEASUREMENTS AND INDICES FOR ALL
PAIRINGS OF THE MAJOR LANGUAGE GROUPS: MALES ONLY

Measurement Number	Variable	Gadsup-Tairora	Gadsup-Auyana	Gadsup-Awa	Tairora-Auyana	Tairora-Awa	Auyana-Awa
0	Weight	(-).120	.420	.654	.540	.774	.233
1	Stature	.351	.699	1.129	.348	.778	.430
2	Trochanteric height	.598	.818	1.042	.220	.445	.225
3	Tibiale height	.272	.428	.508	.156	.236	.080
4	Phyrion height	(-).195	(-).142	.089	.053	.284	.231
5	Humeral length	(-).007	.320	.535	.327	.542	.215
6	Radial length	.389	.715	1.041	.326	.652	.326
7	Sitting height	(-).030	.491	.995	.521	1.024	.503
8	Biacromial width	.060	.274	.797	.214	.738	.524
9	Head height	.206	.529	1.014	.323	.809	.485
10	Hand length	.170	.255	.765	.085	.595	.532
11	Hand width	.186	.085	.796	(-).102	.610	.711
12	Head length	(-).033	.213	.475	.246	.508	.262
13	Head breadth	.087	(-).109	.522	(-).200	.435	.630
14	Basal breadth	.312	(-).083	.312	(-).396	.000	.396
15	Minimum frontal	.042	.208	.104	.167	.062	(-).104
16	Bizygomatic	.060	(-).020	(-).160	(-).080	(-).220	(-).140
17	Bigonial	(-).185	.000	.315	.185	.500	.315
18	Total facial	(-).063	.111	(-).159	.175	(-).095	(-).270
19	Upper facial	.176	.098	.020	(-).078	(-).157	(-).078
20	Mandibular depth	.455	.455	.364	.000	(-).091	(-).091
21	Nasal height	(-).250	(-).136	(-).364	.114	(-).114	(-).227
22	Nasal width	(-).486	(-).086	(-).143	.400	.343	(-).057
23	Nasal depth	(-).630	(-).852	(-).407	(-).222	.222	.444
24	Palatal diameter	(-).088	.265	.382	.353	.471	.118
25	Dorsal arm skinfold	(-).796	(-).141	(-).265	.654	.530	(-).124
26	Subscapular skinfold	.270	.658	.769	.389	.499	.110
27	Circumference, upper arm	.231	.473	1.273	.242	1.042	.800
28	Circumference, calf	.103	.401	.927	.297	.823	.526

TABLE 7 (Continued)

29	Chest girth	.372	.648	1.241	.276	.869	.593
	Indices						
	Trunk/stature	(-).600	(-).333	(-).200	.267	.400	.133
	Cephalic	.120	(-).280	.080	(-).400	(-).040	.360
	Brachial	.576	.636	.848	.061	.273	.212
	Total facial	(-).091	.114	(-).068	.205	.023	(-).182
	Nasal	(-).014	.045	.199	.173	.327	.127
	Totals	8.737	11.541	18.962	8.795	15.531	10.794

Note: A minus sign in parenthesis indicates that the difference was negative.

DZ:MZ, is a measure of its relative heritability.[4] Plotting some measure, or measures, of the relative variability of these traits in the study populations against the heritability estimates should give an idea of the relative roles of hereditary and environmental factors in differentiating the groups within the study area.

Two measures of dispersion between groups were used: one, following the practice of Hiernaux in his study of two Hutu subgroups in Rwanda (1963), was the standardized mean difference between language groups$\left(\dfrac{\bar{x}_1 - \bar{x}_2}{\text{std. deviation}}\right)$ for each variable; the other measure was the F ratio (ratio of the between-groups variance to within-groups variance) over all groups for each measurement. The former technique has the advantage of simplicity and comparability between measurements. The latter measure is related to the criterion of discrimination employed in the multivariate analyses to be found later in this chapter.

Table 7 lists the differences between the various pairings of the major language groups for each of thirty-five variables. Gross trends can be easily spotted in such a table, and consistent clines from Gadsup to Awa through Tairora and Auyana can be seen in stature (1), leg length (2), knee height (3), upper arm length (5), lower arm length (6), sitting height (7), shoulder width (8), head height (9), hand length (10), head length (12), subscapular skinfold (26), circumference of the upper arm (27), circumference of the calf (28), chest girth (29), and brachial index.

A first approximation to the relative importance of high and low heritability factors in differentiating the language groups can be seen from the scatter-diagrams, Figures 1 and 2, in which the MZ:DZ variance ratios from Osborne and DeGeorge are plotted against the mean difference scores for selected pairs of language groups. A negative regression would be expected if a preponderance of variables of low heritability (and therefore greater environmental susceptibility) were creating most of the discrimination between the groups. On the other hand a positive regression would favor an explanation in terms of genetic rather than environmental factors.

Figure 1 shows the relationship between Ontenu and Gadsup for 26 variables. On the basis of linguistic and ethnohistorical evidence these

---

4. An *F* test may be employed to determine the significance of the ratio.

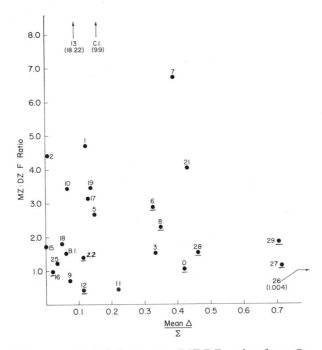

Figure 1. Heritability scores (MZ:DZ ratios from Osborne and DeGeorge) versus mean difference scores between Gadsup and Ontenu males. Linearity measures are underscored.

two groups should be genetically closely related. Tairora and Awa (Fig. 2), on the basis of similar evidence, should be distantly related. The size of the mean differences is greater in the latter case and more significance could be attached to any visible regression. On the whole no strong regression is revealed in either case, the calculated correlations being weakly negative and insignificant.

Head width (measurement 13) was eliminated from the regression assessment due to conflicting evidence concerning the degree of heritability which Osborne and DeGeorge assigned to it (Vandenberg 1962). Most studies concur in assigning it a relatively high genetic component and its inclusion would have enhanced the negative regression, but I remain wary of excessively high values in the light of the low agreement in variance scores for the majority of the dimensions reported by various authors.

Hiernaux's "ecosensitive" (environmentally sensitive) measures can be seen to be scattered generously throughout the lower portion of the

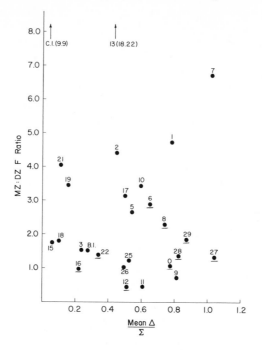

Figure 2. Heritability scores (MZ:DZ ratios
from Osborne and DeGeorge) versus mean
difference scores between Tairora and Awa
males. Linearity measures are underscored.

diagrams. A check of certain linear measures such as stature (1), leg
length (2), tibiale height (3), humeral and radial lengths (5 and 6), sitting height (7), and hand length (10) among the various pairings of
groups reveals an interesting pattern. Gadsup-Ontenu (Fig. 1),
Gadsup-Auyana, and Gadsup-Tairora show no visible regression. A
weak positive trend begins to show up in the Gadsup-Awa pair, be-
coming quite strong in the Auyana-Awa and Tairora-Awa (Fig. 2)
comparisons.

A somewhat different but related test of the same comparison can
be seen in Figure 3 and 4, which consist in plots of the F ratios calculated in this study for each variable over all five groups (including
Ontenu again) against the heritability F ratios. The same lack of significant regression remarked in the preceding figures is also evident in
Figure 3 ($r = .006$). It is once again clear that a small group of
stature variables (1, 2, 7) and radial length (6) plus a set of circumfer-

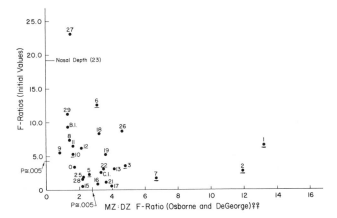

Figure 3. Scatter-diagram of *F* ratios for each variable over four language groups plus Ontenu for males versus MZ:DZ *F* ratios from Osborne and DeGeorge. Linearity measures are underscored. The *P* = .005 level of significance for the *F* ratios is marked on the axes.

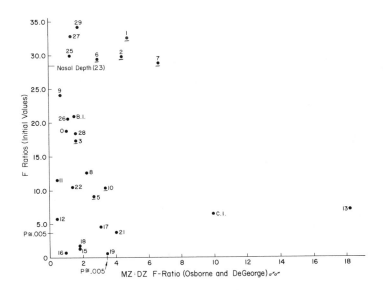

Figure 4. Scatter-diagram of *F* ratios for each variable over four language groups (Ontenu not distinguished) for females versus MZ:DZ *F* ratios for females from Osborne and DeGeorge. Linearity measures are underscored. The *P* = .005 level of significance for the *F* ratios is marked on the axes.

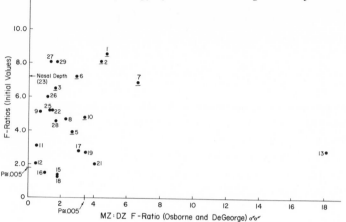

Figure 5. Scatter diagram of *F* ratios for each variable over 29 village-complexes (males only) versus MZ:DZ *F* ratios from Osborne and DeGeorge. Linearity measures are underscored. The *P* = .005 level of significance of the *F* ratios is marked on the axes.

ences and skinfolds (25-29) provide most of the differentiation between groups.

The picture for the females (Fig. 4) is quite different. Here linearity measures, to which Osborne and DeGeorge assign high heritability values, play a minor role in discrimination, four of them failing to show significance. The most variable measures between groups appear to be certain skinfolds and circumferences, widths such as biacromial diameter (8) and hand width (11), and some measures of the head (9, 12, 18, 19), most of which, with the exception of subscapular skinfold (26), have low heritability values in females. Two points are worth noting before leaving the diagrams. In both cases the discriminating power of the nasal depth is very high although no heritability values could be found in the literature.[5] In all cases (mean difference and *F* ratio) lower arm length (6) has greater between-groups variability than upper arm length (5). Hiernaux (1963:581) refers this to an environmental response and cites similar findings by Prevosti.

When the total sample of male subjects is broken down into twenty-nine isolates or village complexes there is a drop in the magnitude of the *F* ratios for the various measures but the scatter-diagram is essentially similar (Fig. 5).

5. Nose salient (not significant in Shapiro and Hulse's 1940 study of Japanese migrants to Hawaii) may reflect the great variability in nasal profile.

In sum, we find that the measures which show the greatest differentiating power in this study are rather evenly divided between variables of high and low heritability. The former group generally consists in linear measures of the postcranial skeleton while the latter include soft tissue measurements, distal limb segments and, in the case of males, head height. Several cautions must be entered before interpreting these results. Low variability in phenotype may be due to lack of genetic variability in the population. Further, heritability estimates based on a middle-class caucasoid sample may not in all respects apply to this particular population. As the ecological and genotypic environments vary so may the response of morphological variables. No complex variable has the immunity to its environment that certain serological loci appear to enjoy. We have already seen that stature, while apparently highly controlled by heredity in a uniform environment, may respond dramatically to environmental stress or beneficence. The long-term response to such stress is a shift in the populaton genotype, but the short-term reaction is to stretch the plastic limits of the phenotype. With the data at hand and the lack of controls (such as, for example, a genuine Awa enclave planted in the middle of Gadsup) inherent in the situation we will, in the long run, only be able to erect further questions.

MULTIVARIATE ANALYSIS OF THE METRICAL DATA

So far I have used simple statistics in a descriptive manner. It is easy to become bemused by the armamentarium of modern statistical science. Electronic computers make the seduction even more likely. Some of the techniques which I will discuss and use are mathematically elegant, logically more "correct" than simpler techniques, and very powerful in the statistical sense. However, as Huizinga (1962: 385) so aptly observed in his charming article on resemblance statistics: "Indeed, if one considers the theoretical assumptions on which the derivation of the D^2 [of Mahalanobis and Rao] is based . . . one may conclude that mathematicians would have hesitated to apply such a subtle method to anthropological data as they are. The attitude (to which respect for Human Problems may be contributory) that it may be enough if the underlying assumptions are 'approximately' correct may remind not a few of the procedure of breaking a fly on the wheel."

In the light of this just criticism one trembles to proceed. However, there are certain heuristic advantages to be gained from the use of discriminant and distance statistics which are basically time and space saving. Such a statement could not have been sensibly uttered before the advent of high-speed computers. Nowadays one hesitates not to avail himself of the facility. What, then, are the advantages of "breaking the fly"?

In the first section I calculated the mean difference scores for each measurement to get a sense of the magnitude and direction of variability in the population. One should not dispense with this step—it gives a feel for the separate measures that will quickly be lost in the more advanced multivariate techniques. Summing the mean differences (Table 7) gives a rough measure of the "biological distance" between the members of the various pairs of groups. Already, however, problems have begun to emerge. Most of the summed difference between groups arises from the adding together of several highly correlated variables, thereby giving excessive weight to what in reality is only one or two composite factors. This in turn obscures the kind of configurational data which enable an expert taxonomist to make his choices. These choices are made by taking into account a set of factors simultaneously and not by summing separate decisions on each separate observation. In addition, if one were to compare, by the same method, each village-complex against every other village complex it would result in 406 separate comparisons, the description of which result would be beyond the patience and abilities of the author or his most diligent readers.

Several techniques currently exist for dealing with these problems, and two of them have been well described in a few articles in the literature of biology and physical anthropology. Bronowski and Long (1952) and Jolicoeur (1959) give particularly lucid accounts of the nature and use of discriminant analysis. Ashton, Healy, and Lipton (1957) pioneered the use of canonical variates in anthropology in an article entitled, significantly, "The Descriptive Use of Discriminant Functions in Physical Anthropology." It is the descriptive use of these statistical methods that concerns me here.

The aim of discriminant analysis and its modifications, such as the D^2 of Mahalanobis and Rao and canonical analysis, is to transform a set of P original variables into a set of k linear functions such that the maximum amount of dispersion between individuals or groups of individuals in the population can be described. Jolicoeur has elegantly illustrated this for discriminant analysis by the use of the following illustration (Fig. 6).

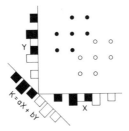

Figure 6. Hypothetical example of discriminatory analysis for two characters. Scatter-diagram and frequency histograms of characters *X* and *Y* and of the transformed axis $K = aX + bY$, which is the discriminant function. (After Jolicoeur 1959:286)

The two populations of white dots and black dots give only weak bimodal distributions when measured along the original axes. By erecting a new axis, $K = aX + bY,$ and projecting the scatter points on it, an optimal separation of the two clusters is obtained. Establishing suitable confidence intervals about the centroids (means) of these clusters allows decisions to be made whether to assign new individuals to one or the other, or neither, of these clusters. This procedure may be logically extended to three or more variables. In the former case, two discriminant functions will be developed which describe a plane of optimum projection of the points in three-dimensional space, and in the latter instance, $P - 1$ discriminant functions describe the dispersion of individuals in P-dimensional space. Canonical analysis is a highly efficient extension of this procedure in which the correlation between characters is minimized and a set of orthogonal axes (canonical variates) developed so that the maximum amount of dispersion between groups is reflected in the first few variates. In many cases this allows an adequate description of the dispersion between the groups to be plotted in two dimensions (the first two canonical variates).

Both of these procedures (plus a D^2 analysis) are contained in a computer program (BMD 07M) developed by the biomedical facility of the University of California at Los Angeles. Partitions of the 888 male and 172 female subjects, as shown in Table 8, were submitted to analysis. This table indicates that in each partition of the sample three different combinations of variables were run as subproblems. The first

TABLE 8

LIST OF VARIOUS COMPUTER RUNS

Run	Partitions	Subproblems	Text Figures	Tables
1. "Tribal" males	4 major language groups and Otenu	a. All 29 variables b. 8 "genetic" variables c. 8 "environmental" variables	8a,b,c 9 10	10 11 12
2. "Tribal" Females	4 major language groups	a. All 29 variables b. 8 "genetic" variables c. 8 "environmental" variables	11a,b 12 13	13 14 15
3. Isolates (males)	29 village-complexes	a. All 29 variables b. 8 "genetic" variables c. 8 "environmental" variables	14a,b,c 	18 19 19

TABLE 9

INDEX NUMBERS OF VARIABLES USED IN SEPARATE COMPUTER RUNS

Runs 1 and 2 (Males)		Run 2 (Females)	
"Genetic" Variables	"Environmental" Variables	"Genetic" Variables	"Environmental" Variables
2	9	2	8
5	12	3	9
6	16	6	10
10	22	13	11
13	25	17	25
17	26	19	27
19	27	21	28
21	28	26	29

subproblem ran all twenty-nine variables regardless of the level of significance. The second and third subproblems ran sets of eight variables of high genetic influence and then eight variables of low genetic and high environmental components (Osborne and DeGeorge 1959: 126-27). In each set of eight variables an attempt was made to include measures which ranged from high to low in their discriminating power in the study population. Certain measures were excluded because of high intercorrelations with variables which were included. Table 9 lists the variables used by their index numbers.

Tables 10-15 give the classification matrices resulting from the stepwise discriminant analysis. The discriminant analysis was about 64 percent successful in assigning males to their own groups (Table 10) when all variables were employed. This figure drops to 36 and 43

TABLE 10

CLASSIFICATION MATRIX OF THE "TRIBAL MALES" RUN: ALL VARIABLES
(By Number of Cases)

	Gadsup	Tairora	Auyana	Awa	Ontenu	Totals*
Gadsup	164	15	19	8	20	226
Tairora	18	182	39	24	24	287
Auyana	28	39	142	30	21	260
Awa	3	8	8	65	6	90
Ontenu	1	3	2	2	17	25
						888

*On the basis of the "Isolate" runs, Binumarien (01) has been included in Gadsup in all subproblems of this run.

TABLE 11

CLASSIFICATION MATRIX OF THE "TRIBAL MALES" RUN: 8 "GENETIC" VARIABLES
(By Number of Cases)

	Gadsup	Tairora	Auyana	Awa	Ontenu	Totals
Gadsup	95	23	27	32	49	226
Tairora	37	82	60	64	44	287
Auyana	47	43	79	62	29	260
Awa	6	12	13	51	8	90
Ontenu	4	5	1	4	11	25
						888

TABLE 12

CLASSIFICATION MATRIX OF THE "TRIBAL MALES" RUN: 8 "ENVIRONMENTAL" VARIABLES
(By Number of Cases)

	Gadsup	Tairora	Auyana	Awa	Ontenu	Totals
Gadsup	136	19	30	8	33	226
Tairora	41	131	36	40	39	287
Auyana	48	58	54	53	47	260
Awa	1	5	15	53	16	90
Ontenu	4	5	3	4	9	25
						888

percent, respectively, for the genetic and environmental subproblems (Tables 11, 12). In order to get a sense of the shift in assignment distributions due to moving from environmental to genetic variables Table 12 was subtracted from Table 11. Results are given in Table 16. Looking down the diagonal of this table the greatest loss of "identity" can be seen in Gadsup and Tairora while Auyana regains some of the integrity it lost in the "environmental" run. Gadsup becomes more closely genetically related to Awa and Ontenu, Tairora to

TABLE 13

CLASSIFICATION MATRIX OF THE "TRIBAL FEMALES" RUN: ALL VARIABLES
(By Number of Cases)

	Gadsup	Tairora	Auyana	Awa	Totals
Gadsup	46	6	3	0	55
Tairora	3	34	3	2	42
Auyana	1	3	25	1	30
Awa	0	2	0	43	45
					172

TABLE 14

CLASSIFICATION MATRIX OF THE "TRIBAL FEMALES" RUN: 8 "GENETIC" VARIABLES
(By Number of Cases)

	Gadsup	Tairora	Auyana	Awa	Totals
Gadsup	30	15	4	6	55
Tairora	9	19	6	8	42
Auyana	1	4	15	10	30
Awa	4	7	12	22	45
					172

TABLE 15

CLASSIFICATION MATRIX OF THE "TRIBAL FEMALES" RUN: 8 "ENVIRONMENTAL"
VARIABLES
(By Number of Cases)

	Gadsup	Tairora	Auyana	Awa	Totals
Gadsup	26	17	9	3	55
Tairora	11	15	10	6	42
Auyana	5	5	17	3	30
Awa	2	2	4	37	45
					172

TABLE 16

MATRIX DIFFERENCES IN ASSIGNMENT BETWEEN "GENETIC" AND "ENVIRONMENTAL"
RUNS: MALES

	Gadsup	Tairora	Auyana	Awa	Ontenu
Gadsup	− 41	+ 4	− 3	+ 24	+ 16
Tairora	− 4	− 49	+ 24	+ 24	+ 5
Auyana	− 1	− 15	+ 25	+ 9	− 18
Awa	+ 5	+ 7	− 2	− 2	− 8
Ontenu	0	0	− 2	0	+ 2

Auyana and Awa. Awa reciprocates by contributing members to Gadsup and Tairora. In the case of females (Tables 13-15) the same subtraction matrix is shown in Table 17.

Gadsup, Tairora, and Auyana give up members to Awa, and Awa reciprocates in rough proportion to the distances between it and the

TABLE 17

MATRIX OF DIFFERENCES IN ASSIGNMENT BETWEEN "GENETIC" AND
"ENVIRONMENTAL" RUNS: FEMALES

	Gadsup	Tairora	Auyana	Awa
Gadsup	+ 4	− 2	− 3	+ 3
Tairora	− 2	+ 4	− 4	+ 2
Auyana	− 4	− 1	− 2	+ 7
Awa	+ 2	+ 5	+ 8	− 15

other three groups. As women are the most mobile aspect of the genetic landscape, it is tempting to assign this result to intermarriage. However, since subjects were included in samples on the basis of their birthplace, this cannot be a reflection of migration in the present generation and must therefore be the result of sex-influenced traits passed down from previous migrants. If the observed pattern were the result of an ecological cline one would expect the signs to be reversed. But this is placing a great burden upon the assumption that we have in any way successfully discriminated between genetically sensitive and environmentally sensitive variables in this population. The three variables which contribute most to the "genetic" discriminant analysis are lower arm length (6), subscapular skinfold (26), and leg length (2), probably the three most ecosensitive of the list. Proceeding to partition the sample along village-complex lines produces the results summarized in Table 18. Assignment of males to their own village-complex was successful in 43 percent of the cases. However, assignment to the "correct" language group took place in 72 percent of the cases and was therefore more successful than the "tribal" run. The data are now being pushed to their limit. The results of the "genetic" and "environmental" subproblems are summarized by listing the diagonal values in Table 19. Some groups (e.g., Batainabura, Waifina, Bairinabuta, etc.) disappear completely on one or the other run. The groups which hold up best are Inkana, Akuna, and Onamuna in Gadsup, Tonkera and Bontaa in Tairora, Indona and Kawaina in Auyana, the three Awa villages (36-38), and Binumarien. This last is interesting since the complex is a Tairora isolate linguistically, but is phenetically (i.e., degree of overall phenotypic similarity) most closely related to the eastern Gadsup.

If Table 18 is interpreted in a manner similar to that employed for Table 2 in Chapter 2, certain clusterings of villages can be discerned. These clusterings have been brought together in the form of a kind of dendritic diagram (Fig. 7). To read the diagram, follow the line or

TABLE 18

CLASSIFICATION MATRIX OF THE "ISOLATE MALES" RUN: ALL VARIABLES
(By Number of Cases)

	02	03	05	06	07	08	01	09	10	11	12	13	14	16	20	22	24	25	26	27	28	31	32	33	34	36	37	38	19
02 Puntibasa	16	7	3					1			1							1	2	1	1	1	1	2	1	1	1	1	2
03 Tompendaka	2	9																	1		1	1	2	2		1	1	1	1
05 Inkana			23	1	2	5	1	1		1								1	1		1	1							
06 Akuna			3	22	4	4	1												1										
07 Onamuna	1	1	3	1	18	2											1		1	1		1			1	1		2	
08 Tompena			5	4	2	12											1				1				1			3	
01 Binumarien				1	2	1	9	1	1			1			1				1		1		1						
09 Batainabura	1	1	4					9	3	3	2	2	1	1	1	1	1	1	2	1	1	1					2		
10 Barabuna								15		3	2	2	2	1			7	1	1	3	13	2	2	1	1	1	2	1	
11 Baieanabuta		1						3	12	4	1	3	4	1	3	1	2	2	1	2	1	15	6	1	2	4	2	1	
12 Bairinabuta		1						3		4	10	2	1	1	2	1	2	6		1	1	5				1	1		
13 Babaraai					1			2	3	3	2	12	3			1	1		1	1		1							
14 Tondona			1		4			1	2	3	1	4	14	2			3		1		1	2					2	2	
16 Tonkera			1					1	1	1	1	1	1	30	5	2			2	1		1				1	1		
20 Bontaa							3	1	1	1	1		1	4	15			1	2			1		1		1	2	5	
22 Avia				1	1					2	2	1	1	1	3	11	1	1	2	3	1	3		2	2	1			1
24 Nankona	1				1			1	1	1							7	2	1	2		3	2	2	2		1		
25 Ofoimpina																	2	6	4										1
26 Waifina	1	1						1							1		2		4		1								
27 Omuna	1							1	1			1					1		1	6	1	1	2			1			
28 Asempa	2	2	1		2		1	1	1		1		3	2	2	2	2	1	1	3	13	2	2	1	1			1	
31 Arora	2	2						1				1					3		1	2	1	15	6	1	2				
32 Indona	1														1				1						2				
33 Anokafa		1	1		1			1							3		1	1	2	1	3	1		5		1			1
34 Kawaina								2		5	5		2		1	1	2		1	4	1	1	2	1	21	1	2	1	
36 Tauna								1		1	1		2				1		1		1	1	2		1	14	2		
37 Ilakia										1	1		3				1		4		1	1	1	1		4	20	3	
38 Mobuta						1																						18	1
19 Ontenu	1				1			2	1		1				1		1			1						1		1	13

Note: Numbers along the horizontal indicate the assignments of male subjects of the particular complex named at the left. Numbers along the vertical are subjects from other complexes assigned to the complex numbered at the top.

TABLE 19
VALUES TAKEN ALONG THE DIAGONAL OF THE CLASSIFICATION
MATRICES FOR SUBPROBLEMS OF THE "ISOLATE" RUN: MALES

Group	"Genetic" Subproblems	"Environ-mental" Subproblems	Group	"Genetic" Subproblems	"Environ-mental" Subproblems
02 Puntibasa (49)	1	10	22 Avia (33)	7	5
03 Tompendaka (25)	4	3	24 Nankona (24)	4	2
05 Inkana (39)	10	6	25 Ofoimpina (10)	3	2
06 Akuna (45)	11	16	26 Waifina (11)	2	0
07 Onamuna (27)	10	11	27 Omuna (15)	3	3
08 Tompena (27)	6	4	28 Asempa (50)	3	5
01 Binumarien (14)	8	6	31 Arora (34)	8	0
09 Batainabura (36)	0	3	32 Indona (12)	2	4
10 Barabuna (30)	2	5	33 Anokafa (23)	1	1
11 Baieanabuta (40)	3	4	34 Kawaina (48)	0	11
12 Bairinabuta (28)	1	0	36 Tauna (28)	3	13
13 Babaraai (30)	6	1	37 Ilakia (37)	8	9
14 Tondona (33)	8	3	38 Mobuta (25)	12	4
16 Tonkera (62)	17	15	19 Ontenu (25)	3	3
20 Bontaa (28)	12	3			
			Total (888)	158	152

Note: Numbers in parentheses are sample sizes.

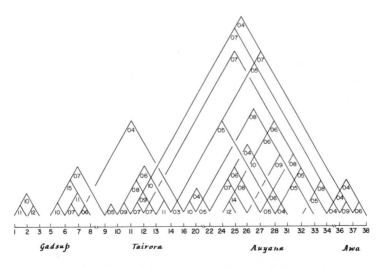

Figure 7. Relationships between village-complexes determined by assignments in the discriminant analysis

lines from a village-complex up to the numbered vertex and then back down to the related complex. The numbers in the vertex indicate the percent of cases crossclassified between the two groups.[6]

The clusters and their interconnections are surprisingly logical in terms of geographical and cultural factors as will be shown in a moment. Prior to a discussion of the results of the discriminant analysis, a look at the canonical plots will assist in forming a picture of the total set of interrelationships between groups as well as affording a rough statistical measure of the significance of their separations.

Figure 8a shows the dispersion of major language groups, and Ontenu, represented by the first two canonical variates (Roman numerals on the axes). The axes are marked in standard deviation units with zero mean for all groups. The points on the graph represent the group means and a circle drawn about the mean with radius of two units would constitute approximately a 95 percent confidence interval. Although it is the purpose of canonical analysis to express the maximum possible dispersion in the fewest number of variates, the success with which this is accomplished varies. The first two canonical variates in the "tribal" male run accounted for 81 percent of the dispersion. For exemplary purposes I have plotted the third and fourth canonical values against the first (Fig. 8b,c). Since the distance along the first axis does not change, the new information in these successive plots is contained in the relative vertical displacement of the points. For instance, Awa, which appears close to Auyana in Figure 8a, becomes strongly separated from it along the third canonical axis. The first three canonical variates account for 96 percent of the dispersion and the fourth (Fig. 8c) accounts for the rest. The fourth axis gives us no new information about the major language groups, but Ontenu now asserts itself as a distinctive entity.

Figures 9 through 13 are the canonical plots corresponding to the discriminant analyses, Tables 11-15. The amounts of dispersion accounted for in these two-variable plots are respectively 85, 94, 83, 94, and 94 percent (the third variable plot for females, Figure 11b, brings that figure to 100 percent). The most persistent pattern to emerge from these graphs is the wide separation of Gadsup and Awa.

The canonical analysis for the twenty-nine isolates was very much less efficient than the preceding analyses and it required four canonical variables to account for 62 percent of the dispersion (Fig. 14a,b,c).

6. This number is the ratio of the number of individuals crossclassified to the sum of the two samples. It is not sensitive to the *direction* of assignment (cf. Table 18).

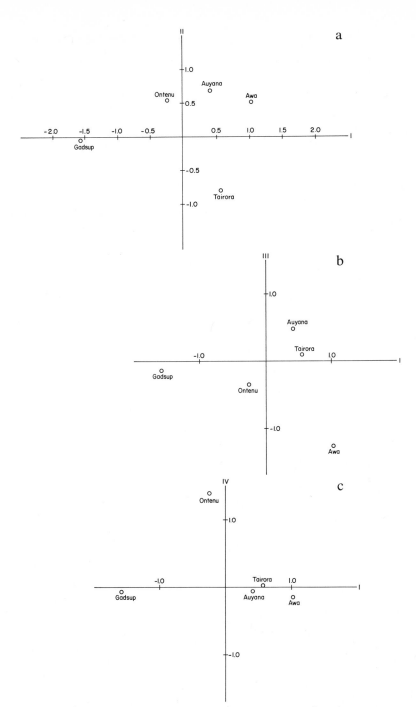

Figure 8a,b,c. Canonical plots of the major language groups (males) for the first four canonical variables: all variables used

The results are instructive. The language groupings maintain their identity and relative placement. Binumarien (01) relates consistently to Gadsup and eventually to the easternmost villages (02, 03). Ontenu falls between Gadsup and Auyana but rather closer to the latter. Gadsup itself divides into two distinct divisions—western (05, 06, 08) and eastern (02, 03) with Omuna (07) moving between them. The third canonical variable clearly breaks Tairora into two parts—the northern group (16, 20) and a southeastern cluster (10, 11, 12, 13, 14)—and seems to have difficulty disentangling itself from Auyana. In Auyana, 32 and 34 are closely associated and on the first two canonical axes are distinguished from the otherwise undifferentiated remainder of the language group. The northern two groups of Awa (36,

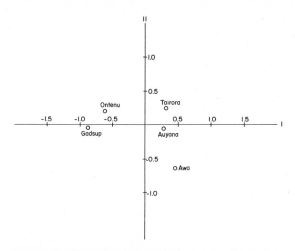

Figure 9. Canonical plot of the major language groups (males) for the first two canonical variables: eight "genetic" variables

37) are more closely associated to each other than to Mobuta (38) which is south of them across the Lamari River. The former in turn seem to be associated with 32 and 34 in Auyana. In general the results of this run correspond with those summarized in Figure 9, and the reader may find it easier to refer to that figure.

While it must be reiterated that on the whole most of the biological distances are apparently due largely to ecosensitive measures, the pattern of clusters of complexes and their relationships among themselves

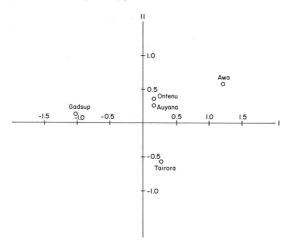

Figure 10. Canonical plot of the major language groups (males) for the first two canonical variables: eight "environmental" variables

in several cases violate the ecological gradient. That is, similarities within and between obvious clusters seem to respond to observed genetic (migration) relationships and are largely borne out by Table 2. The following discussion will attempt to summarize the possible geographical, migrational, and ecological causes for the observed clustering.

Cluster 01, 02, 03. These complexes are ecologically and geographically distinct from the rest of Gadsup. They are located in the lower altitude, heavily forested, eastern margin of the Gadsup area. Intermarriage is high. The Tairora-speaking Binumarien sample may be biased due to small size. Their external relations are with Sasaura (04, sampled only for blood and dental casts) and Akuna (06), but phenetic resemblance to the western Gadsup cluster is apparently weak.

Cluster 05, 06, 08, 07. The western Gadsup complexes occupy a primarily grassland habitat and are heavily intermarried with the exception of Onamuna (07) which exchanges genes mainly with Akuna (06) and has its strongest phenetic resemblance to that village. This cluster is morphologically related to Tairora through Inkana (05)to Batainabura (09), which is the closest Tairora group. Onamuna

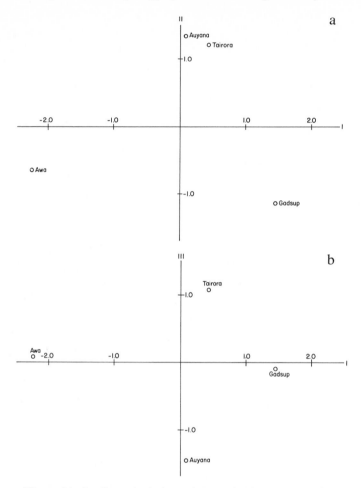

Figure 11a,b. Canonical plots of the major language groups (females) for the first three canonical variables: all variables used

(07) shows a phenetic relationship with Tonkera (16) in Tairora, and this is supported by ethnographic observation. The Gadsup-speaking enclave, Ontenu (19), which is located close to (16) may have originally come from this part of western Gadsup. (Ontenu, not listed in Figure 7, appears to have its greatest phenetic resemblance *in Gadsup* with the members of this western cluster.)

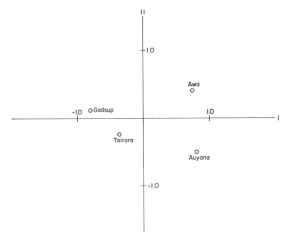

Figure 12. Canonical plot of the major language groups (females) for the first two canonical variables: eight "genetic" variables

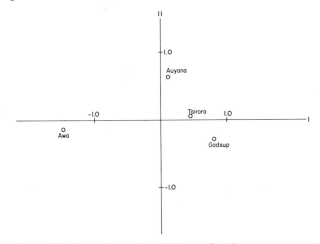

Figure 13. Canonical plot of the major language groups (females) for the first two canonical variables: eight "environmental" variables

Cluster 10, 11, 12, 13, 14. These complexes occupy two parallel valley systems running north and south in the southern portion of the Tairora study area (indicated by the drainage pattern on the map). The habitat of the two valleys is characterized by open grasslands and they are separated by a series of forested hills. While their internal relationship is borne out by the migration pattern, their external phe-

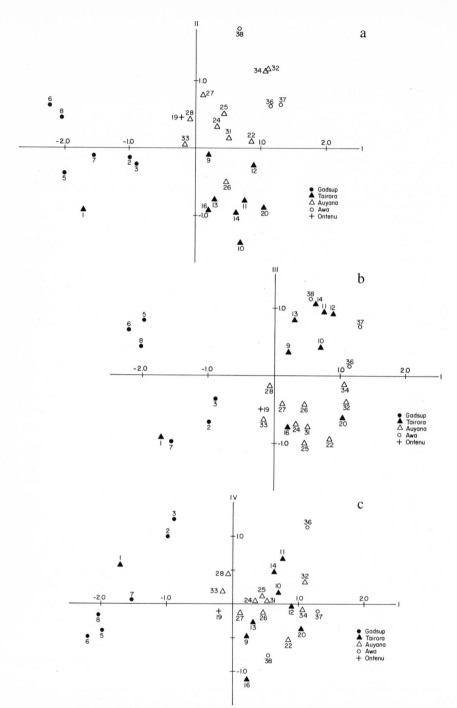

Figure 14a,b,c. Canonical plots of the 29 village-complexes (males) for the first four canonical variables: all variables used

netic relationship to Auyana and Awa is of great interest. In the case of Tondona (14) this is understandable since, as commented in Chapter 2, it is a bilingual complex which has frequent contact with Auyana. Although the preponderance of these contacts are with the eastern Auyana complexes (Table 2) the phenetic resemblance is to central Auyana and northern Awa. Complexes 11 and 12 also tend to resemble southwestern Auyana (Kawaina 34) and northern Awa. A look at Map 1 indicates that travel to the south of the uninhabited (Kratke Range) forest between Auyana and Tairora would bring contact with southern Auyana and northern Awa.

Cluster 16, 20. This northern cluster is very weakly associated with the previous cluster, but contacts Auyana at two points, Avia (22) and Anokafa (33). Tonkera (including Abiera) (16), Ontenu (19), and Bontaa (20) are strung out along a relatively broad, grassy valley which is separated from the other major Tairora complex (above) by rolling hills and a large drainage area which is the remnant of an ancient lake bed. The road which connects these villages leads to the two major trails over the Kratke Range into eastern Auyana. The Auyana terminals of these trails are Anokafa and Avia.

Cluster 24, 25, 26. Auyana is very complex, resulting no doubt from the high internal gene flow and the small size of some of the samples. Avia (22), which occupies the swidden-scarred forests at the head of the Auyana valley, seems to be more closely assignable to the central Auyana cluster (below) than to its neighboring cluster.

Cluster 27, 28, 31. As the valley opens out to the southwest and becomes steeper, the villages tend more and more to occupy ridge-top positions close to the northern wall of the valley until Asempa (28) is reached. At this point the valley broadens dramatically and drops suddenly into a large grassy bowl to the southwest, which native informants have located as the "origin" place for the Auyana. The Arora (31) and Indona (32) complexes occupy the northern side of this bowl and Kawaina (34) the southern rim. The entire pattern of occupation of Auyana resembles a Y with Avia (22) at its base (northeast) and Kawaina and Indona at its tips. Thus, the cluster of Omuna (27)–Asempa (28) is located at the confluence of major trails connecting the various parts of Auyana. Arora (31) appears to be phenetically related to these two. Table 2 supports the conclusion of an extensive migration between (28) and (31) but not for (27) and (31). While this central cluster seems to bear phenetic similarities with villages on all major axes of Auyana, the very high migration values centering on Asempa (28) are not clearly reflected in the discriminant classification. The present migration pattern may be quite recent in origin. Anokafa (33) is phenetically most closely related to the central and previous clusters. The migration pattern reflects this also.

Cluster 32, 34. Kawaina appears to be strongly related to the main body of Auyana and to the neighboring Awa. Indona (32), while showing some affinity for Kawaina and Awa (Tauna 36), seems unrelated to the body of Auyana. Migration figures, however, show a strong contact with the central cluster. The sample from Indona is very small and heavily infused with Fore migrants which may account for the discrepancy.

Cluster 36, 37, 38. The northern two complexes of Awa, Tauna (36) and Ilakia (37), are closely related to one another. Mobuta (38) which is south of the Lamari across a steep gorge shows no similarity to (36) but some affinity with (37). Migration figures reflect this result exactly.

Ontenu (19). From Table 2 Ontenu appears to share similarities with all major groups but most strongly with Puntibasa (02) and Akuna (06) in Gadsup and with the neighboring Tonkera (16) in Tairora. Recent hostilities between Ontenu and the latter complex have apparently not slowed their approximation.

The agreement between the results of the discriminant analysis and inferences drawn from intermarriage and ethnographic data is quite good. The problem of assessing the nature of the forces at work to produce these phenetic clusters is still unsolved, but the fact that migration figures and ethnographic observations of social contact tend to corroborate the morphological map suggests that, at least at the village-complex level, genetic forces (gene flow) may predominate.

To close this chapter some comments on the dental observations and nonmetric morphological observations are in order.

DENTAL TRAITS

Drs. Barksdale and Boyd have performed an excellent and detailed analysis of the metrical and morphological character of the dental casts (see Appendixes III and IV). These casts were obtained from Sausaura (04); Akuna (06); Ontenu (19); Baieanabuta (11); Abiera, in the Tonkera (16) complex; Babaraai (13); Batainabura (09); Tauna (36); and Ilakia (37). Though the sample is small it is representative spatially. In this part I shall only summarize their findings briefly and add some comments from my own field observations.

In general the teeth were large, well spaced in broad arcades, and remarkably free from periodontal and carious complications. Occlusion is good with a strikingly higher frequency of "edge-to-edge" (labiodont) and slight overjet than would be expected in "civilized" populations. Anterior crossbite ("undershot jaw") is also rather high in frequency. This tendency increased towards the south with the Auyana showing the greatest frequency (see Table 21). In line with the general size cline, the Awa have the smallest arcades and teeth. The Awa also show more crowding in the upper and lower anterior dentition, particularly in the latter, and in both cases they are significantly different from the Gadsup. Upper and lower crowding shows a positive correlation (approximately 0.4).

Wear is not extreme and is, of course, correlated with age (average correlation for all groups about 0.6). An unbroken cline of increasing wear from Gadsup to Awa can be seen in Table 21 and the difference between the two ends is significant. Explanations which come to mind are the shift in diet in the northern groups due to the introduction of tinned food and containers for boiling food conveniently,[7] the possible effect of the greater reliance on taro rather than sweet potato in the southern groups, and the reduction of mineral content in seasoned food due to the use of trade salt rather than native salt in the northern groups. An important factor may simply be the reduction in crown area in the smaller-toothed southern people.

Caries was difficult to observe because of the prevalence of betel-chewing in most areas. Advanced caries was much more frequent in Mobuta (Awa) than in the other complexes. Interestingly, the villages of Mobuta (38) and Ilakia (37) included no betel-chewers in the sample and the rate of caries in Awa (particularly in the anterior dentition) was much higher than in the other major language groups. This may in part be due to the ease with which caries could be observed among non betel-chewers, but advanced tooth destruction could be observed in any event and was significantly less frequent with the chewers. Betel combines with dental calculus to form a black coating on the tooth. This, combined with the change in pH of the mouth due to the lime which is chewed with the betel nut, may provide a clue to the observed difference. On the other hand, people with sensitive, carious teeth may incline to pass up the pleasures of the habit. Questioning did not produce any clear response on this point.

---

7. Pottery was rare in precontact times and the customary cooking methods involved using earth ovens or bamboo containers, or placing the food directly on the fire or ashes.

TABLE 20
BETEL-CHEWING BY MAJOR LANGUAGE GROUP*
(In Percent)

	Nonchewers	Recent or Irregular Chewers	Regular Chewers
Gadsup	6	6	88
Tairora	13	21	66
Auyana	33	23	44
Awa	95	2	3

*Women tend much less frequently to be betel-chewers. However, their inclusion in this count does not alter the relative frequencies.

Betel nut grows on a palm which is found in the mixed forests of the lower elevations. Table 20 indicates a sharp gradient in its use and may reflect a trade vector from the Markham-Gadsup region into the interior.

Barksdale and Boyd also attempted, on the basis of their small samples, to assess the amount of the differences between language groups. Boyd, using a combination of palatal and tooth measurements of 149 males, calculated the D^2 distances between pairs of groups (see Appendix IV, Table 93). These are summarized here:

Group Pair	D^2
Gadsup-Tairora	19.36
Gadsup-Auyana	29.53
Gadsup-Awa	33.69
Tairora-Auyana	29.40
Tairora-Awa	19.28
Auyana-Awa	27.07

With the exception of the Gadsup-Tairora distance and possibly the Tairora-Awa relationship, these figures are not greatly at variance with the results of the canonical analysis of body measurements (Figs. 10, 13). Tairora dentition is very similar in size to that of the Gadsup, even slightly exceeding the latter in several dimensions. In most measurements taken singly, however, Tairora is quite different from Awa. Part of the explanation for the discrepancies noted may arise from shape factors concealed in the multivariate method. Another factor could be the high variability of the Tairora samples with respect to each other (see Appendix IV, Table 94). The difficulty of "unpacking" the meaning of discriminant functions and canonical variables makes such inconsistencies difficult to explain, but it is clear that linear size differences were somehow minimized in the Tairora-Awa comparison.

Barksdale employed chi-square tests to reveal the differences in tooth morphology between groups. While this does not yield a distance statistic, the accumulated significant differences (Appendix III, Table 72) favor a wide separation of Gadsup from Awa, somewhat less distinction between Tairora and Awa, and relatively insignificant differences between Auyana and Gadsup and Auyana and Tairora. No other pairings showed significant differences. These results uniformly support the major metrical cline. Though little is known about the genetics of these characters, they are generally presumed to be relatively unresponsive to environmental influence. Except for incisor shoveling and crown variation, no clinal relationships show up in the frequency tables. The differences appear to be random, although their accumulated effect in pair analysis supports the clinal pattern discovered by metric analysis. It may be that many of these traits are genetically simple and, as in the serology, we are dealing with differences produced by random dispersive agencies (drift).

OTHER MORPHOLOGICAL OBSERVATIONS

Anthroposcopic observations are a tricky business. The bland assurance with which frequency charts of the various impressions are published belies the subjective vagaries of the technique. While it is all very well to read textbooks on the subject of attached and free earlobes, the field situation will soon confront the tyro with the task of dividing a continuum into discrete categories. He will do this more or less well on the basis of textual standards or criteria absorbed osmotically from a teacher or colleague, but in the last analysis his scale will be his own. As a consequence the published results are more of a descriptive than an analytic or comparative tool. However, Table 21 represents those observations which, in my judgment, showed enough variability and reliability of observation to merit comment. Significance statistics were obtained for most of them and, while I do not place much confidence in their precision, they serve as a rough guide to the meaningfulness of the observed differences.

Body, beard, and nasal tip hair show a definite and significant cline from the hirsute north to the relatively glabrous south with the Tairorans tending to be hairier than the Gadsup except with respect to body hair. The scales used here and throughout the chart are: O = absent, 1 = very slight to 9 = very strong, frequent, etc. In most cases this ambitious scale has been collapsed to good effect, smoothing the distributions and subjective idiosyncracies which became apparent in the analysis such as a tendency to avoid the number 5 in listing observations.

TABLE 21

FREQUENCY (PERCENT) DISTRIBUTIONS OF VARIOUS ANTHROPOSCOPIC VARIABLES:
MALES ONLY

Variable	Scale	Gadsup		Tairora		Auyana		Awa		Ontenu	
		N	%	N	%	N	%	N	%	N	%
Body hair	0	12	5.7	2	0.7	9	3.4	16	17.8	6	25.0
	1-2	70	33.0	182	60.7	182	69.5	65	72.2	6	25.0
	3-4	76	35.8	87	29.0	52	19.8	8	8.9	3	12.5
	5-6	50	23.6	26	8.7	19	7.3	1	1.1	6	25.0
	7	4	1.9	3	1.0	0	0.0	0	0.0	3	12.5
Beard	0	0	0.0	1	0.3	2	0.8	1	1.1	0	0.0
	1-2	18	8.5	24	8.0	79	30.2	56	62.2	7	29.2
	3-4	101	47.6	101	33.7	128	48.9	29	32.2	6	25.0
	5-6	93	43.9	171	57.0	52	19.8	4	4.4	11	46.8
	7	0	0.0	3	1.0	1	0.4	0	0.0	0	0.0
Midphalangeal hair	0	84	39.6	138	46.0	101	38.6	26	28.9	11	46.8
	1-2	55	25.9	89	29.7	85	32.4	24	26.7	10	41.7
	3-4	38	17.9	65	21.7	63	24.0	33	36.7	3	12.5
	5-6	32	15.1	8	2.7	13	5.0	6	6.7	0	0.0
	7-8	3	1.4	0	0.0	0	0.0	1	1.1	0	0.0
Nasal tip hair	0	181	81.0	229	73.9	217	81.3	91	92.9	22	81.5
	1-2	25	11.4	28	9.0	26	9.7	4	4.1	3	11.1
	3-4	11	5.1	43	13.9	22	8.2	2	2.0	1	3.7
	5-6	5	2.4	10	3.2	2	0.7	1	1.0	1	3.7
Browridges	1	3	1.4	2	0.7	0	0.0	0	0.0	0	0.0
	2-3	58	27.4	71	23.7	33	12.6	23	25.6	1	4.2
	4-5	132	62.3	183	61.0	178	67.9	55	61.1	13	54.2
	6-7	28	13.2	43	14.3	49	18.7	12	13.3	10	41.7
	8	1	0.5	1	0.3	2	0.8	0	0.0	0	0.0
Pterygia	0	109	51.4	65	21.7	87	33.2	2	2.2	12	50.0
	1-2	71	33.5	150	50.0	144	55.0	65	72.2	10	41.7
	3-4	31	14.6	82	27.3	30	11.5	18	20.0	2	8.3
	5-6	1	0.5	3	1.0	1	0.4	5	5.6	0	0.0

TABLE 21 (Continued)

Variable	Scale	Gadsup N	Gadsup %	Tairora N	Tairora %	Auyana N	Auyana %	Awa N	Awa %	Ontenu N	Ontenu %
Bite	U//L	1	0.5	2	0.7	0	0.0	0	0.0	0	0.0
	U//L–U/L	2	1.0	1	0.4	0	0.0	0	0.0	1	4.2
	U/L	65	32.5	47	16.7	50	19.9	16	18.0	13	54.2
	U/L–U-L	47	23.5	117	41.6	60	23.9	20	22.5	0	0.0
	U-L	63	31.5	82	29.2	79	31.5	33	37.1	6	25.0
	U-L–L/U	12	6.0	25	8.9	37	14.7	14	15.7	2	8.3
	L/U	10	5.0	7	2.5	22	8.8	6	6.7	2	8.3
	L/U +	0	0.0	0	0.0	3	1.2	0	0.0	0	0.0
Crowding (lower teeth)	0	83	39.2	135	45.0	133	50.8	28	31.1	7	29.2
	1-2	77	36.3	93	31.0	71	27.1	26	28.9	12	50.0
	3-4	32	15.1	56	18.7	45	17.2	26	28.9	3	12.5
	5-6	16	7.5	15	5.0	12	4.6	10	11.1	1	4.2
	7-8-9	4	1.9	1	0.3	1	0.4	0	0.0	1	4.2
Crowding (upper teeth)	0	108	50.9	143	47.7	134	51.1	40	44.4	12	50.0
	1-2	58	27.4	66	22.0	60	22.9	20	22.2	5	20.8
	3-4	33	15.6	65	21.7	57	21.8	19	21.1	5	20.8
	5-6	11	5.2	21	7.0	9	3.4	11	12.2	1	4.2
	7-8-9	2	0.9	5	1.7	2	0.8	0	0.0	1	4.2
Wear (teeth)	0	0	0.0	3	1.0	3	1.1	2	2.2	0	0.0
	1-2	67	31.6	85	28.3	81	30.9	22	24.4	11	45.8
	3-4	79	37.3	93	31.0	64	24.4	20	22.2	7	29.2
	5-6	56	26.4	62	20.7	53	20.2	28	31.1	3	12.5
	7-8-9	10	4.7	57	19.0	71	27.1	18	20.0	3	12.5
Eye structure striated	0	3	1.4	6	2.0	5	1.9	0	0.0	0	0.0
	1-2	162	76.4	122	40.7	108	41.2	58	64.4	14	58.3
	3-4	39	18.4	133	44.3	109	41.6	28	31.1	9	37.5
	5-6	7	3.3	38	12.7	37	14.1	4	4.4	1	4.2
	7-8	1	0.5	0	0.0	3	1.1	0	0.0	0	0.0
Eye structure cryptose	0	146	68.9	184	61.3	183	69.9	64	71.1	10	41.7
	1-2	41	19.3	57	19.0	38	14.5	14	15.6	7	29.2
	3-4	20	9.4	43	14.3	30	11.5	9	10.0	7	29.2
	5-6	5	2.4	16	5.3	10	3.8	3	3.3	0	0.0
	7-8	0	0.0	0	0.0	1	0.4	0	0.0	0	0.0
Eye structure eroded	0	43	20.3	7	2.3	5	1.9	2	2.2	0	0.0
	1-2	74	34.9	122	40.7	109	41.6	38	42.2	5	20.8
	3-4	83	39.2	163	54.3	137	52.3	45	50.0	17	70.8
	5-6	12	5.7	8	2.7	11	4.2	5	5.6	1	4.2
	7-8	0	0.0	0	0.0	0	0.0	0	0.0	1	4.2

TABLE 21 (Continued)

Variable	Scale	Gadsup		Tairora		Auyana		Awa		Ontenu	
		N	%	N	%	N	%	N	%	N	%
Finger formula	324	31	13.8	48	15.5	9	3.4	4	4.1	1	3.7
	3(4＝2)	58	25.9	102	32.9	61	22.8	23	23.5	7	25.9
	342	135	60.3	160	51.6	197	73.8	71	72.4	19	70.4
Toe formula	123	154	68.7	154	49.7	152	56.9	47	48.0	12	44.4
	213	67	29.9	103	33.2	110	41.2	35	35.7	15	55.6
	(1＝2)3	3	1.3	53	17.1	5	1.9	16	16.3	0	0.0
Handedness	Left	10	4.5	27	8.7	22	8.2	4	4.1	0	0.0
	Right	214	95.5	283	91.3	246	91.9	94	95.9	27	100.0
Earlobes	Attached	99	46.7	166	55.3	144	55.0	33	36.7	6	25.0
	Free	113	53.3	134	44.7	118	45.0	57	63.3	18	75.0

Mid-phalangeal hair is more frequent in Awa and least intense in Tairora (significant) which is contrary to the general hirsuteness trend and may lend some support to the idea that this trait is controlled by an independent allelic series. The assessment of browridge size is very subjective in this study with Auyana showing a significantly greater development than the other three groups. This character had a correlation with age ranging from 0.3 to 0.6.

The incidence and extent of pterygia shows a significant difference between Awa and Gadsup. The trend supports the environmental hypothesis forwarded in Chapter 1 except for Tairora which has a higher rate than Auyana. The dental characters have been discussed above. The scale for the form of occlusion runs from strong overjet (U//L) to strong anterior crossbite (L/U+). It was not possible to examine molar occlusion.

Eye structure (anterior layer of iris) showed considerable variation while eye color did not (consistently medium to dark brown except in "redskins" and albinoes—see below). Striated irises show a highly significant intergroup difference with Gadsup resembling Awa and Tairora close to Auyana. Crypts were relatively rare and the differences insignificant. Eroded pattern frequencies set Gadsup off from the other three groups, which have higher mean rates. No consistent pattern emerges from these data, but the genetics of eye structure is poorly understood.

Finger formula and toe formula are reliable observations, although in the finger pattern the configuration 3-4-2 can be confused for 3(4 = 2) by a light skewing of the fingers; the same holds for 3-2-4 which may make the middle category larger than it should be. Gadsup-Tairora and Auyana-Awa showed no significant difference, all other differences were significant ($P < .025$). Toe formula is much less ambiguous. Auyana had the highest frequency of aristocratic second toes. The Tairora-Awa difference was insignificant, but all other pairs were highly significant ($P < .001$).

Handedness was determined by asking the subject in which hand he held his ax. Seven percent of the sample was left-handed, but no significant differences turned up between groups. Attached earlobes merge easily into the category of "slight free" and a certain amount of imprecision is inevitable. The error in this case probably favors attached earlobes. Tairora-Awa and Auyana-Awa were the only pairs which showed significant differences ($P < .005$).

Hair form showed little variation (medium helical). Balding takes place along with greying in middle age, but no cases of premature balding or greying were noted in the sample. Hair color was dark brown with occasional reddish lights associated with lighter skin color.

Skin color variation was difficult to quantify and subjective measures are virtually useless. Nevertheless, some comment on skin color is required because of the interesting variations which are noted in highland New Guinea. Table 37 in Appendix II lists the Munsell color chip (Munsell Skin Color Charts) numbers for the first twenty-four subjects. The method was so time-consuming that it had to be abandoned, but these figures represent the normal color range (at least for Gadsup). There is a considerable component of red pigment in the skin. Variation in color behaves as if there were two independent systems, one for brown pigments and the other for red. As the brown pigment diminishes, the red is increasingly revealed until a form of melanin albinism takes place in which only the red pigments are left ("redskin"). Four subjects showed this extreme condition and others were observed. The skin is bright rust-color and the eyes tend to light brown or even green. One "redskin" male showed some nystagmus plus a tendency to large melanin spots or freckles on the back.

An extremely redskinned female was observed who, though she had borne at least one child, showed no pigmentation even in the areolar region. Her eyes were light brown and her hair quite reddish gold mixed with brown. With two exceptions these people seem to suffer no undue skin or ocular sensitivity. The two exceptions were males who showed nystagmus, though the degree of light sensitivity they may have experienced is not known.

The "redskin" phenomenon behaves in every way like a complex trait and not like classic albinism. The extreme cases appear simply to be the end of a melanin depigmentation continuum. The problem merits a full-scale study.

Classic albinism also occurs, and several cases were observed in Tairora and Auyana. Not uncommonly it takes the form of white skin with dendritic melanin blotching similar to that reported in African Negroes by Barnicot (1952). Bluish or greenish eyes and, occasionally, nystagmus accompany the condition. In addition six subjects showed piebalding of the skin in various degrees.

4. The Distribution of the Blood Groups

The blood group genes have always held a fascination for the student of ethnogenesis. Their reliability of ascertainment and insensitivity to environmental influence have made them the genetic markers par excellence. The discovery of selection in the blood groups, however, somewhat slowed enthusiasm for reconstructing history on the basis of gene flow. Nevertheless, the isogenic maps which resulted from these earlier studies are still useful over large regions of genetic space. Statements about the presence of S in New Guinea and its absence in Australia, or the observation that New Guinea represents a frequency depression for the gene M are useful as first descriptive approximations. But as the glass is focused on smaller and smaller segments on the genetic landscape, the broad pattern is lost in what begins to look more and more like the Brownian Movement of particles in a seemingly smooth smoke-stream. In a word, drift begins to play a larger role.

Throughout this study we have been attempting to look at a very small piece of genetic space—one whose past behavior in evolutionary terms is poorly understood even in its grosser aspects. The power of our instruments has not been met by a satisfactory resolution of genetic detail. Nowhere is this more apparent than in the case of the blood group genes.

THE SAMPLE

A total sample of 1,163 subjects from twenty-one villages was obtained through cubital venipuncture with Bayer vacuum ampules (8 ml.). The samples were packed in vacuum containers with ice and shipped by air to Sydney, Australia, at the first possible moment. The determinations were done by Dr. R. J. Walsh, then of the Blood Transfusion Service, New South Wales Division, Australian Red Cross. If ice was not available, as sometimes was the case beyond the end of the road, cold river water was placed with the samples and changed frequently until ice could be obtained. This delay was never longer than a day, and most samples arrived in Sydney in good gross condition. Transport times varied from two to ten days, and the fate of such labile groups as P is always a worry. The high homogeneity of the P results (see below) may be an indication of success in this respect.

The blood groups tested were ABO, Rh, MNS, P, Kidd, Tj[a], Fy[a], C[w], Gm[a], Kell, Diego, and haptoglobins and transferrins. Only the first five and the last two showed variation in the sample (Tables 22-29).[1]

ABO (Table 22). No A_2 subgroup was found. The frequency of B is about average to low average for the Eastern Highlands but does not correspond closely with figures reported from this area by Simmons et al. (1961). The two cases of missing B are probably due to inadequate sample size. The B frequencies are much lower than those reported by Giles et al. for the Markham fringe of the study area (1966b). This difference in average frequencies seems to be mainly at the expense of A.

MNS (Table 23). The *S* gene is associated exclusively with *N* and shows relatively low frequencies. *Ms* is interesting in its very low frequency, dropping almost to zero in Awa, especially when compared with lowland frequencies. Except for this, the values of the other alleles are not out of line with those reported for other Eastern Highlands groups.

Rh (Table 24). Only R_1 *(CDe)*, R_2 *(cDE)*, and *Ro (cDe)* genes are present. The variant D[u] appears only in Gadsup in this sample (see Table 29). The frequencies are in accord with both Highland and lowland populations. R_O is very low in frequency especially in Gadsup and Auyana.

P, Kidd (Tables 25, 26). There is very little comparative material

1. The gene frequency calculations were carried out by computer through programs kindly supplied by Dr. Eugene Giles and employing Bernstein's and DeGroot's method for gene frequency and variance in ABO, Mourant's method for MNS, and Boyd's maximum likelihood for Rh. Simple square root and gene counting methods were used for the other loci.

TABLE 22
DISTRIBUTION OF THE ABO BLOOD GROUPS

Village-Complex	Number Tested	O N	O %	A_1 N	A_1 %	B N	B %	A_1B N	A_1B %	p_1	q	r
Gadsup												
02 Puntibasa	53	23	43.40	20	37.74	8	15.09	2	3.77	.2360	.0996	.6644
03 Tompendaka	25	11	44.00	14	56.00	0	...	0	...	.3367	.0000	.6633
04 Sasaura	62	25	40.32	35	56.45	2	3.23	0	...	.3416	.0163	.6421
05 Inkana	53	37	69.81	13	24.53	2	3.77	1	1.89	.1417	.0286	.8296
06 Akuna	63	42	66.67	16	25.40	4	6.35	1	1.59	.1453	.0405	.8142
08 Tompena	27	14	51.85	13	48.15	0	...	0	...	.2799	.0000	.7201
Total	283	152	53.71	111	39.22	16	5.65	4	1.41	.2297	.0360	.7343
Tairora												
09 Batainabura	58	18	31.03	29	50.00	10	17.24	1	1.72	.3160	.1017	.5869
11 Baieanabuta	46	21	45.65	13	28.26	10	21.74	2	4.34	.1795	.1406	.6798
12 Bairinabuta	48	26	54.17	12	25.00	7	14.58	3	6.25	.1694	.1093	.7212
13 Babaraai	44	13	29.55	28	63.64	2	4.55	1	2.27	.4173	.0348	.5479
14 Tondona	43	25	58.14	16	37.21	2	4.65	0	...	.2083	.0236	.7681
16-17 Tonkera, Burauta	50	22	44.00	19	38.00	8	16.00	1	2.00	.2273	.0953	.6774
18 Abiera	39	11	28.21	15	38.46	8	20.51	5	12.82	.2995	.1820	.5184
Total	328	136	41.46	132	40.24	47	14.33	13	3.96	.2539	.0964	.6496
Auyana												
21-22 Amaira/ Avia	59	19	32.20	22	37.29	12	20.34	6	10.17	.2739	.1656	.5604
24 Nankona	45	21	46.67	14	31.11	8	17.78	2	4.44	.1974	.1182	.6844
26-33 "Central Auyana"	73	27	36.99	31	42.47	11	15.07	4	5.48	.2792	.1089	.6119
34 Kawaina	75	39	52.00	17	22.67	13	17.33	6	8.00	.1653	.1342	.7003
Total	252	106	42.06	84	33.33	44	17.46	18	7.14	.2275	.1311	.6414
Awa												
36 Tauna	28	12	42.86	14	50.00	2	7.14	0	...	.2953	.0367	.6680
37 Ilakia	90	39	43.33	36	40.00	13	14.44	2	2.22	.2416	.0878	.6705
38 Mobuta	60	19	31.67	14	23.33	24	40.00	3	5.00	.1554	.2617	.5828
Total	178	70	39.33	64	35.96	39	21.91	5.	2.81	.2200	.1339	.6460
Enclaved group												
19 Ontenu	43	15	34.88	19	44.19	9	20.93	0	...	.2587	.1133	.6275
Ontenu*	55	23	41.82	23	41.82	7	12.73	2	3.64	.2623	.0857	.6520
	98	38	38.78	42	42.86	16	16.33	2	2.04	.2606	.0976	.6417
*Additional Gadsup group**												
Arona	24	14	58.33	5	20.83	5	20.83	0	...	.1111	.1111	.7777
Grand total	1,163	516	44.37	438	37.66	167	14.36	42	3.61	.2343	.0946	.6711

*From the raw data of Watson et al. 1961.

TABLE 23

DISTRIBUTION OF THE MNS BLOOD GROUPS

Village-Complex	Number Tested	Number of Phenotypes						Gene Frequencies		
		NsNs	MsNs	NNS	MMS	MNS	MsMs	Ms	Ns	NS
Gadsup										
02 Puntibasa	53	37	15	0	0	0	1	.1604	.8396	.0000
03 Tompendaka	25	16	7	0	0	0	2	.2200	.7800	.0000
04 Sasaura	62	43	10	7	0	0	2	.1129	.8282	.0589
05 Inkana	53	39	13	0	0	0	1	.1415	.8585	.0000
06 Akuna	63	56	6	1	0	0	0	.0476	.9444	.0080
08 Tompena	27	15	11	0	0	0	1	.2407	.7593	.0000
Total	283	206	62	8	0	0	7	.1343	.8512	.0145
Tairora										
09 Batainabura	58	52	2	4	0	0	0	.1724	.9476	.0351
11 Baieanabuta	46	36	5	5	0	0	0	.0543	.8895	.0561
12 Bairinabuta	48	27	14	4	0	3	0	.1771	.7510	.0719
13 Babaraai	44	33	4	7	0	0	0	.0455	.8713	.0832
14 Tondona	43	28	4	11	0	0	0	.0465	.8157	.1378
16-17 Tonkera, Burauta	50	41	5	3	0	0	1	.0700	.8994	.0306
18 Abiera	39	29	2	8	0	0	0	.0256	.8658	.1085
Total	328	246	36	42	0	3	1	.0625	.8664	.0711
Auyana										
21-22 Amaira/Avia	59	48	1	8	0	1	1	.0339	.8870	.0791
24 Nankona	45	40	5	0	0	0	0	.0556	.9444	.0000
26-33 "Central Auyana"	73	69	2	2	0	0	0	.0137	.9725	.0138
34 Kawaina	75	56	19	0	0	0	0	.1267	.8733	.0000
Total	252	213	27	10	0	1	1	.0595	.9185	.0220
Awa										
36 Tauna	29	26	0	3	0	0	0	.0000	.9469	.0531
37 Ilakia	90	89	0	1	0	0	0	.0000	.9944	.0056
38 Mobuta	60	55	2	3	0	0	0	.0167	.9580	.0253
Total	179	170	2	7	0	0	0	.0056	.9747	.0197
Enclaved group										
19 Ontenu	43	36	5	2	0	0	0	.0581	.9182	.0236
Ontenu*	55	49	5	0	0	1	0	.0545	.9368	.0086
Total	98	85	10	,2	0	1	0	.0561	.9287	.0151
*Additional Gadsup group**										
Arona	24	18	6	0	0	0	0	.1250	.8750	.0000
Grand total	1164	938	143	69	0	5	9	.0713	.8964	.0323

*From the raw data of Watson et al. 1961

for these groups in New Guinea. The frequencies here correspond with the Markham series of Giles, but the frequencies of Jka+ are very low when compared with Western and South Coast New Guinea (Nijenhuis 1961). The sharp drop in Jka− frequencies in Awa is startling but not totally without precedent in the overall sample.

TABLE 24

DISTRIBUTION OF THE RHESUS BLOOD GROUPS

Village-Complex	Number Tested	Number of Phenotypes				Chromosome Frequencies		
		CCDee (R_1R_1)*	CcDEe (R_1R_2)	CcDee (R_1R_0)	ccDEE (R_2R_2)	R_1	R_0	R_2
Gadsup								
02 Puntibasa	53	48	5	0	0	.9528	.0000	.0472
03 Tompendaka	25	23	2	0	0	.9600	.0000	.0400
04 Sasaura	62	59	1	2	0	.9758	.0161	.0081
05 Inkana	53	50	3	0	0	.9717	.0000	.0283
06 Akuna	63	62	1	0	0	.9921	.0000	.0079
08 Tompena	27	27	0	0	0	0000	.0000	.0000
Total	283	269	12	2	0	.9753	.0035	.0212
Tairora								
09 Batainabura	58	56	1	1	0	.9828	.0086	.0086
11 Baieanabuta	46	41	3	1	1	.9348	.0149	.0503
12 Bairinabuta	48	47	1	0	0	.9896	.0000	.0104
13 Babaraai	44	37	6	1	0	.9205	.0114	.0682
14 Tondona	43	36	3	0	0	.9186	.0116	.0698
16-17 Tonkera, Burauta	50	48	1	1	0	.9800	.0100	.0100
18 Abiera	39	36	3	0	0	.9615	.0000	.0385
Total	328	301	21	5	1	.9573	.0081	.0346
Auyana								
21-22 Amaira/Avia	59	50	9	0	0	.9237	.0000	.0763
24 Nankona	45	37	7	1	0	.9111	.0111	.0778
26-33 "Central Auyana"	73	69	4	0	0	.9726	.0000	.0274
34 Kawaina	75	68	7	0	0	.9533	.0000	.0467
Total	252	224	27	1	0	.9444	.0020	.0536
Awa								
36 Tauna	29	23	4	2	0	.8966	.0345	.0690
37 Ilakia	90	87	3	0	0	.9833	.0000	.0167
38 Mobuta	60	41	11	8	0	.8417	.0667	.0917
Total	179	151	18	10	0	.9218	.0279	.0503
Enclaved group								
19 Ontenu	43	31	11	1	0	.8605	.0116	.1279
Ontenu†	55	44	10	0	1	.8909	.0000	.1091
Total	98	75	21	1	1	.8776	.0055	.1169
Additional Gadsup group								
Arona†	24	24	0	0	0	1.0000	.0000	.0000
Grand total	1,164	1,044	99	19	2	.9470	.0081	.0448

*These figures include individuals in Gadsup of $R_1R_1{}^u$ and $R_1{}^uR_1{}^u$ genotypes (see Table 29).

† From the raw data of Watson et al. 1961.

Haptoglobin, transferrin (Tables 27, 28). The results for these groups appear relatively homogeneous with no apparent trends. There is little comparative literature on these groups in New Guinea. Cur-

TABLE 25

DISTRIBUTION OF THE P BLOOD GROUPS

Village-Complex	Number Tested	Number of Phenotypes		Gene Frequencies	
		P −	P +	P_2	P_1
Gadsup					
02 Puntibasa	53	26	27	.7004	.2996
03 Tompendaka	25	12	13	.6928	.3072
04 Sasaura	62	33	29	.7296	.2704
05 Inkana	53	38	15	.8467	.1533
06 Akuna	62	39	23	.7931	.2069
08 Tompena	27	14	13	.7201	.2799
Total	282	162	120	.7579	.2421
Tairora					
09 Batainabura	58	33	25	.7543	.2457
11 Baieanabuta	46	22	24	.6916	.3084
12 Bairinabuta	48	23	25	.6922	.3078
13 Babaraai	44	25	19	.7538	.2462
14 Tondona	43	21	22	.6988	.3012
16-17 Tonkera, Burauta	50	19	31	.6164	.3836
18 Abiera	39	14	25	.5991	.4009
Total	328	157	171	.6919	.3081
Auyana					
21-22 Amaira/Avia	59	24	35	.6378	.3622
24 Nankona	45	23	22	.7149	.2851
26-33 "Central Auyana"	73	36	37	.7022	.2978
34 Kawaina	75	34	41	.6733	.3267
Total	252	117	135	.6814	.3186
Awa					
36 Tauna	29	12	17	.6433	.3567
37 Ilakia	90	51	39	.7528	.2472
38 Mobuta	60	21	39	.5916	.4084
Total	179	84	95	.6850	.3150
Enclaved group					
19 Ontenu	41	18	23	.6626	.3374
Grand total	1,082	538	544	.7051	.2949

tain et al. (1965) report similar gene frequencies for transferrin from the Kainantu study area (based on a few selected villages in Gadsup, Auyana, and Tairora). His reported frequencies for haptoglobin are consistently lower for Hp[1] than those reported here. Giles's data from the Markham (Baumgarten et al. 1968) do not show any appreciable difference with respect to the frequencies of the Kainantu area reported in this study. Curtain's earlier survey (1965) also reported no cases of O.O (or "nil") haptoglobin phenotypes from the Eastern Highlands, whereas the later survey (Baumgarten et al. 1968, Giles's data) and the present results both show instances of this phenotype for every language group in the study area and on the Markham fringe

TABLE 26

DISTRIBUTION OF KIDD (Jk ^{a}) BLOOD GROUPS

Village-Complex	Number Tested	Number of Phenotypes		Gene Frequencies	
		Jk^a −	Jk^a +	JK^a −	JK^a +
Gadsup					
02 Puntibasa	53	25	28	.6868	.3132
03 Tompendaka	25	7	18	.5292	.4709
04 Sasaura*					
05 Inkana	53	13	40	.4953	.5047
06 Akuna	62	17	45	.5236	.4764
08 Tompena	27	11	16	.6383	.3617
Total	220	73	147	.5760	.4240
Tairora					
09 Batainabura*					
11 Baieanabuta	46	13	33	.5316	.4684
12 Bairinabuta	48	18	30	.6124	.3876
13 Babaraai	43	15	28	.5906	.4094
14 Tondona	43	20	23	.6820	.3180
16-17 Tonkera, Burauta	50	21	29	.6481	.3519
18 Abiera	39	23	16	.7679	.2321
Total	269	110	159	.6395	.3605
Auyana					
21-22 Amaira/Avia	59	19	40	.5675	.4325
24 Nankona	45	23	22	.7149	.2851
26-33 "Central Auyana"	73	30	43	.6411	.3589
34 Kawaina	75	30	45	.6325	.3675
Total	252	102	150	.6362	.3638
Awa					
36 Tauna	29	4	25	.3714	.6286
37 Ilakia	90	11	79	.3496	.6504
38 Mobuta*					
Total	119	15	104	.3550	.6450
Enclaved group					
19 Ontenu	17	7	10	.6417	.3583
Grand total	877	307	570	.5917	.4083

* Not tested.

(Wompul, Omisuan, Binumarien, Kusing, and Tumbuna). These apparent discrepancies raise some question concerning the frequencies reported from the *kuru* surveys (Simmons et al. 1961; Curtain et al. 1965; etc.) and possibly with relation to any surveys in a high drift region which are not area-intensive in method.

DISCUSSION

If the village-complex is really a functional isolate then its small size should create a situation in which random sampling errors are influential in determining the frequencies of simple genetic characters,

TABLE 27
DISTRIBUTION OF HAPTOGLOBIN BLOOD GROUPS

Village-Complex	Number Tested	Number of Phenotypes				Gene Frequencies	
		1.1	2.1	2.2	0.0*	Hp^1	Hp^2
Gadsup							
02 Puntibasa	53	31	21	1		.7830	.2170
03 Tompendaka	24	11	13	0	1	.7292	.2708
04 Sasaura	62	19	33	10		.5726	.4274
05 Inkana	53	19	24	10		.5849	.4151
06 Akuna	63	34	25	4		.7381	.2619
08 Tompena	27	9	14	4		.5926	.4074
Total	282	123	130	29	1	.6667	.3333
Tairora							
09 Batainabura	58	39	15	4		.8017	.1983
11 Baieanabuta	45	25	17	3	1	.7444	.2556
12 Bairinabuta	48	18	24	6		.6250	.3750
13 Babaraai	44	26	17	1		.7841	.2159
14 Tondona	43	26	16	1		.7907	.2093
16-17 Tonkera,							
Burauta	50	27	22	1		.7600	.2400
18 Abiera	37	18	17	2	2	.7162	.2838
Total	325	179	128	18	3	.7477	.2523
Auyana							
21-22 Amaira/Avia	59	17	35	7		.5847	.4153
24 Nankona	44	16	23	5	1	.6250	.3750
26-33 "Central Auyana"	71	30	33	8	2	.6549	.3451
34 Kawaina	75	54	20	1		.8533	.1467
Total	249	117	111	21	3	.6928	.3072
Awa							
36 Tauna	29	18	11	0		.8103	.1897
37 Ilakia	85	46	30	9	5	.7176	.2824
38 Mobuta	60	25	29	6	3	.6583	.3417
Total	174	89	70	15	8	.7126	.2874
Enclaved group							
19 Ontenu	39	16	21	2	2	.5513	.4487
Grand total	1,069	524	460	85	17	.7053	.2947

* Not included in calculation.

unless there is damping by strong selective forces or massive gene flow. How much the morphological variables traditionally measured by anthropologists are subject to drift is not known, but a compelling case for sampling variation has been made for blood groups in the recent studies of Simmons et al. (1962) for the Bentinck Islanders of Australia and, more to the point, in the excellent report on drift between two closely related villages in Highland New Guinea by Giles et al. (1966a). The two villages reported by Giles and his colleagues are

TABLE 28
DISTRIBUTION OF TRANSFERRIN BLOOD GROUPS

Village-Complex	Number Tested	Number of Phenotypes			Gene Frequencies	
		CC	CD$_1$	DD	C	D$_1$
Gadsup						
02 Puntibasa	53	33	19	1	.8019	.1981
03 Tompendaka	25	23	2	0	.9600	.0400
04 Sasaura	62	50	11	1	.8952	.1048
05 Inkana	52	33	18	1	.8077	.1923
06 Akuna	63	45	14	4	.8254	.1746
08 Tompena	27	9	14	4	.5926	.4074
Total	282	193	78	11	.8227	.1773
Tairora						
09 Batainabura	58	44	12	2	.8621	.1379
11 Baieanabuta	46	34	12	0	.8696	.1304
12 Bairinabuta	48	39	9	0	.9063	.0937
13 Babaraai	44	36	8	0	.9091	.0909
14 Tondona	43	29	14	0	.8372	.1628
16-17 Tonkera, Burauta	50	43	7	0	.9300	.0700
18 Abiera	38	30	8	0	.8947	.1053
Total	327	255	70	2	.8869	.1131
Auyana						
21-22 Amaira/Avia	59	45	12	2	.8644	.1356
24 Nankona	45	39	6	0	.9333	.0667
26-33 "Central Auyana"	73	59	14	0	.9041	.0959
34 Kawaina	75	61	14	0	.9067	.0933
Total	252	204	46	2	.9008	.0992
Awa						
36 Tauna	29	22	7	0	.8793	.1207
37 Ilakia	90	69	19	2	.8722	.1278
38 Mobuta	63	43	20	0	.8413	.1587
Total	182	134	46	2	.8626	.1374
Enclaved group						
19 Ontenu	41	32	9	0	.8902	.1098
Grand total	1,084	818	249	17	.8695	.1305

located on the periphery of the present study area and are linguistically related to it. Despite the apparent common origin of the two villages, two miles removed from one another, radical differences for gene frequencies were observed in three out of the four blood group loci tested (ABO, MNS, and P; Rh was not significantly different). The size of the two villages is also comparable to the average population size noted for the villages of the present study.

The most powerful forces promoting drift in the Highlands are, in addition to the relative isolation of various small villages and hamlet-clusters, the founding of new villages by small groups of people displaced by warfare, crop failure (cf. Meggitt 1958), or internal disputes, and the tendency of these new groups to grow relatively rapidly thus concealing the small beginnings of the recent past. The effect of small initial numbers may be offset, however, by the practice of smaller isolates receiving a greater proportion of migrants than larger isolates which have produced enough exogamous units within themselves to become more self-sufficient in the acquisition of mates (Littlewood 1966; Meggitt 1962).

The marshaling of circumstantial evidence for drift is necessary since the materials at hand do not permit a clear-cut demonstration of the fact. Drift, however, is probably the best explanation for the erratic distribution of gene frequencies. The few clines which appear between major language groups (*B*, or *q*, in ABO; R_1 in Rh; and *Ms* in MNS) are weak or unconvincing in view of the internal heterogeneity of the village frequencies. The only exception is *Ms* which runs from a high of 13.4 percent in Gadsup to virtual extinction in Awa. A plot against altitude of Giles's data for *Ms* from the Markham (1966b) reveals an extension of this cline to the higher frequencies at the lower elevation. The proportion of this chromosome rises again to the west of the study area and to the south of Anga (see Simmons et al. 1961). The gradient seems real enough, dropping quickly in eastern Tairora, Auyana, and Awa, but Kawaina provides a notable break, arguing once again for the operation of random factors.

The D^u variant of Rh, first revealed in this area by Watson et al. (1961), is confined in this study to the Gadsup area (Table 29). In the original study Watson found cases in Auyana, Tairora, and Agarabi as well as Gadsup. Giles et al. (1966b) found high frequencies of the gene on the eastern periphery of Gadsup and pointed out that twenty-seven of the twenty-eight individuals discovered in the two studies were located in an area only twenty-five by thirty-five miles square. The present data reinforce this impression and locate the highest frequencies in the central and eastern Gadsup region.

One of the most erratic of all the loci reported in this study is the Kidd blood group, which drops suddenly in the frequency of the Jk^b gene in Awa. At least two different donors provided anti-sera during the period of testing and this may have biased the accuracy of the determination. However, the low value for Inkana (05) was obtained

TABLE 29

DISTRIBUTION OF THE D^u VARIANT OF Rh IN THE GADSUP LANGUAGE AREA

Village-Complex	Number Tested	Phenotypes				Chromosome Frequency	
		$CCDee + CCDD^uee$ $(R_1R + R_1R_1{}^u)$		CCD^uD^uee $(R_1{}^uR_1{}^u)$		R_1	$R_1{}^u$
		N	%	N	%		
02 Puntibasa	53	47	88.68	1	1.89	.8153	.1375
03 Tompendaka	25	23	92.00	0	. . .	.9600	.0000
04 Sasaura	62	51	82.26	8	12.90	.6166	.3592
05 Inkana	53	44	83.02	6	11.32	.6352	.3365
06 Akuna	63	59	93.65	3	4.76	.7739	.2182
08 Tompena	27	25	92.59	2	7.41	.7278	.2722
Arona*	24	20	83.33	4	16.67	.5917	.4083
Total	307	269	87.62	24	7.81	.6958	.2795

* From the raw data of Watson et al. 1961.

early in the field period and the low values for Awa near the end of the study.

In the face of this variability what reliance can be placed on pooled estimates of gene frequencies? For purposes of assessing genetic changes over large, even continental areas, such estimates are better than relying on a single village or two to represent a whole language area. The gene frequencies reported by Simmons et al. (1961) for "Auyana," "Awa," and so on, bear little relationship to the average figures or in some cases to the pattern of village frequencies reported here. This is not a matter of repeatability of sampling (cf. Watson's Ontenu figures versus mine in Tables 22, 23, 24) but rather a result of picking one village to represent a larger entity. Table 30 presents the results of a series of homogeneity tests (after Neel and Schull 1954) run for seven blood group loci. Such a test asks the question of whether the samples included could have been selected from the same universe. This is clearly not the case in about half the cells of the table. Rh, Haptoglobin, P, Kidd, and Transferrin demonstrate less heterogeneity than ABO and MN. The nonsignificant result for MN in Awa is probably due to the fact that the *n* gene is virtually fixed in that group. Giles et al. (1966b) reports similar results for language groups in the Morobe District where, however, Kidd appears to be much less variable and P much more so.

Gadsup shows the least homogeneity (four out of five loci). This may be a reflection of the polarization between east and west apparent

TABLE 30

HOMOGENEITY TESTS FOR SEVEN BLOOD GROUP LOCI

Locus	Gadsup		Tairora		Auyana		Awa	
	Chi-Square	Probability	Chi-Square	Probability	Chi-Square	Probability	Chi-Square	Probability
ABO	35.65	.001	34.15	.001	8.61	N.S.	29.42	.001
MN	17.73	.005	28.33	.001	18.99	.001	4.13	N.S.
Rh	not calcu-lated	N.S.	12.80	N.S.	4.44	N.S.	10.28	.050
Haptoglobin	19.64	.005	11.39	N.S.	27.49	.001	4.45	N.S.
Transferrin	31.03	.005	5.58	N.S.	2.85	N.S.	0.86	N.S.
Kidd	7.91	.050	9.44	.050	3.85	N.S.	1.62	N.S.
P	3.69	N.S.	4.53	N.S.	0.95	N.S.	4.39	N.S.

Note: In the case of ABO and Rh, the alleles A, B and R_1, R_2 were used in the test and in that order.

in the migrational and metrical data (Chapters 2 and 3), but inspection of the blood frequencies themselves reveals no corresponding dichotomy. Auyana and Awa appear the least variable. In the former the two significant results (for MN and Haptoglobin) seem to rest largely on the aberrant frequencies in Kawaina (34), the most isolated of the major segments of that language group. In Awa the two significant heterogeneity levels (ABO and Rh) again depend upon one village, Mobuta (38) where $B(q)$ takes the highest value in the study area and R_1 the lowest. Mobuta is more isolated than its neighbors to the north both in absolute terms and relative to the northern Awa groups.

It is tempting to speculate on the possible role of various evolutionary agencies in producing homogeneity and heterogeneity. Many loci are fixed in this area as well as in surrounding parts of highland and lowland New Guinea (Giles et al. 1966b). In this study extensive testing (but not total) for Tj[a], Fy[a], C[w], Kell, and Diego produced all positives for the first two loci and all negatives for the last three. Gm[a] showed positive results with the exception of three subjects.[2] Certain alleles such as S in MNS and Ro in the Rh appear to be close to extinction and did not turn up in several samples, although no language

2. Field nos. 307 (Puntibasa 02), 590-11 (Nankona 24), and 1100-39 (Ilakia 37).

group was completely devoid of them. Selection cannot of course, be eliminated as a cause of the observed pattern, but drift (in addition to errors in small field samples) is an efficient cause of extinction for low frequency alleles. Theoretically, the operation of drift alone over long periods of time should reduce within-groups variability (by extinction and fixation) and increase between-groups variability (by dispersing gene frequencies and, ultimately, by the arbitrary fixation of alternate alleles). Gene flow and selection can upset the course of such dispersive tendencies and, within a relatively small genetic space, reduce the intergroup variability. Where such variability is low and allelic frequencies are characterized by values nearer the middle rather than the limits of their range, selection for a balanced or transitional polymorphism may be hypothetically indicated.

With regard to selection, the question we must ask is whether the study area is a genetically large or a genetically small space. That is, are ecological conditions different enough between, say, Awa and Gadsup to have produced by selection a noticeable genetic variation? The selective landscape is complicated by pockets of disease (e.g., goitre, malaria), and the possibility of localized epidemics in the past —dysentery, for example, although Charles Nelson (personal communication, 1966) suggests that bacillary dysentery first entered the Highlands as late as the 1940's. Nutritional stresses occasioned by warfare or crop failure may also have complicated the selective picture. I have already discussed the acculturational gradient in the study area, and changes in selective pressure which are associated with this cline (see Chap 1, note 4) should produce directional and relatively smooth genetic changes from Gadsup to Awa.

Gene flow has the tendency to reduce genetic variability between proximate groups and increase it over longer genetic distances (measured by the strength and frequency of intervening isolate boundaries). In any event, it is not a question of selection versus drift, gene flow versus selection, and so forth, but of the *relative* strength of these agencies. Where drift is very high, especially in small founder populations, selection may have little influence unless it is extremely intense. None of the loci tested here are subject to high selective pressures (comparable to the hemoglobins, for example), although all have been suggested at one time or another to be susceptible to selective agencies, the evidence for some groups being quite impressive (Race and Sanger 1962). As a consequence, drift may be expected to play a large role in generating the observed variability.

In an attempt to discover the general trends of differentiation between the language groups, another version of an homogeneity test was employed. This method is the one developed by Sangvhi (1953) for comparing pairs of populations by chi-square methods. Table 31 shows the results of this test. Sangvhi also proposed the use of the sum of the chi-square values divided by the total degrees of freedom as a form of distance statistic (Table 31 lists only the total chi-squares in the right-hand column).[3] Of all the loci ABO, MN, and Kidd show the greatest degree of differentiation between groups. From the foregoing discussion and the results of the earlier homogeneity test it is apparent that we are including, in the summed chi-square, variables which are very different in their heterogeneity patterns. In order to attempt to get more information out of the table, the variables were divided into two sets: a high heterogeneity set (ABO, MN, and Haptoglobin), and a high homogeneity set (Rh, Transferrin, and P). Kidd is problematic, but the peculiar frequencies in the rather small Awa sample tempt me to eliminate it.

TABLE 31

VALUES OF CHI-SQUARE FOR INTERGROUP DIFFERENCES
WITH RESPECT TO BLOOD GROUPS

Group Pair	Blood Groups							Total X^2 (D.F. = 13)
	ABO	MN	Rh	P	Kidd	Hapto-globin	Trans-ferrin	
Gadsup-Tairora	6.51a	5.82a	.78	1.64	1.36	2.80	3.48	22.29
Gadsup-Auyana	11.76d	6.68c	4.46	2.42	1.06	2.80	5.12	34.30
Gadsup-Awa	12.68d	24.20e	6.84b	2.00	11.30e	1.00	2.22	60.24
Tairora-Auyana	1.80	.04	3.52	.08	.02	1.32	.30	7.08
Tairora-Awa	2.36	9.94d	3.36	.02	19.88e	.78	.44	36.78
Auyana-Awa	2.50	8.88c	6.18	.02	18.72e	.52	1.46	38.28

Statistical significance—a: P < .10; b: P < .05; c: P < .025; d: P < .01; e: P < .005.

Note: This is not a sensitive chi-square method, and the statements of "significance" should be used only for rough ranking purposes.

Table 32 lists the resulting summed chi-squares divided by their respective degrees of freedom. Only two patterns emerge: the rather large differences between Gadsup and both Auyana and Awa, and the

3. The temptation to use chi-square as a distance measure in the manner of Sanghvi (1953) and Pollitzer (1958) is probably not legitimate. I have used the statistic here as a measure of relative strength of difference between paired groups and not as a distance measure.

TABLE 32

SUMMED CHI-SQUARE VALUES, DIVIDED BY DEGREES OF FREEDOM, FOR BLOOD
GROUPS SHOWING HIGH HETEROGENEITY AND HIGH HOMOGENEITY

	ABO/MN/ Haptoglobin	Rh/Transferrin/P	All Groups (including Kidd)
Gadsup-Tairora	2.16	1.18	1.71
Gadsup-Auyana	3.03	2.40	2.64
Gadsup-Awa	5.41	2.21	4.63
Tairora-Auyana	.45	.78	.54
Tairora-Awa	1.87	.76	2.83
Auyana-Awa	1.70	1.53	2.94

consistent closeness of Tairora and Auyana. Both findings conform to the results of the discriminant analysis of metrical variables and to the separation of groups (particularly females) created by the first two canonical variables. On the basis of the migrational data (Table 2) I am inclined to think that this similarity between Auyana and Tairora is due to gene flow between these two adjacent groups. In a similar fashion the larger differences in the table may be explained on the basis of reduced gene flow between Gadsup and Auyana and Gadsup and Awa. Ethnographic evidence, as well as the results of the migrational and discriminant analyses, supports this contention. If the results of the Kidd locus are excluded, the difference between Gadsup and Tairora is seen to be greater than that between Tairora and its two neighbors, Auyana and Awa. Ethnohistorical accounts of hostility between the first two groups may account for such dissimilarity.

I hesitate to push the results any further. What kind of distance measure chi-square values constitute is a moot point, especially when dealing with monofactorial traits and random dispersive agencies. I think that one may safely pay attention to patterns of consistently wide difference and close similarity, but beyond this one's own hypotheses and the accumulation of circumstantial evidence are too liable to bias refined conclusions.

5. Summary and Conclusions

Physical anthropological monographs traditionally marshal their descriptive materials for an outward, comparative look at other ethnic entities. This study has taken similar materials and attempted to look inward, into the labyrinth, to see if the history of a relatively small area can be disentangled through an understanding of biological differences. The focus is not narrow enough to shed light upon specific microevolutionary agencies, nor is it broad enough to generalize about problems of highland entry, relationships to the greater Southwest Pacific, and the like. It is a middle-range focus on the order of Pollitzer's study of the Charleston Negro (1958) and the many Indian studies of caste relationships such as those of Majumdar et al. (1949, 1958), Sangvhi (1953), and most recently, Karve and Mulhotra (1968). The impetus for the study was the larger ethnographic question of the causes and results of the fission of formerly unitary human communities into two or more culturally distinctive entities.

The methods employed were borrowed here and there from earlier attempts of other workers on the basis of their suitability to the materials at hand and their agreeableness to my own imperfect understanding of statistics. Since the methods are not new, the only assuredly novel aspect of this work is the presentation of data on an hitherto unexamined people.

The application of distance measures to these data, however, is not without methodological interest. The early efforts of such workers as Czekanowski, Pearson, Morant, Mahalanobis, and Rao suffered a partial eclipse with the advent of the new philosopher's stone—serology. A few individuals, working with serologically recalcitrant populations of teeth, fossils, and burials, utilized and improved upon the earlier techniques, and, with the dimming of the serological passion and the rise of computing technology, a new interest in traditional questions and data has emerged. The new phase, scarcely two decades old, is marked by a clear sense of experimentation and a groping for the biological sense of the staitstical results (see, especially, Hiernaux 1956, 1963, and Howells 1966b). The nature of both the data and the method has been called into question, and occasionally one hears dim but desperate pleas for standardization of technique—a sure sign of growth.

Tomorrow will hopefully bring a better methodology and tomorrow may provide better data, but at the moment this study can best be looked upon as an experiment in present techniques. Though I have professed to simplify the descriptive burden I am conscious of the fact that the reader has been asked to struggle through some very turgid presentation. The data must speak for themselves as to their relevance or uniqueness, depending upon the reader's particular interests. I shall only attempt here to summarize the results of the tests of difference between the various study groups.

The only nonbiological basis at present for an assessment of distance between groups in the Kainantu Language Family are the lexicostatistical and phonostatistical figures of McKaughan and Wurm, cited by McKaughan (1964, 1972). In general, he finds that Tairora is clearly the most divergent of the four major languages, while Gadsup, Auyana, and Awa are similar enough to each other to be placed in a subgroup which he calls Gauwa. The present position of Tairora, which completely interdicts Gadsup and Auyana, is seen as the result of a later intrusion. No ethnohistorical evidence refutes this view and there is some to support it. It is interesting, then, to compare the biological distances with the linguistic ones. Table 33 gives difference measures for phonostatistics, lexicostatistics, canonical distance using males only, canonical distance for females, the sum of mean metrical differences for males (from Table 7), and the chi-square results from the blood data. The ranking of the distances (0 for closest to 5 for farthest) accompanies each list simply to facilitate inspection, and, in the same vein, an average of the biological rankings is presented.

The two sets of data, linguistic and biological, agree quite well within themselves but are highly discordant with one another. The rankings obscure the magnitude of differences in several cases but

TABLE 33

Summary of Various Distance Measures and Their Rankings

Group Pair	Phonological Mean Degrees of Difference		Lexicostatistical Percentage, Cognate Difference*		Canonical Distance: Males		Canonical Distance: Females		Mean Difference: Males		Blood Total Chi-Square		Rank Average for Biological Distance
Gadsup-Tairora	3.30	(2)	51.4	(4)	2.25	(4)	2.73	(1)	8.74	(0)	1.71	(1)	1.5
Gadsup-Auyana	2.78	(1)	40.0	(1)	2.23	(3)	3.16	(2)	11.54	(3)	2.64	(2)	2.5
Gadsup-Awa	3.41	(3)	48.2	(2)	2.89	(5)	3.79	(5)	18.96	(5)	4.63	(5)	5.0
Tairora-Auyana	3.76	(4)	52.7	(5)	1.56	(0)	2.56	(0)	8.80	(1)	0.54	(0)	0.25
Tairora-Awa	4.08	(5)	51.2	(3)	1.94	(2)	3.42	(3)	15.53	(4)	2.83	(3)	3.0
Auyana-Awa	2.70	(0)	40.1	(0)	1.86	(1)	3.44	(4)	10.79	(2)	2.94	(4)	2.75

Note: Number in parentheses shows rank.

* This figure is the average percentage of the probable shared cognates of McKaughan's (1964) Lists I and II subtracted from 100 percent.

† The canonical distance was calculated as the square root of the sum of the squares of the distances on each canonical axis.

demonstrate the pattern very nicely. In the linguistic data there is good agreement on the closest pairs—Auyana-Awa and Gadsup-Auyana. The two pairs farthest from each other are Tairora-Auyana and Tairora-Awa. In the biological list the most striking contrast is found in the consistent closeness of Tairora-Auyana. In every case the biological distance between Gadsup and Awa is the greatest. The other consistent pattern to emerge from the biological list finds the top two pairs (Gadsup-Tairora, Gadsup-Auyana) similar in magnitude and the bottom two pairs (Tairora-Awa, Auyana-Awa) likewise similar in the degree of difference. Fluctuations in rank make further refinement too ambitious, but there does seem to be a tendency for the Gadsup-Auyana distance to be greater than the Gadsup-Tairora distance, in strong contrast to the linguistic evidence.

If we look within the biological list itself we see that the mean difference list compares least favorably with the others and that the male canonical values are not concordant in detail with the female and blood lists. The correlation between the latter two lists is striking ($r = .963$, $P < .01$). The male canonical list is more poorly correlated with the blood list ($r = .80$, $P = .05$) and shows even less association with the female list ($r = .61$). The mean difference values in turn have a low correlation with the male canonical figures ($r = .69$) and, if truth can be measured by consensus, appear to be the poorest discriminators of the lot. Needless to say, such an assertion is not testable in the present case, and the high level of agreement on the major differences and similarities is the most interesting feature of the biological variables.

In spite of the earlier caveats about the vagaries of blood group behavior, they have, in the last analysis, supported the metrical findings. The groups which contributed most to the chi-square—ABO, MNS, and Kidd—are three of the four most heterogeneous in the study area. If the hypothesis is correct that drift is the primary cause of such heterogeneity for the blood groups, then the question arises as to the cause of similar differences in the metrical variables. The one clear factor which correlates the two is distance, not language. Whether this distance is geographic, topographic, nutritional, acculturational, or something else cannot be determined at present. Time cannot be separated from space, especially where population movements are relatively slow and fragmentary (Birdsell 1950), and drift-responsive loci may be a better measure of such space-time than the more inertial polygenic loci. In sum, space with its attendant environmental gradients could have produced the plastic and selective clines in morphological variables while drift, through time of separation and founder effects, dispersed the frequencies of the environmentally insulated traits. The blood group genes do not, in general, evidence clines but they do show striking dispersal.

If the morphological variables are space-dependent in a uniform way, and they seem to be, then the problem of language barriers and discordances remains to be tackled. Two suggestions come to mind. The first of these is that environmental factors override linguistic differences and that immigrants of roughly the same genetic make-up, living under the same conditions would come to resemble their hosts, just as immigrants to the New World have approached the norms of the recipient population. The Tairora may be responding in this fashion. A further study of the Tairora of the extreme south (who appear to be shorter in stature) might throw light on this conjecture.

The other suggestion is that the gene flow rates reported here between the major language groups are not accurate representations of the historical reality. Gene flow may have operated effectively across language boundaries for some time in such a manner as to produce a zone of transition between the taller Markham peoples and the shorter populations in Anga (Kukukuku) to the south of Awa. This possibility is quite intriguing, but depends for its reasonableness upon the acquisition of morphological data from these two polar areas.

To summarize these ideas briefly we may hypothesize, on theoretical grounds, the probable operation of the following agents in creating the observed diversity:

1. For polygenic loci and environmentally sensitive traits an ecological gradient from northeast to southwest would result in a selection gradient. The first response to such a cline would be plastic, that is, primarily phenotypic without genotypic shifts. The present evidence may simply reflect this.

2. For these same traits, a true genetic cline may be in evidence due to the selective gradient. Attempts to distinguish genetic from plastic change failed in this study in the sense that traits with high heritability scores from twin studies were not positively correlated with the dicriminant power of these same variables (Chap. 3). Conversely, however, it is not demonstrated that a genetic cline does not exist for two reasons: (A) the plastic and genetic responses for the same variable will be in the same direction and are not separable by the methods employed in this study, and (B) the meaningfulness of herita-

bility scores used in this study (and in general) is still questionable in terms of both validity and reliability.

3. Genetically simple traits which are not responding to strong selective forces or gene flow conditions will tend, under the present demographic situation, to increase in intergroup variability (i.e., dispersion of allelic frequencies) due to the stochastic nature of drift. This can produce rapid divergence in gene frequencies just as the ecological gradient produces a relatively swift plastic divergence; the former will, however, be nonclinal in appearance while the latter may appear clinal. Both of these results could be inferred from the present data.

4. Both simple and complex genetic traits could be influenced by a gene flow gradient across the study region generated by widely differing external groups at the poles of the cline (in this case the Anga versus the Markham peoples). The fact that smooth clines in the blood groups are not readily apparent diminishes slightly the force of this suggestion. Two factors cloud this interpretation: (A) the Anga region is biologically and ethnographically very poorly known, and (B) drift may operate rapidly enough to disrupt gradient formation in the monofactorial traits.

5. Regardless of what interpretation is placed on the results, the most prominent fact that emerges is the consistent discordance between the cultural-linguistic and the biological evidence. Since the demographic data indicate that language (both language, *sensu stricto,* and dialect) does produce breaks in the gene flow pattern we cannot conclude that that agency was primarily accountable for the submergence of Tairora's biological individuality vis-à-vis the other language groups. But, it is enough to suggest that plastic (if not selective) and random forces (drift) may override the distinctions imposed by demographic isolation, and indeed, in the case of drift, can be augmented by such barriers. Language distance may not, in many cases, be correlated with biological distance, but it is not necessary to invoke gene flow across linguistic boundaries to account for the fact (cf. Livingstone 1963; Howells 1966b).

6. It is most likely that all of these forces have been at work in producing the observed result, and a case could be made for short-term microevolutionary agencies predominating. The genetic affinities implied by the lexicostatistical data are not thereby denied—they are simply covered over.

In conclusion I should like to point out that New Guinea is an excellent area in which to test some of the ideas which are re-emerging in physical anthropology. With increasing acculturation the time for such studies grows short.

Appendix I: Field Methods and Techniques

It is frequently the case that the comparability of data from different studies is unknown simply because the authors have neglected to make explicit the particular mode of gathering the observations (Coon 1939:241-45). Since all observations within this study were made by a single observer the problem of comparability or "personal equation" within the study area was minimized except insofar as continued practice tended to reduce variation. Nevertheless, since one of the purposes of the study was to provide descriptive materials for other workers it is necessary to discuss my own idiosyncracies.[1] Not only will such a discussion aid others in selecting comparable data, it should also provide a basis for critical assessment of the present study and a dismal warning concerning some of the difficulties to be encountered in the field.

My previous experience at the outset consisted in one summer's work collecting anthropometric and anthroposcopic material among the Nez Perce Indians of Idaho. Serological samples had also been collected, and dental casting technique was learned at the expense of several classes of nervous freshmen students. Anthropometric techniques generally followed the methods of Hooton (1946) which in turn derive from Martin (1928). In the following discussion the sequence of descriptions follows that of the actual field protocol.

1. Careful readers will note the absence of any reference to bi-iliac diameter. This can only be laid to youthful incompetence. By the time I decided to consider it the sample was well started and, mindful of the computer's reluctance to negotiate missing data, I relegated its loss to the realm of neurotic self-recrimination for the remainder of the study.

NEW GUINEA MICROEVOLUTION PROJECT

Field No. ....

Blood ....
Dental ....

Name .... Place .... Date ....
Own Tribe .... Own Hamlet ....
Age .... Sex .... Birthplace .... Birth Order ....
Father .... Fa's Birthplace ....
Mother .... Mo's Birthplace ....
MoMo .... MoFa .... FaMo .... FaFa ....
Spouses ....
Bros .... Sis ....
Children ....
Med. History .... Reel .... Frames ....

1. Weight .... E.					
2. __Stature .... E.					
3. Troch. Ht. .... E.					
4. __Tib. Ht.					
5. Sphy. Ht.					
6. __Humeral					
7. Radial .... E.					
8. __Sitting .... E.					
9. Biacromial .... E.					
10. __Head Ht.					
11. Hand L.					
12. __Hand W.					
13. Head L.					
14. __Head B.					
15. Basal B.					
16. __Min. Fron.					
17. Bizygomatic					
18. __Bigonial					
19. Tot. Fac.					
20. __Up. Fac.					
21. Mand. D.					
22. __Nasal H.					
23. Nasal B.					
24. __Nasal D.					
25. Palatal D.					
26. Bicanine D.					
27. Biincisor D.					
28. __Skinfolds					
a. Dors. Arm					
b. **subscap.**					
29. __Circumferences					
a. Up. Arm					
b. Calf					
30. **chest girth**					
31.					
32.					

Hirsuitness

	Abs.	Sm.	+	+ +	+ + +
Body.					
Beard.					
N. Tip.					
Trag.					
2d Pha.					
Carun.					

Hair form
1. Str.
2. L. Wave
3. D. Wave
4. Loose Helical
5. Medium Helical
6. Tight Helical

Widow's Peak
1. Abs.   Sm.   +   + +   + + +

Baldness

	Front.	Occip.
	Abs.	Abs.
	Sm.	Sm.
	+	+
	+ +	+ +
	+ + +	+ + +
	Compl.	

Grayness

	Head	Beard
	Abs.	Abs.
	Sm.	Sm.
	+	+
	+ +	+ +
	+ + +	+ + +

Texture (Head)
Fine + Coarse Wiry

Browridges
Abs.   Sm.   +
+ +   + + +

Type
Med.   Div.   Front.

Nasal Profile
Concave,   Straight
Convex (high, low)
Tip Snub.

Eye Folds

	Ex.	Med.	Int.
Abs.			
Sm.			
+			
+ +			

Chin
Abs.   Med.   Bilateral
Sm.   +   + +   + + +

Prognathism

	Alv.	M-F	Tot.
Abs.			
Sm.			
+			
+ +			
+ + +			

Comments:

(FINGERPRINTS)

Pigmentation

Skin

Munsell

Exposed..............................

Unexposed..........................

Comments

Head Hair

Melanin	*Red-Gold*
White	Abs.
Ash-Bl.	Golden
Lt. Brn.	+
Med. "	+ +
Dk. "	+ + +
Black	

Hair Whorl

Clock, Counter, Dbl.

Eyes

Status

1. Pure Lt.
2. Mixed
3. Homo. Dark
4. Dark 2-tone

Structure

1. Striated
2. Cryptose
3. Eroded
4. Ridged
5. Scallop & Edge
6. Scalloped

Color Pattern

1. Even
2. Color Crypt
3. Zoned
4. Dbl. Zoned

Arci Senilis.......................

Cloudiness

....

Background

1. Lgt. Bl.-Gray
2. Med. Blue (Dk)
3. Med. Gray (Dk)
4. Green
5. Dk. Green
6. Light Brown
7. Med. Brown
8. Dark Brown
9. "Black"

Detail Color

1. White-Gray
2. Yellow
3. Orange
4. Red-Brown
5. Med. Brown
6. Dark Brown

Detail Area

V. sm. + ++ +++

Specks

Abs. No. Pres.................

Handedness

Rt. Lf. Ambi.

Finger formula

....

Toe formula

....

Thumb. Hyp. Ext.

Degrees.............................

Helix

Flat Sl. roll

\+ ++

Darwin's pt.

Rt............ Lf............

Tubercle

Rt............ Lf............

Lobe

None

Soldered

Attached

Free (+ ++ +++)

Dental Eruption Complete Partial

Loss

8 7 6 5 4 3 2 1 | 1 2 3 4 5 6 7 8
8 7 6 5 4 3 2 1 | 1 2 3 4 5 6 7 8

Un-erupt

8 7 6 5 4 3 2 1 | 1 2 3 4 5 6 7 8
8 7 6 5 4 3 2 1 | 1 2 3 4 5 6 7 8

Caries

8 7 6 5 4 3 2 1 | 1 2 3 4 5 6 7 8
8 7 6 5 4 3 2 1 | 1 2 3 4 5 6 7 8

Shovel-shape

3 2 1 | 1 2 3
3 2 1 | 1 2 3

Bite U//L U/L U-L L/U

Anomalous Cusps Bolk's..

Carabelli.. Other..........................

Supernumerary ....

Missing.. *Crowding*..........................

Comments:

RT | 1 | 2 | 3 | 4

(FINGERPRINTS)

Figure 15. Field data blank used by the New Guinea Micro-evolution Project

The subject's name, the place and date of observation, and the subject's own major language group and current place of residence were recorded. An age estimation was made followed by an error term (e.g., ± 5 years, etc.) to indicate how good the guess might be. The subject's place of birth was determined by employing either one or both of the following pidgin questions: "Yu kamapim long wanem ples?" or "Mama i-karim yu long wanem ples?" The response could usually be verified as referring to a definite group of dwellings by direct observation and was reinforced by consensus. Birth order was recorded but siblings who died young were probably differentially remembered reducing the accuracy of this datum.

Parents' and grandparents' names and birthplaces were obtained although the informant's memory began to sag at the second ascending generation and bystanders were often called in to supply the missing grandparent. Spouses' names were obtained, in order, as well as the names of living and dead siblings until recording the latter became too time-consuming (after about three-hundred subjects had been interviewed). Finally, the number and sex of living and dead children were recorded.

A series of two, full-length, black and white photographs (front and side views) were taken with a 35 mm. reflex camera using a 135 mm. telephoto lens to reduce parallax. A high-speed film was found to be most satisfactory because its gray-scale range was wider and the effect of shadow on dark skin was minimized. Posing of the subjects was casual and a backdrop was not needed due to the short depth-of-field of the telephoto.

Weight was measured by a Seabeck scale using a bamboo tripod and a cargo-box lid for a platform.

Stature was taken by anthropometer, with a cargo-box as a level platform and with the subject instructed to look at the horizon.

Trochanteric, tibiale, and *sphyrion* heights were taken with the anthropometer, with the subject in the same position. Landmarks were palpated and the measurements taken with the thumb in position on the landmark.

Humeral and *radial* lengths were obtained with the anthropometer as sliding caliper. A felt-pen was used for landmarks. *Acromion* was the most difficult landmark to determine in this series.

Biacromial width, hand length (from the base of the palm), and *hand width* were taken with the anthropometer as sliding caliper. Missing terminal phalangeal segments due to mourning practices sometimes complicated the hand length measure. (Upon the death of a relative, it is the custom to remove one or more segments of the fingers of young females.)

Head height was measured from *tragion* to *vertex* by the anthropometer used as sliding caliper (Hooton 1946:758). Since I had no assistant to check the orientation of the caliper a clip-on device employing two spirit-levels at right angels to each other and to the axis of the caliper was devised to assure approximation to the vertical. The subject was told to look at the horizon. While I had little faith in the measure it turned out to be one of the more effective discriminating variables (Chap. 3).

All vertical dimensions were obtained from the left side of the subject unless deformity or injury made this impossible.

Head length and *head breadth* were measured in the conventional manner with the spreading caliper.

Basal breadth was measured with the spreading caliper as the maximum distance between the supramastoid sulci.

Minimum frontal was taken with the spreading caliper as the minimum separation of the temporal line above the orbits. Since this feature was well defined on most subjects the measurement was felt to be quite reliable.

Bizygomatic and *bigonial* diameters were taken at their maxima by spreading caliper.

Total facial height was measured by sliding caliper from nasion (taken as the angle of the nasal root and the pronounced glabellar protrusion) to gnathion. Edentulous condition was noted in this as in other measures which included the teeth.

Upper facial height was taken to prosthion without moving the upper arm of the sliding caliper from the previous position.

Nasal height was measured, in a similar manner, to subnasale. Since the tip of the nose often dropped as a result of a pierced septum it was necessary to lift the tip with the sliding arm of the caliper.

Nasal breadth was taken by sliding caliper as the maximum separation of the alae.

Nasal depth was measured from pronasale to the crease of the ala by sighting along the caliper. Due to the possible deformity of the nasal tip by the practice of nose-piercing, the reliability of this measure is suspect. However, it turned out to be a powerful factor in the discriminant analysis (Chap. 3).

Palatal (molar), bicanine, and *biincisor* diameters were measured as the maximum separation of the labial or distal aspects of the teeth involved. Cases of extreme crowding or tooth rotation were noted.

Skinfold thickness was measured by means of the Lange skinfold caliper at the inferior angle of the scapula and at a point midway on the dorsal aspect of the upper arm.

Circumferences of upper arm, calf, and chest were taken with steel tape rule. The arm circumference was measured at the same level as the skinfold observation and the calf at its maximum width. Chest girth was taken at the inferior border of the pectorals in males and at the inferior crease of the breasts in females.

The anthroposcopic observations are highly subjective and probably only useful for purposes of the present study. Skin color is a very interesting phenomenon in highland New Guinea and an attempt was made to employ the Munsell Skin Color Charts to get some objective measure of it. Problems of lighting, cleansing the skin, and manipulating the book itself became so time-consuming that it was abandoned after the first twenty-four subjects and a subjective evaluation was recorded instead.

Fingerprints were taken directly on the data cards which seemed convenient at the time but discouraged the later manipulation of the cards for fear of blurring the images. The whole process up to this point took about twenty-five minutes per subject. All data cards were photographed in the field to provide a duplicate record.

Serological samples were obtained at the termination of a stay in a given village since it was often necessary to walk upwards of a day to get to a source of ice, much less to transportation by air to the coast and on to Australia. The method used was cubital venipuncture, with 8 ml. Bayer vacuum ampules without additives. The ampules were then placed in thermos jugs and immersed in cold river water if ice was not available immediately. No samples were lost due to spoilage between the field and Sydney, but the effect on some of the more labile groups such as P is not known.

A special session was usually reserved for making dental casts. Large trays were required and two people could be run at one time. An alginate material served for the impression, and the molds were poured up with dental stone immediately. In this manner few trays were required, the dimensional accuracy of the casts was assured, and any errors could be immediately corrected by taking a second impression. Interestingly enough none of the 218 subjects exhibited any tension or gagging reflex. With practice, the taking of dental impressions is a fairly rapid and easy process. Considering the relatively small number of casts series which have been made on populations untouched by dental therapy and prosthesis, it is to be regretted that such permanent data are not more routinely acquired.

Appendix II: Other Morphological Data

TABLE 34

MEANS AND STANDARD DEVIATIONS FOR 29 MEASUREMENTS FOR MALES IN THE 29 VILLAGE-COMPLEXES

Measurement No.	Variable	Village-Complex											
		02 (N = 49)		03 (N = 25)		05 (N = 39)		06 (N = 45)		07 (N = 27)		08 (N = 27)	
		$\bar{x}$	S.D.	$\bar{x}$	S.D.	$\bar{x}$	S.D.	$\bar{x}$	S.D.	$\bar{x}$	S.D.	$\bar{x}$	S.D.
1	Stature	159.57	6.04	159.23	4.50	156.75	4.34	157.90	7.83	159.47	6.41	156.7	5.66
2	Trochanteric height	825.2	40.8	824.3	33.7	809.3	31.5	832.4	54.0	826.3	46.0	818.2	38.1
3	Tibiale height	434.8	22.3	435.3	17.6	421.0	15.7	439.2	28.5	442.3	23.5	429.6	25.2
4	Sphyrion height	67.3	5.9	67.9	5.7	62.4	5.1	63.5	7.4	65.7	6.7	64.2	5.6
5	Humeral length	293.3	15.7	292.4	13.4	294.5	11.7	297.7	15.6	292.7	15.3	298.1	15.8
6	Radial length	251.5	13.7	249.2	10.9	251.2	10.6	253.4	17.2	254.4	12.9	252.0	12.0
7	Sitting height	812.1	24.7	811.2	26.1	800.6	27.3	798.3	36.8	802.5	36.3	790.0	30.4
8	Biacromial width	369.6	15.9	364.8	13.5	361.5	15.2	361.3	18.3	371.6	15.5	361.3	16.1
9	Head height	116.5	5.7	113.7	6.6	117.2	6.6	116.7	8.7	112.9	7.2	113.6	6.9
10	Hand length	187.2	9.1	185.0	6.8	182.9	5.5	182.8	13.3	189.6	10.0	184.7	8.5
11	Hand width	97.3	4.9	96.4	4.2	97.8	4.3	98.4	7.3	99.6	5.5	96.9	3.8
12	Head length	196.5	5.9	196.3	6.7	196.9	4.2	197.3	8.2	199.3	6.1	195.8	6.8
13	Head breadth	145.1	4.3	144.0	3.8	147.4	5.2	145.2	5.4	146.7	4.0	145.2	4.5
14	Basal breadth	129.6	4.1	128.4	2.9	130.6	4.2	130.0	5.0	130.4	4.1	129.6	5.2
15	Minimum frontal	100.3	4.5	100.3	4.9	102.7	4.7	103.0	6.0	102.6	5.4	102.0	4.6
16	Bizygomatic	141.2	4.7	140.8	5.0	141.0	4.2	140.9	5.6	140.9	5.1	140.4	5.5
17	Bigonial	103.3	5.6	102.2	5.5	105.8	4.8	103.0	6.2	105.1	4.2	103.0	6.3
18	Total facial	116.2	5.8	115.8	4.9	118.2	5.1	117.5	7.1	117.4	6.9	117.4	5.5
19	Upper facial	68.7	4.8	68.2	5.1	70.9	4.8	70.8	5.0	69.4	5.6	71.5	4.8
20	Mandibular depth	41.0	2.6	40.0	3.0	42.5	2.7	42.9	3.7	42.5	3.2	43.2	2.7
21	Nasal height	50.2	4.6	50.0	3.8	49.8	3.5	49.5	4.4	49.4	4.2	49.9	4.4
22	Nasal width	45.1	2.9	45.2	3.3	47.8	2.6	47.7	2.6	47.1	3.1	46.6	3.8
23	Nasal depth	32.2	2.1	31.3	2.4	30.9	2.1	32.0	2.8	31.6	2.9	30.9	2.6
24	Palatal diameter	68.3	3.0	67.4	3.4	68.8	2.6	68.2	3.0	68.4	2.8	67.7	2.4
25	Dorsal arm skinfold	43.3	8.8	43.5	7.6	46.7	10.9	43.4	8.9	43.8	11.8	42.8	7.6
26	Subscapular skinfold	95.0	21.9	92.6	23.3	117.7	30.2	120.6	39.7	96.4	25.9	109.8	22.5
27	Circumference, upper arm	263.7	17.4	263.6	17.6	269.8	12.3	269.0	22.3	281.3	17.9	271.6	18.5
28	Circumference, calf	334.5	25.1	335.9	20.9	329.6	20.6	328.7	25.6	337.8	23.9	335.6	26.1
29	Chest girth (xiphoid)	856.5	34.6	853.9	35.4	859.3	31.7	856.8	50.0	877.4	49.3	866.8	42.4

Measurement No.	20 (N = 28)		22 (N = 33)		24 (N = 24)		25 (N = 10)		26 (N = 11)		27 (N = 15)		28 (N = 50)	
	$\bar{x}$	S.D.	$\bar{x}$	S.D.	$\bar{x}$	S.D.	$\bar{x}$	S.D.	$\bar{x}$	S.D.	$\bar{x}$	S.D.	$\bar{x}$	S.D.
1	159.93	5.50	155.80	5.58	152.25	5.34	153.03	4.39	152.88	6.35	152.31	7.31	154.95	6.67
2	829.4	38.3	797.2	34.7	771.7	33.6	774.0	25.1	777.8	34.6	787.7	43.2	798.7	37.8
3	439.4	20.6	424.9	20.7	410.5	18.6	415.2	13.3	407.0	21.9	418.8	28.1	424.7	21.5
4	71.0	5.7	67.1	4.8	67.0	5.7	66.1	3.5	66.6	3.6	65.9	3.3	65.7	4.9
5	307.3	13.6	296.8	13.0	284.1	11.7	287.4	10.6	285.4	14.9	288.7	18.9	290.1	12.1
6	253.5	14.1	243.9	13.6	239.1	11.0	242.3	10.0	240.1	10.4	239.9	14.9	244.4	12.0
7	810.1	26.3	791.8	27.9	784.6	34.8	774.7	27.6	789.5	23.9	770.7	35.4	795.8	37.4
8	375.3	17.2	363.7	13.9	357.0	15.5	356.7	10.8	361.4	17.8	357.1	19.2	363.6	16.0
9	113.4	6.5	112.6	5.1	112.9	5.1	111.7	5.5	112.6	7.7	112.6	5.9	111.5	7.5
10	191.4	9.0	184.6	7.9	181.1	7.7	184.1	4.0	180.7	6.8	182.1	9.1	183.5	9.1
11	99.3	4.9	100.3	4.0	98.1	4.8	98.0	4.0	97.1	5.4	96.6	5.8	98.0	4.9
12	197.9	5.1	197.7	6.6	197.8	6.2	195.8	5.2	195.8	7.2	195.6	5.2	195.9	6.0
13	145.5	4.3	147.8	3.4	147.7	4.0	145.7	4.9	145.4	5.2	144.2	6.1	145.5	3.8
14	129.8	5.0	130.3	4.6	131.4	4.8	131.3	3.5	127.6	4.9	129.2	5.4	130.7	4.5
15	103.6	4.7	102.7	4.1	101.2	4.6	100.9	4.2	99.6	5.0	100.5	4.1	100.8	5.1
16	141.6	4.1	143.5	5.2	141.5	4.8	143.4	5.3	141.9	5.2	139.3	6.8	140.8	4.5
17	107.6	5.1	106.8	5.4	103.8	5.0	106.2	4.0	102.9	4.4	102.2	5.3	101.8	5.2
18	117.7	5.3	116.7	6.4	116.4	7.1	117.4	4.3	113.6	4.5	113.9	4.3	117.4	7.2
19	68.2	4.5	69.5	4.8	69.8	5.6	69.2	2.9	66.5	4.1	68.0	3.6	70.6	5.8
20	40.0	3.2	40.9	3.5	40.5	4.0	39.9	2.3	40.0	2.9	40.0	2.3	40.8	3.1
21	50.5	3.3	51.1	4.2	50.7	5.6	50.2	3.6	47.9	3.1	48.9	3.2	50.8	5.4
22	48.8	2.9	48.2	4.0	46.4	3.7	46.8	4.6	47.4	2.4	46.5	2.9	46.4	2.7
23	34.0	2.2	35.5	3.3	34.0	2.4	33.8	2.8	33.4	3.0	32.6	3.2	32.6	2.5
24	69.0	4.4	68.4	3.2	66.8	3.0	67.3	3.0	65.9	3.3	67.0	2.3	68.6	3.7
25	54.1	9.0	46.6	10.4	45.7	8.3	40.5	6.7	53.8	16.3	42.5	12.5	43.2	9.0
26	97.3	17.4	91.1	19.3	93.3	17.8	83.9	18.5	101.6	39.0	88.1	18.5	85.0	13.7
27	266.2	14.4	267.2	14.1	262.2	17.7	258.4	20.6	268.1	9.4	257.3	24.0	263.9	13.4
28	336.4	18.7	328.9	19.0	321.3	21.1	321.3	25.2	331.7	16.2	324.4	26.9	330.1	19.2
29	852.1	32.1	840.2	27.9	834.6	43.8	838.1	31.7	840.5	36.4	823.7	53.4	840.3	28.8

Village-Complex

	01 (N = 14)		09 (N = 36)		10 (N = 30)		11 (N = 40)		12 (N = 28)		13 (N = 30)		14 (N = 33)		16 (N = 62)	
	$\bar{x}$	S.D.	$\bar{x}$	S.D.	$\bar{x}$	S.D.	$\bar{x}$	S.D.	$\bar{x}$	S.D.	$\bar{x}$	S.D.	$\bar{x}$	S.D.	$\bar{x}$	S.D.
	161.47	5.40	154.42	7.01	156.04	6.10	154.70	6.91	154.18	5.83	152.47	5.60	153.92	6.15	158.22	4.95
	836.9	41.0	793.4	40.1	789.3	38.3	789.0	51.0	791.8	40.0	774.9	37.2	788.3	38.2	819.1	31.3
	446.4	22.4	418.8	20.3	416.9	21.5	420.3	25.8	426.0	20.6	410.4	18.7	416.9	19.4	432.9	18.6
	66.4	6.0	63.4	4.6	66.6	4.6	64.1	5.8	63.3	5.5	65.3	5.9	66.4	4.6	68.5	4.3
	295.6	16.9	291.9	15.3	292.5	13.8	292.2	18.8	291.4	16.6	289.4	13.6	293.5	15.0	299.2	15.2
	256.5	13.5	244.1	11.6	241.8	13.7	241.3	16.2	241.2	13.3	239.9	12.4	243.6	17.2	254.7	13.5
	811.7	23.2	788.3	44.6	817.2	30.5	808.2	29.5	806.5	34.5	797.7	26.7	805.5	28.6	800.4	29.6
	363.6	13.4	361.8	14.6	362.0	13.4	359.8	17.9	359.5	15.6	357.7	17.6	360.5	17.4	371.1	13.7
	120.1	5.0	112.6	7.1	116.8	4.2	113.3	5.5	114.2	5.7	115.9	5.1	110.9	5.2	113.9	5.4
	185.8	8.3	181.5	7.9	183.5	9.3	181.8	10.1	181.8	9.7	177.4	7.0	182.0	11.0	186.6	8.2
	98.0	3.8	97.6	5.6	97.5	5.5	95.5	4.9	96.8	4.4	94.6	5.6	96.5	4.9	99.5	4.4
	195.7	5.9	199.1	5.6	198.9	5.9	194.9	5.2	197.3	5.4	197.0	6.3	195.6	5.5	197.6	5.6
	143.0	4.5	146.2	4.0	145.6	3.8	145.5	5.2	144.5	5.1	146.5	4.1	144.7	4.6	144.8	4.3
	127.7	3.9	128.9	5.5	129.1	5.2	126.9	4.2	128.1	4.5	127.3	5.0	126.8	5.1	129.3	4.4
	101.5	3.8	102.4	4.5	100.8	5.0	101.1	4.5	101.8	7.8	102.4	4.4	100.7	4.9	100.7	4.9
	138.9	4.1	142.4	6.4	140.6	3.5	139.9	4.5	140.8	5.6	139.3	4.7	141.0	5.9	140.5	5.1
	104.3	4.6	103.7	5.4	104.4	4.3	103.0	4.9	106.3	5.8	103.2	4.4	103.2	4.5	106.1	5.2
	115.7	7.5	119.2	6.4	115.9	5.0	118.7	5.8	117.8	7.0	115.6	7.0	119.8	8.5	116.5	5.0
	66.9	4.4	70.6	4.8	68.7	4.1	71.4	4.5	70.5	5.3	68.7	4.9	70.6	6.7	66.3	4.4
	40.0	4.4	41.8	3.8	39.7	4.2	40.2	3.1	40.1	3.5	40.4	2.8	39.8	3.2	41.6	3.6
	49.1	4.0	50.5	4.7	51.4	3.5	53.1	3.8	50.9	5.3	50.4	4.7	52.7	5.3	49.3	3.9
	46.4	2.3	48.4	3.1	48.4	3.8	46.7	3.7	49.6	4.8	47.5	3.2	46.8	3.2	49.9	3.6
	31.4	2.2	33.8	2.8	32.8	2.4	33.1	2.5	33.8	2.8	32.1	3.2	32.5	2.5	34.0	2.1
	69.4	3.3	68.6	3.1	69.4	4.5	68.5	3.7	68.4	3.2	67.3	3.0	67.7	3.4	68.5	3.9
	45.9	14.7	52.5	11.6	55.8	10.7	53.6	12.1	51.3	12.8	51.7	13.4	52.1	6.8	54.5	15.3
	95.6	24.2	104.3	22.6	92.5	18.8	98.1	26.3	95.7	20.8	101.2	22.5	106.0	23.8	101.9	22.5
	270.5	19.2	264.4	17.4	268.6	15.5	258.1	17.1	258.1	15.4	259.4	14.6	263.2	14.1	272.5	17.7
	338.9	19.8	331.2	22.6	333.6	24.2	328.6	20.1	320.9	21.3	323.3	22.5	328.3	21.0	335.1	20.6
	874.9	36.8	847.0	30.4	836.7	37.6	834.9	35.1	832.4	43.5	832.3	37.2	840.2	40.2	860.4	37.1

	31 (N = 34)		32 (N = 12)		33 (N = 23)		34 (N = 48)		36 (N = 28)		37 (N = 37)		38 (N = 25)		19 ((N = 25)	
	$\bar{x}$	S.D.	$\bar{x}$	S.D.	$\bar{x}$	S.D.	$\bar{x}$	S.D.	$\bar{x}$	S.D.	$\bar{x}$	S.D.	$\bar{x}$	S.D.	$\bar{x}$	S.D.
	154.41	4.86	154.43	5.02	155.74	6.50	150.68	5.93	154.36	4.90	150.56	4.82	147.37	5.00	157.48	5.81
	792.0	34.2	808.5	46.8	800.8	40.7	784.9	40.5	803.2	36.0	778.3	30.3	759.4	28.8	823.2	38.0
	417.4	19.0	435.8	24.8	424.4	23.5	418.7	23.5	425.0	16.9	419.6	17.0	408.5	12.9	437.1	20.5
	65.2	4.8	66.7	6.1	65.3	5.6	64.8	6.4	66.0	4.9	65.0	5.4	62.3	5.1	66.2	5.0
	291.1	12.5	291.2	18.3	290.1	16.7	288.8	13.2	294.9	13.5	286.7	13.3	277.6	12.9	297.2	17.8
	239.5	9.7	244.9	18.5	245.8	16.6	238.1	13.1	241.8	13.2	235.2	10.9	234.3	11.0	253.2	12.8
	788.5	27.3	783.1	29.6	795.6	31.0	774.6	28.2	788.6	29.0	767.4	28.6	750.8	32.9	789.7	29.5
	362.8	16.8	366.6	12.3	360.0	19.1	354.9	12.7	357.7	17.0	352.6	20.0	343.4	13.0	359.1	16.1
	112.3	5.5	110.6	5.8	112.3	7.5	110.7	6.4	108.5	7.8	108.9	6.1	108.4	9.2	115.0	6.9
	182.7	7.2	183.3	8.9	184.2	7.9	181.2	9.1	183.6	10.0	176.9	7.4	173.3	7.1	184.6	10.0
	96.9	3.7	96.5	5.1	96.7	4.9	94.7	4.6	93.9	5.3	92.7	4.9	92.6	4.4	96.5	4.4
	193.7	6.0	193.4	5.6	194.0	5.6	196.0	5.5	193.9	5.9	193.5	6.1	195.2	7.0	196.3	6.2
	147.9	5.4	145.5	4.5	146.2	4.8	144.7	3.9	144.1	3.9	143.7	4.5	141.4	4.1	146.0	5.0
	129.9	4.7	129.2	3.7	130.7	4.5	129.7	4.7	127.3	4.9	128.0	4.8	129.8	5.4	129.9	5.1
	99.9	4.5	99.3	2.9	101.8	4.6	100.3	4.0	101.4	3.6	101.8	4.6	100.5	4.2	101.8	4.5
	140.9	5.3	143.8	3.8	139.7	4.9	139.1	3.8	142.0	5.7	142.5	4.4	140.2	5.7	141.0	4.3
	104.0	5.0	104.3	5.7	103.7	4.6	103.5	5.7	102.9	5.9	102.0	6.4	101.2	5.9	103.0	4.7
	116.0	4.6	120.7	9.8	115.8	6.5	115.9	6.2	119.0	5.4	118.0	6.8	117.3	6.7	116.8	8.1
	69.2	3.4	72.9	8.2	67.8	4.2	69.2	5.3	71.0	4.0	69.1	4.4	69.4	4.7	69.2	6.3
	40.7	2.5	41.4	2.8	40.6	4.3	40.4	2.1	40.5	2.7	40.6	3.3	41.9	2.6	41.8	3.4
	50.5	4.0	52.3	6.2	49.7	3.6	49.9	4.5	52.4	3.8	51.7	3.8	49.9	3.2	51.7	5.6
	47.1	2.7	49.3	4.0	46.8	3.4	46.1	3.2	45.0	3.5	48.9	3.3	46.8	3.2	47.0	3.6
	34.6	2.0	35.8	2.2	33.4	2.0	34.1	2.0	33.4	2.2	33.0	2.9	31.4	2.6	33.5	1.9
	67.1	3.5	68.4	3.1	66.8	3.7	66.0	2.9	65.7	3.3	67.6	3.3	67.3	2.2	68.7	3.3
	47.5	8.9	42.4	9.5	46.7	13.6	46.7	9.4	47.4	8.5	48.1	7.8	45.2	10.5	43.6	8.9
	97.4	19.4	84.5	14.5	92.0	20.1	88.7	15.8	85.1	17.0	89.8	20.3	87.2	20.2	81.9	16.7
	262.7	13.9	319.8	14.4	263.1	19.2	250.5	17.4	245.1	18.2	247.9	17.2	242.5	15.1	255.9	17.2
	325.9	21.7	319.8	19.4	331.8	22.7	309.5	22.9	312.9	17.7	311.5	18.3	310.4	24.0	322.4	26.2
	834.4	33.0	841.6	28.4	848.3	32.5	813.8	39.5	830.9	35.4	813.7	30.9	778.0	48.7	831.4	40.7

TABLE 35

MEANS AND STANDARD DEVIATIONS FOR 36 MEASUREMENTS AND INDICES FOR FEMALES

Measurement No.	Variable	Gadsup (N = 55) x̄	Gadsup S.D.	Tairora (N = 42) x̄	Tairora S.D.	Auyana (N = 30) x̄	Auyana S.D.	Awa (N = 45) x̄	Awa S.D.	Grand Mean (N = 172)	Overall S.D.
0	Weight	114.3	12.7	117.9	13.1	108.8	9.6	110.1	12.6	113.1	12.7
1	Stature	148.95	4.75	149.41	6.06	146.31	4.84	145.32	4.97	147.65	5.41
2	Trochanteric height	764.3	33.4	769.2	46.7	746.6	29.5	754.3	35.5	759.8	37.0
3	Tibiale height	402.0	20.7	401.7	25.2	388.5	16.9	394.8	17.4	397.7	20.5
4	Sphyrion height	59.2	5.7	59.6	5.7	60.2	5.6	58.1	4.0	59.2	5.5
5	Humeral length	273.3	12.8	276.0	17.0	269.2	11.4	269.4	14.6	272.2	14.4
6	Radial length	229.7	12.5	228.6	15.5	217.3	11.6	217.5	10.4	224.1	13.9
7	Sitting height	757.5	27.3	757.0	25.9	752.3	22.5	745.7	30.5	753.4	27.3
8	Biacromial width	328.9	14.2	332.2	16.5	329.8	8.1	319.1	14.8	327.3	14.9
9	Head height	110.4	7.0	109.0	6.0	107.0	6.0	105.4	6.5	108.1	6.7
10	Hand length	172.3	9.0	176.0	8.5	171.4	7.8	168.6	9.4	172.1	9.1
11	Hand width	88.6	4.6	88.7	5.4	88.9	4.3	85.1	4.4	87.7	4.9
12	Head length	187.0	5.3	190.2	5.0	186.5	5.2	185.7	5.1	187.4	5.4
13	Head breadth	138.9	3.9	138.7	4.5	138.8	3.7	136.7	3.8	138.3	4.1
14	Basal breadth	122.7	4.3	121.4	5.5	123.3	3.6	119.5	3.3	121.6	4.5
15	Minimum frontal	98.5	4.4	97.8	3.6	97.6	4.2	98.5	4.1	98.2	4.1
16	Bizygomatic	130.8	4.3	131.2	4.1	130.9	3.7	132.1	4.6	131.3	4.2
17	Bigonial	96.7	5.5	96.5	5.3	97.5	5.8	96.2	3.9	96.6	5.1
18	Total facial	106.9	4.7	109.8	4.8	105.4	4.5	105.5	3.5	107.0	4.7
19	Upper facial	65.7	4.5	66.2	3.7	63.7	3.9	63.5	3.8	64.9	4.1
20	Mandibular depth	38.8	2.9	38.7	2.4	36.7	1.7	37.4	2.4	38.0	2.6
21	Nasal height	45.8	3.2	46.5	3.6	45.4	3.4	45.4	2.8	45.8	3.2
22	Nasal width	42.0	2.9	43.6	3.4	43.3	2.6	42.4	2.8	42.7	3.0
23	Nasal depth	27.7	2.5	31.2	2.7	30.1	2.5	28.5	1.9	29.1	2.8
24	Palatal diameter	64.7	2.8	65.7	3.8	62.9	3.2	64.0	2.4	64.4	3.2
25	Dorsal arm skinfold	82.7	38.1	79.2	26.1	66.9	24.6	72.6	32.9	76.4	32.0
26	Subscapular skinfold	165.9	69.6	132.0	50.9	103.8	40.5	129.7	49.7	137.3	59.5
27	Circumference, upper arm	247.1	16.6	243.1	13.3	236.7	12.9	223.6	14.6	238.1	17.3
28	Circumference, calf	311.1	19.8	310.1	16.4	306.1	15.1	304.2	16.8	308.2	17.5
29	Chest girth (xiphoid)	798.1	43.9	794.0	33.6	774.8	21.3	760.5	32.3	783.2	38.4
	Indices										
	Trunk/stature	50.9	1.6	50.7	1.6	51.4	1.2	51.3	1.9	51.1	1.6
	Cephalic index	74.3	2.3	72.9	2.5	74.5	2.7	73.7	2.3	73.8	2.5
	Brachial index	84.1	3.5	82.9	3.1	80.7	2.8	80.8	2.8	82.3	3.4
	Head height/head length	59.0	3.3	57.3	3.3	57.4	3.4	56.7	2.8	57.7	3.3
	Biacromical sitting height	43.4	1.6	43.9	1.7	43.9	1.3	42.8	1.9	43.5	1.7
	Total facial index	81.6	3.8	83.5	3.9	80.5	3.8	79.8	3.6	81.4	4.0
	Nasal index	92.1	10.1	94.3	10.7	95.9	9.6	93.5	7.2	93.7	9.5

TABLE 36

WITHIN-GROUP CORRELATION BETWEEN MEASUREMENTS USED IN THE DISCRIMINANT ANALYSIS

Measurement Number	1	2	3	4	5	6	7	8	9	10	11	12	13
1 Stature	1.000	.898	.772	.467	.824	.798	.594	.580	.189	.701	.584	.302	.075
2 Trochanteric height	.905	1.000	.865	.426	.770	.817	.398	.515	.166	.636	.529	.278	.035
3 Tibiale height	.841	.895	1.000	.406	.672	.742	.301	.507	.073	.548	.476	.196	.034
4 Sphyrion height	.453	.394	.402	1.000	.306	.350	.344	.381	.047	.399	.440	.145	.003
5 Humeral length	.786	.813	.734	.339	1.000	.757	.385	.452	.039	.589	.450	.174	.027
6 Radial length	.783	.813	.770	.343	.767	1.000	.330	.535	.093	.616	.535	.267	.027
7 Sitting height	.755	.552	.513	.399	.481	.459	1.000	.538	.183	.432	.434	.336	.205
8 Biacromial width	.652	.604	.542	.394	.533	.555	.538	1.000	.211	.511	.410	.261	.198
9 Head height	.300	.210	.176	.111	.185	.155	.364	.211	1.000	.119	.085	.394	.209
10 Hand length	.757	.722	.687	.452	.637	.693	.560	.569	.203	1.000	.622	.170	.127
11 Hand width	.491	.414	.403	.325	.358	.416	.448	.399	.240	.547	1.000	.304	.075
12 Head length	.332	.266	.252	.237	.255	.237	.317	.299	.312	.333	.315	1.000	.334
13 Head breadth	.196	.115	.111	.102	.122	.074	.231	.243	.298	.179	.176	.415	1.000
14 Basal breadth	.287	.254	.244	.213	.244	.236	.224	.302	.169	.264	.228	.388	.464
15 Minimum frontal	.211	.177	.191	.143	.188	.145	.226	.201	.262	.237	.201	.375	.415
16 Bizygomatic	.327	.263	.273	.282	.294	.248	.296	.434	.139	.345	.290	.410	.476
17 Bigonial	.292	.236	.249	.276	.218	.209	.266	.332	.167	.295	.280	.239	.296
18 Total facial	.233	.188	.215	.174	.201	.176	.219	.226	.119	.254	.193	.320	.215
19 Upper facial	.134	.112	.162	.106	.149	.117	.151	.152	.088	.156	.117	.242	.169
20 Mandibular depth	.249	.214	.209	.192	.201	.185	.228	.250	.171	.247	.250	.341	.218
21 Nasal height	.089	.066	.117	.083	.120	.074	.091	.086	.014	.116	.064	.149	.110
22 Nasal width	.137	.114	.141	.093	.138	.152	.054	.144	.056	.162	.184	.285	.194
23 Nasal depth	.169	.153	.183	.112	.162	.124	.126	.146	.116	.205	.152	.194	.129
24 Palatal diameter	.323	.268	.263	.206	.218	.249	.306	.339	.225	.283	.248	.268	.220
25 Dorsal arm skinfold	.241	.202	.188	.130	.190	.164	.274	.216	.227	.232	.207	.186	.172
26 Subscapular skinfold	.062	.073	.056	.007	.094	.044	.086	.123	.081	.044	.066	.162	.210
27 Circumference, upper arm	.354	.257	.257	.272	.199	.267	.381	.476	.189	.374	.436	.310	.284
28 Circumference, calf	.510	.415	.401	.381	.312	.338	.493	.571	.277	.470	.462	.295	.274
29 Chest girth (xiphoid)	.595	.543	.525	.386	.487	.525	.490	.675	.231	.573	.458	.353	.299

	14	15	16	17	18	19	20	21	22	23	24	25	26	27	28	29
1	.282	.225	.426	.278	.147	.013	.035	.175	.186	.189	.343	.095	.002	.322	.499	.573
2	.275	.239	.406	.311	.082	-.040	.041	.071	.220	.141	.336	.095	.009	.291	.470	.535
3	.252	.110	.349	.315	.090	-.048	.028	.100	.153	.124	.311	.052	.016	.227	.363	.513
4	.193	.112	.236	.377	.154	.062	.042	.230	.241	.201	.347	.007	-.019	.218	.458	.330
5	.192	.142	.389	.308	.108	.052	.017	.159	.134	.086	.354	-.031	-.092	.151	.299	.500
6	.256	.165	.412	.287	.110	.004	.029	.065	.226	.110	.273	.096	.055	.274	.374	.532
7	.202	.177	.258	.356	.144	-.005	-.032	.169	.175	.227	.247	.251	.209	.450	.493	.448
8	.359	.172	.407	.318	.204	.015	.122	.121	.250	.121	.354	.140	.222	.400	.441	.581
9	.103	.323	.049	.056	.128	-.064	.100	.010	.069	.103	.009	.181	.161	.165	.194	.176
10	.249	.155	.396	.356	.099	-.086	.041	.113	.120	.089	.248	.153	.065	.314	.447	.482
11	.250	.206	.350	.451	.144	-.002	-.009	.106	.151	.212	.381	.173	.104	.351	.444	.379
12	.349	.402	.290	.165	.183	.068	.147	.112	.177	.185	.179	.212	.257	.316	.344	.369
13	.451	.405	.450	.075	.248	.058	.176	.049	.106	.049	.099	.127	.168	.177	.271	.231
14	1.000	.267	.535	.310	.136	-.032	.061	-.019	.079	.119	.304	.121	.106	.170	.318	.263
15	.290	1.000	.469	.190	.099	-.007	.154	-.057	.127	.193	.283	.302	.261	.318	.347	.269
16	.523	.400	1.000	.373	.206	.046	.200	.024	.209	.197	.445	.279	.230	.421	.464	.550
17	.355	.237	.417	1.000	.106	-.052	-.097	-.016	.103	.188	.373	.156	.095	.244	.298	.273
18	.218	.198	.346	.189	1.000	.658	.469	.525	.173	.378	.171	.140	.096	.311	.244	.341
19	.142	.166	.257	.123	.843	1.000	.324	.615	.072	.210	.180	.015	-.016	.110	.033	.090
20	.182	.191	.298	.200	.608	.487	1.000	.144	.144	.145	.174	.127	.140	.199	.134	.184
21	.164	.098	.240	.071	.679	.708	.227	1.000	-.012	.359	.125	-.046	-.065	.095	.145	.160
22	.220	.152	.257	.238	.131	.045	.181	-.032	1.000	.178	.303	.020	.064	.227	.248	.237
23	.176	.132	.211	.160	.378	.314	.170	.393	.229	1.000	.105	.159	.128	.204	.251	.150
24	.244	.217	.371	.318	.253	.234	.280	.111	.154	.139	1.000	.004	.013	.203	.285	.272
25	.113	.139	.118	.158	.024	-.037	.120	-.093	.073	.115	.108	1.000	.756	.654	.397	.392
26	.135	.130	.162	.141	.124	.054	.200	-.002	.156	.160	.051	.479	1.000	.624	.360	.394
27	.238	.200	.384	.333	.170	.074	.274	-.008	.207	.118	.306	.305	.245	1.000	.678	.646
28	.213	.249	.367	.274	.177	.117	.256	.038	.077	.113	.328	.317	.163	.666	1.000	.546
29	.292	.269	.460	.373	.302	.210	.353	.138	.180	.199	.352	.286	.277	.662	.679	1.000

Note: Figures above the diagonal are for females (N = 172), those below for males (N = 888).

TABLE 37

MUNSELL SKIN COLOR VALUES FOR 24 SUBJECTS FROM AKUNA (06)

Males				Females		
Subject Number	Exposed	Unexposed		Subject Number	Exposed	Unexposed
1	2.5YR 3/4	5YR 4/4		4	5YR 3/4	7.5YR 4/4
2	2.5YR 3/4	2.5YR 5/4		8	2.5YR 3/4	5YR 4/4
3	5YR 4/4	5YR 4/4		9	5YR 4/6	2.5YR 5/4
6	5YR 3/4	5YR 4/4		10	7.5YR 4/4	7.5YR 5/4
7	2.5YR 3/4	2.5YR 5/4		12	5 YR 3/4	5YR 4/4
11	2.5YR 3/6	7.5YR 4/4		15	2.5YR 3/4	5YR 4/4
13	2.5YR 3/4	7.5YR 5/4		16	5YR 4/4	5YR 4/4
14	2.5YR 3/4	5YR 3/4		21	2.5YR 3/4	7.5YR 4/4
17	2.5YR 3/6	5YR 5/4		22	5YR 3/6	7.5YR 5/4
18	2.5YR 3/4	5YR 5/4		23	5YR 3/4	7.5YR 5/4
19	2.5YR 3/4	5YR 4/4		24	5YR 3/4	5YR 4/6
20	2.5YR 3/4	7.5YR 5/4				
25	2.5YR 3/6	5YR 4/4				

Note: Exposed skin was taken at the forehead, unexposed skin on the medial aspect of the upper arm.

Appendix III: A Descriptive and Comparative Investigation of Dental Morphology

JOHN THOMAS BARKSDALE, D.D.S.

INTRODUCTION

The changing dentition of man has been a subject of study by physical anthropologists for many years.[1] The changes are toward less complicated tooth patterns and smaller measurements than were found in early man. Studies of various racial groups throughout the world reveal that there is much variability in the rate of change of the dentition (Dahlberg 1945). It is accepted theory that many morphologic features of the dentition such as form, cusp numbers, and groove patterns are genetically determined. In view of this, it would seem that various races would show certain similarities in their dentitions just as they do in other genetically controlled features.

However, the value of the dentition in classifying contemporary races is not known. Related populations have been studied but the degree of similarity between morphologic patterns of the dentition has not been fully determined. Much work has been done on contemporary Mongoloids and the results are encouraging. The marked shovel-shape incisor and low incidence of Carabelli's anomaly seem to be a morphologic pattern for Mongoloid dentitions. Much information, however, remains to be collected for other racial groups (Moorrees 1957).

1. This study is based upon a thesis submitted in partial fulfillment of the requirements for the degree of Master of Science in dentistry, University of Washington, 1966. I wish to thank Dr. Robert A. Littlewood for the use of his collection of dental casts and other information. I am grateful to Dr. Benjamin C. Moffett for his interest and guidance in the preparation of this paper and to Mr. Dean Auve of the dental photography department.

The work of Campbell (1925), describing in detail the dentition of the Australian aboriginal, is similar to the present investigation. Campbell concluded that the crown form and cusp number for these people are probably more primitive from an evolutionary viewpoint than those found in any other living racial group. More recently, a study by Pedersen (1949) defined the dentition of the East Greenland Eskimoes very thoroughly and substantiated their Mongoloid ancestry. Pedersen urged that similar dental studies be extended to other aboriginal groups.

Dahlberg (1949), a major contributor to the field of dental anthropology, has studied the dentition of the American Indian, presenting valuable information about the concept of dentition and primary and secondary characters. Tratman (1950) compared the Indo-European racial stocks with Mongoloid people of southeast Asia. His data on the Mongoloid group conformed very closely to Pedersen's (1949) findings on the East Greenland Eskimo. On the basis of his study of these two limited samples, Tratman felt that his findings could be applied to the racial groups as being basically characteristic. In a detailed study of the Aleut dentition, Moorrees (1957) compared the dental traits in two closely genetically related Aleut populations, hoping to associate these characteristics with the racial origin of the population being studied. His results were handicapped by small sample size.

Results of these investigations will be reviewed in the discussion section of this study.

MATERIALS AND METHODS

The sample for this study consists of 218 sets of dental casts prepared by Littlewood from natives in the Eastern Highlands of New Guinea. Dental impressions were made in the field using an irreversible hydrocolloid material (alginate). The impressions were immediately poured up in dental stone to insure as accurate a model of the dentition as is possible. The hard dental stone provides a durable three-dimensional record in sufficient detail for a study of tooth morphology. The fact that no dental treatment was available to the natives is important because the casts represent natural morphological patterns instead of artifically restored surfaces.

The casts were made in eighteen villages within the four language groups included in this study. These villages were grouped into isolates on the basis of gene flow data. Since the subjects are all adults, no data are available concerning the deciduous dentition. Males ac-

TABLE 38
NUMBER AND DISTRIBUTION OF DENTAL CASTS

Group	All	Females	Males
*Gadsup**	74	10	64
Sasaura Isolate†	40	3	37
Sasaura Village			
Akuna Isolate	20	2	18
Akuna Village			
Amomunta Village			
Ontenu Isolate	14	5	9
Ontenu Village			
*Tairora**	70	2	68
Baieanabuta Isolate†	31	0	31
Baira Village			
Orena Village			
Abiera Isolate	14	2	12
Abiera Village			
Ontabura Village			
Babaraai Isolate	13	0	13
Nompia Village			
Ontura Village			
Batainabura Isolate	12	0	12
Batainabura Village			
*Auyana**	22	4	18
Auyana Isolate	18	4	14
Terendapa Village			
Wotempa Village			
Asempa Village			
Omuna Village			
Kawaina Isolate	4	0	4
Kawaina Village			
*Awa**	52	22	30
Ilakia Isolate†	30	17	13
Ilakia Village			
Tauna Isolate	22	5	17
Tauna Village			
Total	218	38	180

* These language groups were compared by using the chi-square test.
† These isolates were compared by using the chi-square test.

count for 82 percent of the casts. The distribution of casts, according to language group, isolate, village, and sex, is shown in Table 38.

The dental characteristics selected for study represent those previously used to evaluate various populations. Therefore, the data can be compared with the findings of other investigators. In order to insure greater accuracy and objectivity the series of plaques devised by Dahlberg (1957) from the Zoller Laboratory of Dental Anthropology, University of Chicago, were used wherever possible to classify tooth characters. Dahlberg produced these three-dimensional plaques as a step toward standardization of tooth character classification, since many of the publications on comparative morphology of the human dentition use different methods for evaluation.

The casts were evaluated without any knowledge of which language group or isolate they represented. All observations were double checked. A time interval of three weeks was allowed between the first and second observations in order to increase objectivity in evaluating features. Observations were not recorded for severely decayed or abraded teeth.

The dental traits are discussed under the following headings.

1. *Shovel-Shape of the Maxillary Incisors* (Plate 5)

Hrdlicka's (1920) subjective scale for grading the degree of shovel-shape has been used by practically all authors. Moorrees (1957) modi-fied this system to include five degrees of expression for this trait. The latter method was used by this investigator because it is more objective than previous techniques. The system of gradation is as follows.

Marked shovel: the marginal ridges are excessively prominent and when seen in a transverse section appear to fold or roll over the lingual surface similar to the letter C.

Shovel: the enamel rim with the enclosed fossa is well-developed.

Semishovel: the enamel rim is distinct but the enclosed fossa is shallow.

Trace shovel: the enamel rim is distinct but it cannot be classed as semishovel.

Absent shovel: the trace of rim and fossa is faint or absent so as not to deserve special attention.

2. *Variations of the Crown of the Maxillary Lateral Incisor* (Plate 6)

The following observations were made for the crown of the maxillary lateral incisor.

Lingual cusps: the variation of the cingulum which presents a definite cusp.

Peg-shaped: the size of the crown is abnormally reduced and the crown is malformed.

Missing: a subjective observation without x-rays, but it was recorded in casts where it appeared that the tooth was never present.

Normal: teeth that are of normal size and shape.

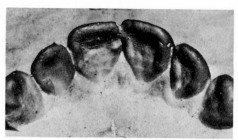

a. Absent shovel

b. Trace shovel

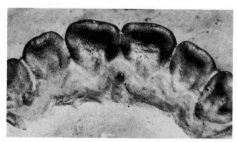

c. Semishovel

d. Shovel

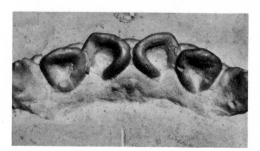

e. Marked shovel

Plate 5. Examples of shovel-shape of the maxillary incisors (Dahlberg)

a. Lingual cusp

b. Peg-shaped

Plate 6. Examples of variations of the crown of the maxillary lateral incisor (Dahlberg)

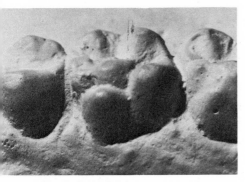

a. Pronounced tubercle

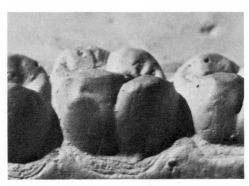

b. Slight tubercle

c. Groove and pit

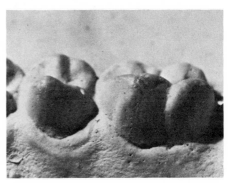

d. Groove

e. Absent

Plate 7. Examples of Carabelli's anomaly of the maxillary first molars (Dahlberg)

3. *Carabelli's Anomaly of the Maxillary First Molars* (Plate 7)

This accessory cusp of the mesiolingual cusp (protocone) of maxillary first molars appears in a variety of forms. The scale for grading this trait is similar to that used by other authors.

Pronounced tubercle: a large cusp.

Slight tubercle: a small palpable cusp.

Groove: a groove or furrow where a cusp would be.

Groove and pit: a groove or furrow with a definite pit.

Absent: a mesiolingual cusp with no manifestation of the anomaly.

4. *Cusp Numbers of the Maxillary Molars* (Plate 8)

The number of cusps occurring in the maxillary molars are quite variable in modern man. The distolingual cusp (hypocone) is the most recently acquired structure in the evolution of the upper molars, and it is also the most variable part of the tooth. The following four classes were used:

4: the presence of four well-developed main cusps.

$4-$: the distolingual cusp is reduced in size.

$3+$: the distolingual cusp reduced in size to small cuspule.

3: three main cusps, distolingual cusp completely absent.

5. *Cusp Numbers and Groove Patterns of the Mandibular Molars* (Plate 9)

Occlusal surface patterns of the mandibular molars are commonly used for classifying tooth morphology. In the system proposed by Hellman (1928) the numbers of cusps and groove patterns are interdependent. A plus $(+)$ is formed when the mesiobuccal cusp (protoconid) is in contact with the distolingual cusp (entoconid). The mesiobuccal cusp is of similar size to the mesiolingual cusp (metaconid). When this arrangement is modified slightly the buccal cusp (hypoconid) is in contact with the mesiolingual cusp, and a Y pattern is observed. Jorgensen (1955) reported another arrangement of the occlusal grooves when the mesiobuccal cusp contacts the distolingual cusp. This is symbolized by the letter X. The data were recorded in the following manner.

$Y4$: a Y groove pattern occurring with four cusps.

$Y5$: a Y groove pattern occurring with five cusps.

$Y6$: a Y groove pattern occurring with six cusps.

$+3$: a $+$ groove pattern occurring with three cusps.

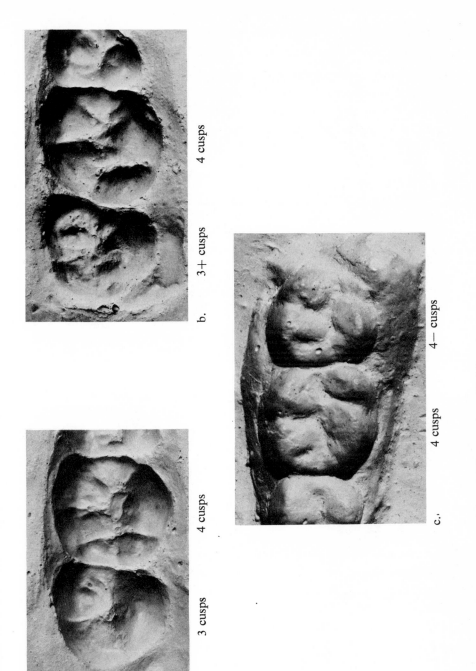

a. 3 cusps   4 cusps

b. 3+ cusps   4 cusps

c. 4 cusps   4— cusps

Plate 8. Examples of cusp numbers of the maxillary molars (Dahlberg)

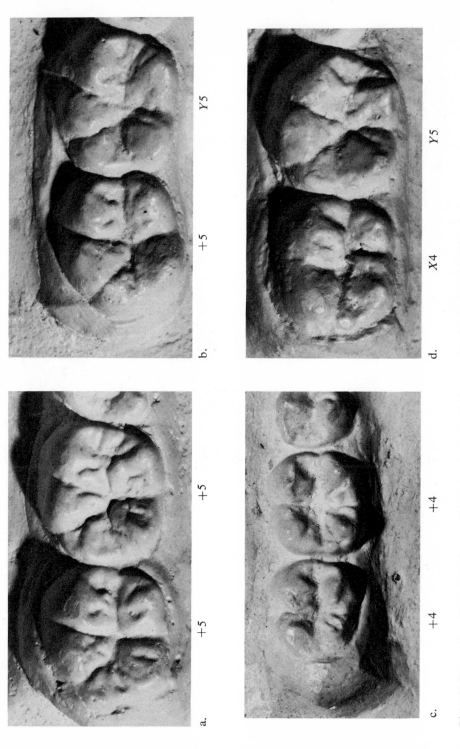

Plate 9. Examples of cusp numbers and groove patterns of the mandibular molars (Dahlberg)

+ 4: a + groove pattern occurring with four cusps.
+ 5: a + groove pattern occurring with five cusps.
+ 6: a + groove pattern occurring with six cusps.
X4: an X groove pattern occurring with four cusps.
X5: an X groove pattern occuring with five cusps.

6. *Cusp Numbers of the Mandibular Premolars*

A cusp is defined as having an independent apex, however slight (Kraus 1951). The mandibular premolar has two or three cusps in most instances. The second premolar has three cusps more commonly than the first premolar which usually has two cusps. Occasionally four and five cusps are seen on premolars (Ludwig 1957). These data were tabulated by classifying the teeth as having two, three, four, or five cusps.

7. *Supernumerary Cusps*

A supernumerary cusp may be defined as an extra cusp present on the tooth in an area where cusps are not normally found. The locations studied are as follows:

Paramolar cusps of the maxillary molars, found on the mesial part of the buccal surface of maxillary molars.

Protostylids, occurring on the mesial part of the buccal surface of mandibular molars. This cusp is a subgroup of the paramolar group as defined by Dahlberg (1950) (Plate 10, *top*).

Occlusal cusps, found on the occlusal aspect of molars and premolars.

8. *Supernumerary Teeth*

Hyperodontia is a term which describes an increase in the number of teeth over the usual figure. Several examples of this condition were found in the anterior and the posterior teeth.

The above data were tabulated on UniSort cards. One card was used for each set of dental casts. The cards were then sorted and these data accumulated for each of the language groups (Gadsup, Tairora, Auyana, Awa) and the three largest isolate samples (Sasaura, Baieana-buta, Ilakia). The following statistical analyses were made:

1. Frequency and percentage distribution for dental traits of the tribes and isolates. These data were separated for sex differences.

2. Chi-square tests were used to compare the frequency distributions of traits for the tribes and isolates.

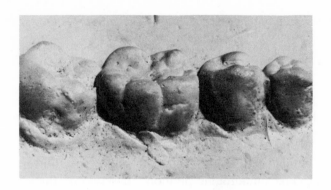

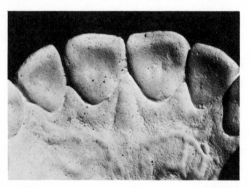

a. Absent shovel

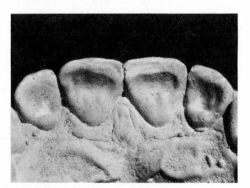

b. Trace shovel

c. Semishovel

Plate 10. *Top:* Example of the protostylid type of supernumerary cusp on the mandibular first molar (Dahlberg). *Middle and bottom:* Examples of shovel shape of the maxillary incisors in the Eastern Highlands natives

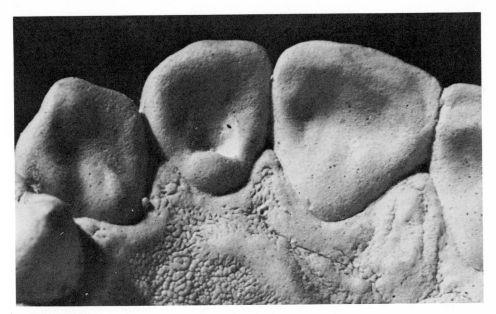

a. Lingual cusp

b. Peg-shaped

Plate 11. Examples of variations of the crown of the maxillary lateral incisor in the Eastern Highlands natives

RESULTS

When the data for right and left teeth were compared, no statistically significant difference was found. Therefore, an average value for the two sides was used in analyzing these data. Sex differences in dental morphology were analyzed for Awa, which provided the largest ratio of females (22) to males (30); however, no statistically significant differences were found. The results of chi-square tests for language groups and isolates were recorded only when they were significant. Tables 71 and 72 present summaries of significantly different chi-square tests for the language groups and isolates, respectively.

1. *Shovel-Shape of the Maxillary Incisors* (Tables 39-42; Plate 10a,b,c,)

Figures in the tables, for the shovel-shaped incisors of the natives of the Eastern Highlands region, are based on the number of individuals rather than individual teeth. Differences between antimeres were not encountered.

Incisors with the marked shovel and shovel gradations were not encountered and therefore are not included in the tables. Absent shovel for the central incisors was observed 63 percent of the time. Trace shovel was present 31 percent of the time and a semishovel was noted for 6 percent of the individuals studied. The lateral incisor presented the absent shovel in 50 percent of the individuals with trace shovel and semishovel being present in 44 percent and 6 percent of the respective subjects.

Chi-square tests showed significant differences for shovel-shape of the central incisors between Gadsup and Awa. The lateral incisor presented significant differences when comparing shovel-shape for Gadsup and Awa, and Tairora and Awa. Isolate comparisons revealed significant differences for Sasaura and Ilakia.

2. *Variations of the Crown of the Maxillary Lateral Incisor* (Tables 43-45; Plate 11)

The normal lateral incisor was seen in 78 percent of the individuals studied. The variation which presents a lateral incisor with a lingual cusp was found to be present 18 percent of the time. The peg-shaped and missing lateral incisors were each noted in 2 percent of the individuals studied.

Chi-square tests presented significant differences in the following language group comparisons: Gadsup and Auyana, and Gadsup and

TABLE 39
Shovel-Shape of the Maxillary Central Incisors: Frequency (Percent) Array for Language Groups

	Total			Gadsup			Tairora		
	All	Female	Male	All	Female	Male	All	Female	Male
Semishovel	5.9 (11)	6.9 (2)	5.7 (9)	6.2 (4)	0.0 (0)	7.3 (4)	7.5 (5)	50.0 (1)	6.2 (4)
Trace shovel	31.4 (59)	41.4 (12)	29.6 (47)	24.6 (16)	10.0 (1)	27.3 (15)	31.3 (21)	50.0 (1)	30.8 (20)
Absent Shovel	62.8 (118)	51.7 (15)	64.8 (103)	69.2 (45)	90.0 (9)	65.5 (36)	61.2 (41)	0.0 (0)	63.1 (41)
Total	(188)	(29)	(159)	(65)	(10)	(55)	(67)	(2)	(65)

	Auyana			Awa		
	All	Female	Male	All	Female	Male
Semishovel	5.3 (1)	0.0 (0)	6.3 (1)	2.7 (1)	7.1 (1)	0.0 (0)
Trace shovel	21.1 (4)	33.3 (1)	18.8 (3)	48.6 (18)	64.3 (9)	39.1 (9)
Absent shovel	73.7 (14)	66.7 (2)	75.0 (12)	48.6 (18)	28.6 (4)	60.9 (14)
Total	(19)	(3)	(16)	(37)	(14)	(23)

Note: The figures in parentheses refer to the number of individuals studied.

TABLE 40
Shovel-Shape of the Maxillary Lateral Incisors: Frequency (Percent) Array for Language Groups

	Total			Gadsup			Tairora		
	All	Female	Male	All	Female	Male	All	Female	Male
Semishovel	6.6 (13)	9.4 (3)	6.0 (10)	5.8 (4)	0.0 (0)	6.8 (4)	7.5 (5)	50.0 (1)	6.2 (4)
Trace shovel	43.9 (87)	53.1 (17)	42.2 (70)	31.9 (22)	20.0 (2)	33.9 (20)	38.8 (26)	50.0 (1)	38.5 (25)
Absent shovel	49.5 (98)	37.5 (12)	51.8 (86)	62.3 (43)	80.0 (8)	59.3 (35)	53.7 (36)	0.0 (0)	55.4 (36)
Total	(198)	(32)	(166)	(69)	(10)	(59)	(67)	(2)	(65)

	Auyana			Awa		
	All	Female	Male	All	Female	Male
Semishovel	10.0 (2)	0.0 (0)	11.8 (2)	4.8 (2)	11.8 (2)	0.0 (0)
Trace shovel	50.0 (10)	66.7 (2)	47.1 (8)	69.0 (29)	70.6 (12)	68.0 (17)
Absent shovel	40.0 (8)	33.3 (1)	41.2 (7)	26.2 (11)	17.6 (3)	32.0 (8)
Total	(20)	(3)	(17)	(42)	(17)	(25)

Note: The figures in parentheses refer to the number of individuals studied.

TABLE 41
SHOVEL-SHAPE OF THE MAXILLARY LATERAL INCISORS:
FREQUENCY (PERCENT) ARRAY FOR ISOLATES

	Sasaura			Baieanabuta			Ilakia		
	All	Female	Male	All	Female	Male	All	Female	Male
Semishovel	7.9 (3)	0.0 (0)	8.6 (3)	6.7 (2)	0.0 (0)	6.7 (2)	4.3 (1)	7.1 (1)	0.0 (0)
Trace shovel	26.3 (10)	0.0 (0)	28.6 (10)	36.7 (11)	0.0 (0)	36.7 (11)	73.9 (17)	71.4 (10)	77.8 (7)
Absent shovel	65.8 (25)	100.0 (3)	62.9 (22)	56.7 (17)	0.0 (0)	56.7 (17)	21.7 (5)	21.4 (3)	22.2 (2)
Total	(38)	(3)	(35)	(30)	(0)	(30)	(23)	(14)	(9)

Note: The figures in parentheses refer to the number of individuals studied.

TABLE 42

CHI-SQUARE TESTS FOR COMPARISON OF FREQUENCY DISTRIBUTIONS:
SHOVEL-SHAPE OF THE MAXILLARY INCISORS FOR PAIRED GROUPS

	Groups	χ^2	Degrees of Freedom	Probability
Central incisors	*Language groups* Gadsup-Awa			
	Females	8.9037	2	.011
	Males	2.4670	2	N.S.
	All	6.2757	2	.045
	Isolates: None			
Lateral incisors	*Language groups* Gadsup-Awa			
	Females	10.2926	2	.005
	Males	8.8915	2	.012
	All	14.9047	2	.001
	Tairora-Awa			
	Females	2.1207	2	N.S.
	Males	6.9339	2	.030
	All	9.5137	2	.008
	Isolates Sasaura-Ilakia			
	Females	6.6786	2	.037
	Males	7.4251	2	.025
	All	13.2615	2	.001

Awa. Isolate comparisons presenting significant chi-square values were Baieanabuta and Ilakia, and Sasaura and Ilakia.

3. *Carabelli's Anomaly of the Maxillary First Molars* (Tables 46, 47; Plate 12)

The groove was the most common expression of Carabelli's anomaly and was present in 41 percent of the individuals studied. Other expressions were present in the following percentages; absent (27 percent), slight tubercle (13 percent), groove and pit (13 percent), and pronounced tubercle (6 percent).

4. *Cusp Numbers for the Maxillary Molars* (Tables 48-53; Plate 13)

The findings for the maxillary first molars are not included because they presented four cusps 100 percent of the time, and would not contribute any additional information if tabulated. Other authors (Moorrees 1957; Pedersen 1949) have noted this finding.

The maxillary second molars presented a 4 − number of cusps in 85

TABLE 43
VARIATIONS OF THE CROWN OF THE MAXILLARY LATERAL INCISORS: FREQUENCY (PERCENT) ARRAY FOR LANGUAGE GROUPS

	Total			Gadsup			Tairora		
	All	Female	Male	All	Female	Male	All	Female	Male
Lingual cusp	18.0 (38)	25.7 (9)	16.5 (29)	12.3 (9)	10.0 (1)	12.7 (8)	13.2 (9)	50.0 (1)	12.1 (8)
Peg-shaped	2.4 (5)	5.7 (2)	1.7 (3)	0.0 (0)	0.0 (0)	0.0 (0)	1.5 (1)	0.0 (0)	1.5 (1)
Missing	1.9 (4)	0.0 (0)	2.3 (4)	1.4 (1)	0.0 (0)	1.6 (1)	1.5 (1)	0.0 (0)	1.5 (1)
Normal	77.7 (164)	68.6 (24)	79.5 (140)	86.3 (63)	90.0 (9)	85.7 (54)	83.8 (57)	50.0 (1)	84.8 (56)
Total	(211)	(35)	(176)	(73)	(10)	(63)	(68)	(2)	(66)

	Auyana			Awa		
	All	Female	Male	All	Female	Male
Lingual cusp	19.0 (4)	0.0 (0)	22.2 (4)	32.7 (16)	35.0 (7)	31.0 (9)
Peg-shaped	14.3 (3)	33.3 (1)	11.1 (2)	2.0 (1)	5.0 (1)	0.0 (0)
Missing	0.0 (0)	0.0 (0)	0.0 (0)	4.1 (2)	0.0 (0)	6.9 (2)
Normal	66.7 (14)	66.7 (2)	66.7 (12)	61.2 (30)	60.0 (12)	62.1 (18)
Total	(21)	(3)	(18)	(49)	(20)	(29)

Note: The figures in parentheses refer to the number of individuals studied.

TABLE 44

Variations in the Crown of the Maxillary Lateral Incisors: Frequency (Percent) Array for Isolates

	Sasaura			Baieanabuta			Ilakia		
	All	Female	Male	All	Female	Male	All	Female	Male
Lingual cusp	17.5 (7)	33.3 (1)	16.2 (6)	3.3 (1)	0.0 (0)	3.3 (1)	37.9 (11)	37.5 (6)	38.5 (5)
Peg-shaped	0.0 (0)	0.0 (0)	0.0 (0)	3.3 (1)	0.0 (0)	3.3 (1)	0.0 (0)	0.0 (0)	0.0 (0)
Missing	0.0 (0)	0.0 (0)	0.0 (0)	3.3 (1)	0.0 (0)	3.3 (1)	3.4 (1)	0.0 (0)	7.7 (1)
Normal	82.5 (33)	66.7 (2)	83.8 (31)	90.0 (27)	0.0 (0)	90.0 (27)	58.6 (17)	62.5 (10)	53.8 (7)
Total	(40)	(3)	(37)	(30)	(0)	(30)	(29)	(16)	(13)

Note: The figures in parentheses refer to the number of individuals studied.

TABLE 45

CHI-SQUARE TESTS FOR COMPARISON OF FREQUENCY DISTRIBUTIONS:
VARIATIONS OF THE CROWN OF THE MAXILLARY LATERAL INCISORS
FOR PAIRED GROUPS

Groups	X²	Degrees of Freedom	Probability
Language groups			
Gadsup-Auyana			
Females	3.7818	2	N.S.
Males	8.7662	3	.032
All	12.0161	3	.007
Gadsup-Awa			
Females	2.9196	2	N.S.
Males	6.7487	2	.033
All	10.6956	3	.015
Isolates			
Baieanabuta-Ilakia			
Females	0.0000	1	N.S.
Males	10.3241	3	.015
All	11.5924	3	.009
Sasaura-Ilakia			
Females	0.0188	1	N.S.
Males	6.1445	2	.045
All	5.3923	2	N.S.

percent of the second molars studied. The other patterns found were as follows: 3+ cusps (8 percent), 3 cusps (5 percent), and 4 cusps (2 percent).

Chi-square tests showed significant differences when comparing the maxillary right second molar for the following language groups: Gadsup and Awa, and Tairora and Awa. The Sasaura and Ilakia isolates also presented significant differences for the maxillary right second molar. The maxillary left second molar presented a significant chi-square value for the Gadsup and Awa.

The maxillary third molars presented the following percentages for the number of cusps: 3+ cusps (46 percent), 4− cusps (46 percent), and 3 cusps (8 percent).

5. *Cusp Numbers and Groove Patterns for the Mandibular Molars* (Tables 54-63; Plate 14)

The mandibular first molar presented a Y5 pattern in 55 percent of the teeth evaluated. The second most frequently observed pattern was the +5 arrangement which occurred 25 percent of the time. Other patterns observed were: +4 (7 percent), Y4 (5 percent), Y6 (4 per-

TABLE 46

CARABELLI'S ANOMALY OF THE MAXILLARY RIGHT FIRST MOLAR: FREQUENCY (PERCENT) ARRAY FOR LANGUAGE GROUPS

	Total			Tairora		
	All	Female	Male	All	Female	Male
Pronounced tubercle	6.7 (14)	0.0 (0)	8.1 (14)	10.3 (7)	0.0 (0)	10.6 (7)
Slight tubercle	12.5 (26)	13.9 (5)	12.2 (21)	14.7 (10)	0.0 (0)	15.2 (10)
Groove	41.3 (86)	33.3 (12)	43.0 (74)	44.1 (30)	50.0 (1)	43.9 (29)
Groove & pit	13.0 (27)	11.1 (4)	13.4 (23)	8.8 (6)	0.0 (0)	9.1 (6)
Absent	26.4 (55)	41.7 (15)	23.3 (40)	22.1 (15)	50.0 (1)	21.2 (14)
Total	(208)	(36)	(172)	(68)	(2)	(66)

	Gadsup			Awa		
	All	Female	Male	All	Female	Male
Pronounced tubercle	5.6 (4)	0.0 (0)	6.5 (4)	4.3 (2)	0.0 (0)	7.7 (2)
Slight tubercle	8.3 (6)	10.0 (1)	8.1 (5)	19.6 (9)	20.0 (4)	19.2 (5)
Groove	44.4 (32)	30.0 (3)	46.8 (29)	28.3 (13)	30.0 (6)	26.9 (7)
Groove & pit	19.4 (14)	20.0 (2)	19.4 (12)	13.0 (6)	10.0 (2)	15.4 (4)
Absent	22.2 (16)	40.0 (4)	19.4 (12)	34.8 (16)	40.0 (8)	30.8 (8)
Total	(72)	(10)	(62)	(46)	(20)	(26)

	Auyana		
	All	Female	Male
Pronounced tubercle	4.5 (1)	0.0 (0)	5.6 (1)
Slight tubercle	4.5 (1)	0.0 (0)	5.6 (1)
Groove	50.0 (11)	50.0 (2)	50.0 (9)
Groove & pit	4.5 (1)	0.0 (0)	5.6 (1)
Absent	36.4 (8)	50.0 (2)	33.3 (6)
Total	(22)	(4)	(18)

Note: The figures in parentheses refer to the number of individuals studied.

TABLE 47

CARABELLI'S ANOMALY OF THE MAXILLARY LEFT FIRST MOLAR: FREQUENCY (PERCENT) ARRAY FOR LANGUAGE GROUPS

	Total			Gadsup			Tairora		
	All	Female	Male	All	Female	Male	All	Female	Male
Pronounced tubercle	5.8 (12)	5.4 (2)	5.9 (10)	5.7 (4)	0.0 (0)	6.7 (4)	3.0 (2)	0.0 (0)	3.1 (2)
Slight tubercle	13.1 (27)	13.5 (5)	13.0 (22)	10.0 (7)	10.0 (1)	10.0 (6)	16.7 (11)	0.0 (0)	17.2 (11)
Groove	41.3 (85)	35.1 (13)	42.6 (72)	50.0 (35)	50.0 (5)	50.0 (30)	42.4 (28)	50.0 (1)	42.2 (27)
Groove & pit	13.1 (27)	8.1 (3)	14.2 (24)	14.3 (10)	10.0 (1)	15.0 (9)	13.6 (9)	0.0 (0)	14.1 (9)
Absent	26.7 (55)	37.8 (14)	24.3 (41)	20.0 (14)	30.0 (3)	18.3 (11)	24.2 (16)	50.0 (1)	23.4 (15)
Total	(206)	(37)	(169)	(70)	(10)	(60)	(66)	(2)	(64)

	Auyana			Awa		
	All	Female	Male	All	Female	Male
Pronounced tubercle	4.5 (1)	0.0 (0)	5.6 (1)	10.4 (5)	9.5 (2)	11.1 (3)
Slight tubercle	4.5 (1)	0.0 (0)	5.6 (1)	16.7 (8)	19.0 (4)	14.8 (4)
Groove	31.8 (7)	50.0 (2)	27.8 (5)	31.3 (15)	23.8 (5)	37.0 (10)
Groove & pit	13.6 (3)	0.0 (0)	16.7 (3)	10.4 (5)	9.5 (2)	11.1 (3)
Absent	45.5 (10)	50.0 (2)	44.4 (8)	31.3 (15)	38.1 (8)	25.9 (7)
Total	(22)	(4)	(18)	(48)	(21)	(27)

Note: The figures in parentheses refer to the number of individuals studied.

a. Pronounced tubercle

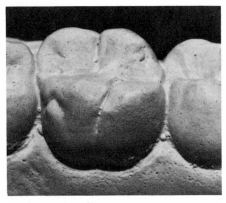

b. Slight tubercle

c. Groove

d. Groove and pit

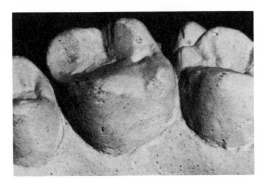

e. Absent

Plate 12. Examples of Carabelli's anomaly of the maxillary first molars in the Eastern Highlands natives

TABLE 48

CUSP NUMBERS OF THE MAXILLARY RIGHT SECOND MOLAR:
FREQUENCY (PERCENT) ARRAY FOR LANGUAGE GROUPS

	Total			Gadsup			Tairora		
	All	Female	Male	All	Female	Male	All	Female	Male
4 cusps	2.0 (4)	0.0 (0)	2.4 (4)	0.0 (0)	0.0 (0)	0.0 (0)	1.5 (1)	0.0 (0)	1.6 (1)
4− cusps	84.8 (173)	83.3 (30)	85.1 (143)	86.1 (62)	55.6 (5)	90.5 (57)	87.9 (58)	50.0 (1)	89.1 (57)
3+ cusps	8.8 (18)	16.7 (6)	7.1 (12)	13.9 (10)	44.4 (4)	9.5 (6)	4.5 (3)	50.0 (1)	3.1 (2)
3 cusps	4.4 (9)	0.0 (0)	5.4 (9)	0.0 (0)	0.0 (0)	0.0 (0)	6.1 (4)	0.0 (0)	6.3 (4)
Total	(204)	(36)	(168)	(72)	(9)	(63)	(66)	(2)	(64)

	Auyana			Awa		
	All	Female	Male	All	Female	Male
4 cusps	0.0 (0)	0.0 (0)	0.0 (0)	6.8 (3)	0.0 (0)	13.0 (3)
4− cusps	81.8 (18)	100.0 (4)	77.8 (14)	79.5 (35)	95.2 (20)	65.2 (15)
3+ cusps	13.6 (3)	0.0 (0)	16.7 (3)	4.5 (2)	4.8 (1)	4.3 (1)
3 cusps	4.5 (1)	0.0 (0)	5.6 (1)	9.1 (4)	0.0 (0)	17.4 (4)
Total	(22)	(4)	(18)	(44)	(21)	(23)

Note: The figures in parentheses refer to the number of individuals studied.

TABLE 49

CUSP NUMBERS OF THE MAXILLARY RIGHT SECOND MOLAR:
FREQUENCY (PERCENT) ARRAY FOR ISOLATES

	Sasaura			Baieanabuta			Ilakia		
	All	Female	Male	All	Female	Male	All	Female	Male
4 cusps	0.0 (0)	0.0 (0)	0.0 (0)	3.4 (1)	0.0 (0)	3.4 (1)	8.0 (2)	0.0 (0)	22.2 (2)
4− cusps	90.0 (36)	66.7 (2)	91.9 (34)	89.7 (26)	0.0 (0)	89.7 (26)	80.0 (20)	93.8 (15)	55.6 (5)
3 + cusps	10.0 (4)	33.3 (1)	8.1 (3)	3.4 (1)	0.0 (0)	3.4 (1)	8.0 (2)	6.3 (1)	11.1 (1)
3 cusps	0.0 (0)	0.0 (0)	0.0 (0)	3.4 (1)	0.0 (0)	3.4 (1)	4.0 (1)	0.0 (0)	11.1 (1)
Total	(40)	(3)	(37)	(29)	(0)	(29)	(25)	(16)	(9)

Note: The figures in parentheses refer to the number of individuals studied.

TABLE 50

CUSP NUMBERS OF THE MAXILLARY LEFT SECOND MOLAR: FREQUENCY (PERCENT) ARRAY FOR LANGUAGE GROUPS

	Total			Gadsup			Tairora		
	All	Female	Male	All	Female	Male	All	Female	Male
4 cusps	2.9 (6)	0.0 (0)	3.6 (6)	2.9 (2)	0.0 (0)	3.3 (2)	1.5 (1)	0.0 (0)	1.6 (1)
4− cusps	84.9 (174)	86.1 (31)	84.6 (143)	87.1 (61)	66.7 (6)	90.2 (55)	81.8 (54)	50.0 (1)	82.8 (53)
3+ cusps	6.8 (14)	11.1 (4)	5.9 (10)	8.6 (6)	22.2 (2)	6.6 (4)	9.1 (6)	50.0 (1)	7.8 (5)
3 cusps	5.4 (11)	2.8 (1)	5.9 (10)	1.4 (1)	11.1 (1)	0.0 (0)	7.6 (5)	0.0 (0)	7.8 (5)
Total	(205)	(36)	(169)	(70)	(9)	(61)	(66)	(2)	(64)

	Auyana			Awa		
	All	Female	Male	All	Female	Male
4 cusps	0.0 (0)	0.0 (0)	0.0 (0)	6.3 (3)	0.0 (0)	11.1 (3)
4− cusps	90.5 (19)	100.0 (4)	88.2 (15)	83.3 (40)	95.2 (20)	74.1 (20)
3+ cusps	4.8 (1)	0.0 (0)	5.9 (1)	2.1 (1)	4.8 (1)	0.0 (0)
3 cusps	4.8 (1)	0.0 (0)	5.9 (1)	8.3 (4)	0.0 (0)	14.8 (4)
Total	(21)	(4)	(17)	(48)	(21)	(27)

Note: The figures in parentheses refer to the number of individuals studied.

cent), +6 (2 percent), and one *X5* which was observed for one mandibular right first molar.

The mandibular second molar had a +4 pattern approximately 72 percent of the time. Other observations were: *X4* (11 percent), +5 (10 percent), +6 (1 percent), *X5* (1 percent). In addition a *Y5* was observed for one mandibular left second molar, and an *X6* for one mandibular right second molar. The chi-square tests presented significant differences for the right second molar between Gadsup and Awa as well as Sasaura and Baieanabuta, and Sasaura and Ilakia isolates. The left second molar presented a significant difference when comparing the Sasaura and Ilakia isolates.

TABLE 51

CHI-SQUARE TESTS FOR COMPARISON OF FREQUENCY DISTRIBUTIONS:
CUSP NUMBERS OF THE MAXILLARY SECOND MOLARS FOR PAIRED GROUPS

	Groups	χ^2	Degrees of Freedom	Probability
Right maxillary second molar	*Language groups* Gadsup-Awa			
	Females	7.1429	1	.007
	Males	21.0125	3	.001
	All	13.9000	3	.003
	Tairora-Awa			
	Females	4.7069	1	.028
	Males	8.3705	3	.038
	All	2.5918	3	N.S.
	Isolates Sasaura-Ilakia			
	Females	1.9675	1	N.S.
	Males	13.5358	3	.004
	All	5.0452	3	N.S.
Left maxillary second molar	*Language groups* Gadsup-Awa			
	Females	4.8474	2	N.S.
	Males	13.3968	3	.004
	All	6.0462	3	N.S.
	Isolates: None			

TABLE 52

Cusp Numbers of the Maxillary Right Third Molar: Frequency (Percent) Array for Language Groups

	Total			Gadsup			Tairora		
	All	Female	Male	All	Female	Male	All	Female	Male
4 − cusps	45.1 (65)	53.3 (8)	44.2 (57)	44.7 (21)	50.0 (3)	43.9 (18)	49.1 (27)	0.0 (0)	49.1 (27)
3 + cusps	45.8 (66)	40.0 (6)	46.5 (60)	44.7 (21)	33.3 (2)	46.3 (19)	43.6 (24)	0.0 (0)	43.6 (24)
3 cusps	9.0 (13)	6.7 (1)	9.3 (12)	10.6 (5)	16.7 (1)	9.8 (4)	7.3 (4)	0.0 (0)	7.3 (4)
Total	(144)	(15)	(129)	(47)	(6)	(41)	(55)	(0)	(55)

	Auyana			Awa		
	All	Female	Male	All	Female	Male
4 − cusps	47.4 (9)	33.3 (1)	50.0 (8)	34.8 (8)	66.7 (4)	23.5 (4)
3 + cusps	47.4 (9)	66.7 (2)	43.8 (7)	52.2 (12)	33.3 (2)	58.8 (10)
3 cusps	5.3 (1)	0.0 (0)	6.3 (1)	13.0 (3)	0.0 (0)	17.6 (3)
Total	(19)	(3)	(16)	(23)	(6)	(17)

Note: The figures in parentheses refer to the number of individuals studied.

TABLE 53

CUSP NUMBERS OF THE MAXILLARY LEFT THIRD MOLAR: FREQUENCY (PERCENT) ARRAY FOR LANGUAGE GROUPS

Total

	All		Female		Male	
4 − cusps	46.9	(67)	62.5	(10)	44.9	(57)
3 + cusps	46.9	(67)	31.3	(5)	48.8	(62)
3 cusps	6.3	(9)	6.3	(1)	6.3	(8)
Total	(143)		(16)		(127)	

Auyana

	All		Female		Male	
4 − cusps	52.9	(9)	100.0	(1)	50.0	(8)
3 + cusps	41.2	(7)	0.0	(0)	43.8	(7)
3 cusps	5.9	(1)	0.0	(0)	6.3	(1)
Total	(17)		(1)		(16)	

Gadsup

	All		Female		Male	
4 − cusps	42.0	(21)	50.0	(3)	40.9	(18)
3 + cusps	54.0	(27)	50.0	(3)	54.5	(24)
3 cusps	4.0	(2)	0.0	(0)	4.5	(2)
Total	(50)		(6)		(44)	

Awa

	All		Female		Male	
4 − cusps	56.0	(14)	66.7	(6)	50.0	(8)
3 + cusps	32.0	(8)	22.2	(2)	37.5	(6)
3 cusps	12.0	(3)	11.1	(1)	12.5	(2)
Total	(25)		(9)		(16)	

Tairora

	All		Female		Male	
4 − cusps	45.1	(23)	0.0	(0)	45.1	(23)
3 + cusps	49.0	(25)	0.0	(0)	49.0	(25)
3 cusps	5.9	(3)	0.0	(0)	5.9	(3)
Total	(51)		(0)		(51)	

Note: The figures in parentheses refer to the number of individuals studied.

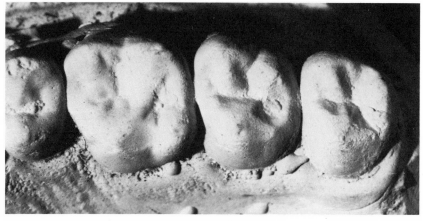

a.   4 cusps   3 cusps   3 cusps

b.   4 cusps   4— cusps   4— cusps

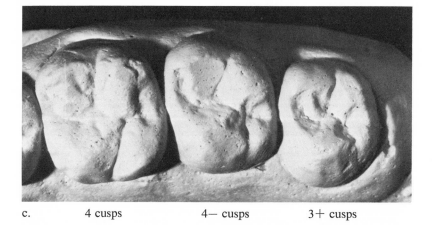

c.   4 cusps   4— cusps   3+ cusps

Plate 13. Examples of cusp numbers of the maxillary molars in the Eastern Highlands natives

TABLE 54

Cusp Numbers and Groove Patterns of the Mandibular Right First Molar: Frequency (Percent) Array for Language Groups

	Total						Gadsup						Tairora					
	All		Female		Male		All		Female		Male		All		Female		Male	
Y4	5.0	(10)	6.5	(2)	4.8	(8)	5.6	(4)	10.0	(1)	4.9	(3)	3.1	(2)	0.0	(0)	3.1	(2)
Y5	54.3	(108)	41.9	(13)	56.5	(95)	49.3	(35)	30.0	(3)	52.5	(32)	58.5	(38)	100.0	(1)	57.8	(37)
Y6	5.0	(10)	6.5	(2)	4.8	(8)	5.6	(4)	10.0	(1)	4.9	(3)	7.7	(5)	0.0	(0)	7.8	(5)
+4	7.0	(14)	16.1	(5)	5.4	(9)	8.5	(6)	10.0	(1)	8.2	(5)	3.1	(2)	0.0	(0)	3.1	(2)
+5	26.1	(52)	25.8	(8)	26.2	(44)	25.4	(18)	30.0	(3)	24.6	(15)	26.2	(17)	0.0	(0)	26.6	(17)
+6	2.0	(4)	3.2	(1)	1.8	(3)	4.2	(3)	10.0	(1)	3.3	(2)	1.5	(1)	0.0	(0)	1.6	(1)
X5	0.5	(1)	0.0	(0)	0.6	(1)	1.4	(1)	0.0	(0)	1.6	(1)	0.0	(0)	0.0	(0)	0.0	(0)
Total		(199)		(31)		(168)		(71)		(10)		(61)		(65)		(1)		(64)

	Auyana						Awa					
	All		Female		Male		All		Female		Male	
Y4	9.1	(2)	0.0	(0)	11.1	(2)	4.9	(2)	6.3	(1)	4.0	(1)
Y5	50.0	(11)	0.0	(0)	61.1	(11)	58.5	(24)	56.3	(9)	60.0	(15)
Y6	0.0	(0)	0.0	(0)	0.0	(0)	2.4	(1)	6.3	(1)	0.0	(0)
+4	22.7	(5)	75.0	(3)	11.1	(2)	2.4	(1)	6.3	(1)	0.0	(0)
+5	18.2	(4)	25.0	(1)	16.7	(3)	31.7	(13)	25.0	(4)	36.0	(9)
+6	0.0	(0)	0.0	(0)	0.0	(0)	0.0	(0)	0.0	(0)	0.0	(0)
X5	0.0	(0)	0.0	(0)	0.0	(0)	0.0	(0)	0.0	(0)	0.0	(0)
Total		(22)		(4)		(18)		(41)		(16)		(25)

Note: The figures in parentheses refer to the number of individuals studied.

TABLE 55
CUSP NUMBERS AND GROOVE PATTERNS OF THE MANDIBULAR LEFT FIRST MOLAR: FREQUENCY (PERCENT) ARRAY FOR LANGUAGE GROUPS

	Total			Gadsup			Tairora		
	All	Female	Male	All	Female	Male	All	Female	Male
Y4	5.7 (11)	6.5 (2)	5.5 (9)	5.7 (4)	10.0 (1)	5.0 (3)	4.7 (3)	0.0 (0)	4.8 (3)
Y5	55.7 (108)	48.4 (15)	57.1 (93)	52.9 (37)	40.0 (4)	55.0 (33)	56.3 (36)	50.0 (1)	56.5 (35)
Y6	4.1 (8)	3.2 (1)	4.3 (7)	2.9 (2)	0.0 (0)	3.3 (2)	6.3 (4)	0.0 (0)	6.5 (4)
+4	7.2 (14)	19.4 (6)	4.9 (8)	8.6 (6)	10.0 (1)	8.3 (5)	3.1 (2)	50.0 (1)	1.6 (1)
+5	24.2 (47)	19.4 (6)	25.2 (41)	24.3 (17)	30.0 (3)	23.3 (14)	26.6 (17)	0.0 (0)	27.4 (17)
+6	3.1 (6)	3.2 (1)	3.1 (5)	5.7 (4)	10.0 (1)	5.0 (3)	3.1 (2)	0.0 (0)	3.2 (2)
Total	(194)	(31)	(163)	(70)	(10)	(60)	(64)	(2)	(62)

	Auyana			Awa		
	All	Female	Male	All	Female	Male
Y4	9.5 (2)	0.0 (0)	11.8 (2)	5.1 (2)	6.7 (1)	4.2 (1)
Y5	47.6 (10)	0.0 (0)	58.5 (10)	64.1 (25)	66.7 (10)	62.5 (15)
Y6	0.0 (0)	0.0 (0)	0.0 (0)	5.1 (2)	6.7 (1)	4.2 (1)
+4	19.0 (4)	75.0 (3)	5.9 (1)	5.1 (2)	6.7 (1)	4.2 (1)
+5	23.8 (5)	25.0 (1)	23.5 (4)	20.5 (8)	13.3 (2)	25.0 (6)
+6	0.0 (0)	0.0 (0)	0.0 (0)	0.0 (0)	0.0 (0)	0.0 (0)
Total	(21)	(4)	(17)	(39)	(15)	(24)

Note: The figures in parentheses refer to the number of individuals studied.

CUSP NUMBERS AND GROOVE PATTERNS OF THE MANDIBULAR RIGHT SECOND MOLAR: FREQUENCY (PERCENT) ARRAY FOR LANGUAGE GROUPS

	Total			Gadsup			Tairora		
	All	Female	Male	All	Female	Male	All	Female	Male
Y4	4.1 (8)	3.1 (1)	4.3 (7)	1.4 (1)	0.0 (0)	1.7 (1)	7.6 (5)	0.0 (0)	7.8 (5)
+4	73.8 (144)	84.4 (27)	71.8 (117)	79.7 (55)	70.0 (7)	81.4 (48)	69.7 (46)	100.0 (2)	68.8 (44)
+5	8.7 (17)	3.1 (1)	9.8 (16)	5.8 (4)	10.0 (1)	5.1 (3)	9.1 (6)	0.0 (0)	9.4 (6)
+6	1.0 (2)	0.0 (0)	1.2 (2)	0.0 (0)	0.0 (0)	0.0 (0)	1.5 (1)	0.0 (0)	1.6 (1)
X4	10.8 (21)	6.3 (2)	11.7 (19)	11.6 (8)	10.0 (1)	11.9 (7)	10.6 (7)	0.0 (0)	10.9 (7)
X5	1.0 (2)	0.0 (0)	1.2 (2)	0.0 (0)	0.0 (0)	0.0 (0)	1.5 (1)	0.0 (0)	1.6 (1)
X6	0.5 (1)	3.1 (1)	0.0 (0)	1.4 (1)	10.0 (1)	0.0 (0)	0.0 (0)	0.0 (0)	0.0 (0)
Total	(195)	(32)	(163)	(69)	(10)	(59)	(66)	(2)	(64)

	Auyana			Awa		
	All	Female	Male	All	Female	Male
Y4	0.0 (0)	0.0 (0)	0.0 (0)	5.3 (2)	6.3 (1)	4.5 (1)
+4	77.3 (17)	100.0 (4)	72.2 (13)	68.4 (26)	87.5 (14)	54.5 (12)
+5	9.1 (2)	0.0 (0)	11.1 (2)	13.2 (5)	0.0 (0)	22.7 (5)
+6	4.5 (1)	0.0 (0)	5.6 (1)	0.0 (0)	0.0 (0)	0.0 (0)
X4	9.1 (2)	0.0 (0)	11.1 (2)	10.5 (4)	6.3 (1)	13.6 (3)
X5	0.0 (0)	0.0 (0)	0.0 (0)	2.6 (1)	0.0 (0)	4.5 (1)
X6	0.0 (0)	0.0 (0)	0.0 (0)	0.0 (0)	0.0 (0)	0.0 (0)
Total	(22)	(4)	(18)	(38)	(16)	(22)

Note: The figures in parentheses refer to the number of individuals studied.

TABLE 57

CUSP NUMBERS AND GROOVE PATTERNS OF THE MANDIBULAR RIGHT SECOND MOLAR: FREQUENCY (PERCENT) ARRAY FOR ISOLATES

	Sasaura			Baieanabuta			Ilakia		
	All	Female	Male	All	Female	Male	All	Female	Male
Y4	0.0 (0)	0.0 (0)	0.0 (0)	3.6 (1)	0.0 (0)	3.6 (1)	4.3 (1)	0.0 (0)	10.0 (1)
+4	80.6 (29)	66.7 (2)	81.8 (27)	60.7 (17)	0.0 (0)	60.7 (17)	73.9 (17)	92.3 (12)	50.0 (5)
+5	0.0 (0)	0.0 (0)	0.0 (0)	17.9 (5)	0.0 (0)	17.9 (5)	8.6 (2)	0.0 (0)	20.0 (2)
+6	0.0 (0)	0.0 (0)	0.0 (0)	0.0 (0)	0.0 (0)	0.0 (0)	0.0 (0)	0.0 (0)	0.0 (0)
X4	19.4 (7)	33.3 (1)	18.2 (6)	17.9 (5)	0.0 (0)	17.9 (5)	8.6 (2)	7.7 (1)	10.0 (1)
X5	0.0 (0)	0.0 (0)	0.0 (0)	0.0 (0)	0.0 (0)	0.0 (0)	4.3 (1)	0.0 (0)	10.0 (1)
X6	0.0 (0)	0.0 (0)	0.0 (0)	0.0 (0)	0.0 (0)	0.0 (0)	0.0 (0)	0.0 (0)	0.0 (0)
Total	(36)	(3)	(33)	(28)	(0)	(28)	(23)	(13)	(10)

Note: The figures in parentheses refer to the number of individuals studied.

TABLE 58

Cusp Numbers and Groove Patterns of the Mandibular Left Second Molar: Frequency (Percent) Array for Language Groups

	Total			Gadsup			Tairora		
	All	Female	Male	All	Female	Male	All	Female	Male
Y4	5.0 (10)	2.9 (1)	5.5 (9)	1.4 (1)	0.0 (0)	1.6 (1)	7.6 (5)	0.0 (0)	7.8 (5)
Y5	0.5 (1)	2.9 (1)	0.0 (0)	0.0 (0)	0.0 (0)	0.0 (0)	0.0 (0)	0.0 (0)	0.0 (0)
+4	69.8 (139)	80.0 (28)	67.3 (111)	77.5 (55)	70.0 (7)	78.7 (48)	60.6 (40)	100.0 (2)	59.4 (38)
+5	10.6 (21)	5.7 (2)	12.1 (20)	9.9 (7)	20.0 (2)	8.2 (5)	13.6 (9)	0.0 (0)	14.1 (9)
+6	1.5 (3)	0.0 (0)	1.8 (3)	0.0 (0)	0.0 (0)	0.0 (0)	3.0 (2)	0.0 (0)	3.1 (2)
X4	11.1 (22)	5.7 (2)	12.1 (20)	9.9 (7)	0.0 (0)	11.5 (7)	12.1 (8)	0.0 (0)	12.5 (8)
X5	1.5 (3)	2.9 (1)	1.2 (2)	1.4 (1)	10.0 (1)	0.0 (0)	3.0 (2)	0.0 (0)	3.1 (2)
Total	(199)	(35)	(165)	(71)	(10)	(61)	(66)	(2)	(64)

	Auyana			Awa		
	All	Female	Male	All	Female	Male
Y4	4.8 (1)	0.0 (0)	5.9 (1)	7.3 (3)	5.3 (1)	9.1 (2)
Y5	0.0 (0)	0.0 (0)	0.0 (0)	2.4 (1)	5.3 (1)	0.0 (0)
+4	71.4 (15)	75.0 (3)	70.6 (12)	70.7 (29)	84.2 (16)	59.1 (13)
+5	9.5 (2)	0.0 (0)	11.8 (2)	7.3 (3)	0.0 (0)	13.6 (3)
+6	4.8 (1)	0.0 (0)	5.9 (1)	0.0 (0)	0.0 (0)	0.0 (0)
X4	9.5 (2)	25.0 (1)	5.9 (1)	12.2 (5)	5.3 (1)	18.2 (4)
X5	0.0 (0)	0.0 (0)	0.0 (0)	0.0 (0)	0.0 (0)	0.0 (0)
Total	(21)	(4)	(17)	(41)	(19)	(22)

Note: The figures in parentheses refer to the number of individuals studied.

TABLE 59

Cusp Numbers and Groove Patterns of the Mandibular Left Second Molar: Frequency (Percent) Array for Isolates

	Sasaura			Baieanabuta			Ilakia		
	All	Female	Male	All	Female	Male	All	Female	Male
Y4	0.0 (0)	0.0 (0)	0.0 (0)	3.4 (1)	0.0 (0)	3.4 (1)	7.7 (2)	0.0 (0)	18.2 (2)
Y5	0.0 (0)	0.0 (0)	0.0 (0)	0.0 (0)	0.0 (0)	0.0 (0)	0.0 (0)	0.0 (0)	0.0 (0)
+4	81.6 (31)	66.7 (2)	82.9 (29)	51.7 (15)	0.0 (0)	51.7 (15)	76.9 (20)	93.3 (14)	54.5 (6)
+5	5.3 (2)	33.3 (1)	2.0 (1)	17.2 (5)	0.0 (0)	17.2 (5)	3.8 (1)	0.0 (0)	9.1 (1)
+6	0.0 (0)	0.0 (0)	0.0 (0)	3.4 (1)	0.0 (0)	3.4 (1)	0.0 (0)	0.0 (0)	0.0 (0)
X4	13.2 (5)	0.0 (0)	14.3 (5)	20.7 (6)	0.0 (0)	20.7 (6)	11.5 (3)	6.7 (1)	18.2 (2)
X5	0.0 (0)	0.0 (0)	0.0 (0)	3.4 (1)	0.0 (0)	3.4 (1)	0.0 (0)	0.0 (0)	0.0 (0)
Total	(38)	(3)	(35)	(29)	(0)	(29)	(26)	(15)	(11)

Note: The figures in parentheses refer to the number of individuals studied.

TABLE 60

Cusp Numbers and Groove Patterns of the Mandibular Right Third Molar: Frequency (Percent) Array for Language Groups

	Total All		Total Female		Total Male		Gadsup All		Gadsup Female		Gadsup Male		Tairora All		Tairora Female		Tairora Male	
Y4	0.8	(1)	0.0	(0)	0.9	(1)	2.4	(1)	0.0	(0)	2.8	(1)	0.0	(0)	0.0	(0)	0.0	(0)
Y5	3.1	(4)	0.0	(0)	3.6	(4)	4.8	(2)	0.0	(0)	5.6	(2)	2.0	(1)	0.0	(0)	2.0	(1)
+3	3.1	(4)	0.0	(0)	3.6	(4)	2.4	(1)	0.0	(0)	2.8	(1)	4.1	(2)	0.0	(0)	4.1	(2)
+4	24.0	(31)	52.9	(9)	19.6	(22)	26.2	(11)	50.0	(3)	22.2	(8)	18.4	(9)	0.0	(0)	18.4	(9)
+5	34.9	(45)	23.5	(4)	36.6	(41)	23.8	(10)	33.3	(2)	22.2	(8)	49.0	(24)	0.0	(0)	49.0	(24)
+6	1.6	(2)	0.0	(0)	1.8	(2)	2.4	(1)	0.0	(0)	2.8	(1)	0.0	(0)	0.0	(0)	0.0	(0)
X4	8.5	(11)	5.9	(1)	8.9	(10)	4.8	(2)	0.0	(0)	5.6	(2)	8.2	(4)	0.0	(0)	8.2	(4)
X5	20.9	(27)	17.6	(3)	21.4	(24)	28.6	(12)	16.7	(1)	30.6	(11)	16.3	(8)	0.0	(0)	16.3	(8)
X6	3.1	(4)	0.0	(0)	3.6	(4)	4.8	(2)	0.0	(0)	5.6	(2)	2.0	(1)	0.0	(0)	2.0	(1)
Total		(129)		(17)		(112)		(42)		(6)		(36)		(49)		(0)		(49)

	Auyana All		Auyana Female		Auyana Male		Awa All		Awa Female		Awa Male	
Y4	0.0	(0)	0.0	(0)	0.0	(0)	0.0	(0)	0.0	(0)	0.0	(0)
Y5	7.1	(1)	0.0	(0)	8.3	(1)	0.0	(0)	0.0	(0)	0.0	(0)
+3	0.0	(0)	0.0	(0)	0.0	(0)	4.2	(1)	0.0	(0)	6.7	(1)
+4	28.6	(4)	100.0	(2)	16.7	(2)	29.2	(7)	44.4	(4)	20.0	(3)
+5	21.4	(3)	0.0	(0)	25.0	(3)	33.3	(8)	22.2	(2)	40.0	(6)
+6	0.0	(0)	0.0	(0)	0.0	(0)	4.2	(1)	0.0	(0)	6.7	(1)
X4	7.1	(1)	0.0	(0)	8.3	(1)	16.7	(4)	11.1	(1)	20.0	(3)
X5	28.6	(4)	0.0	(0)	33.3	(4)	12.5	(3)	22.2	(2)	6.7	(1)
X6	7.1	(1)	0.0	(0)	8.3	(1)	0.0	(0)	0.0	(0)	0.0	(0)
Total		(14)		(2)		(12)		(24)		(9)		(15)

Note: The figures in parentheses refer to the number of individuals studied.

TABLE 61

Cusp Numbers and Groove Patterns of the Mandibular Left Third Molar: Frequency (Percent) Array for Language Groups

	Total			Gadsup			Tairora		
	All	Female	Male	All	Female	Male	All	Female	Male
Y4	0.8 (1)	0.0 (0)	0.0 (1)	0.0 (0)	0.0 (0)	0.0 (0)	2.3 (1)	0.0 (0)	2.3 (1)
Y5	3.1 (4)	0.0 (0)	3.7 (4)	4.8 (2)	0.0 (0)	5.7 (2)	4.5 (2)	0.0 (0)	4.5 (2)
+3	4.7 (6)	0.0 (0)	5.5 (6)	2.4 (1)	0.0 (0)	2.9 (1)	6.8 (3)	0.0 (0)	6.8 (3)
+4	23.6 (30)	50.0 (9)	19.3 (21)	33.3 (14)	57.1 (4)	28.6 (10)	9.1 (4)	0.0 (0)	9.1 (4)
+5	31.5 (40)	22.2 (4)	33.0 (36)	23.8 (10)	28.6 (2)	22.9 (8)	47.7 (21)	0.0 (0)	47.7 (21)
+6	2.4 (3)	0.0 (0)	2.8 (3)	2.4 (1)	0.0 (0)	2.9 (1)	0.0 (0)	0.0 (0)	0.0 (0)
X4	5.5 (7)	5.6 (1)	5.5 (6)	4.8 (2)	0.0 (0)	5.7 (2)	2.3 (1)	0.0 (0)	2.3 (1)
X5	24.4 (31)	22.2 (4)	24.8 (27)	21.4 (9)	14.3 (1)	22.9 (8)	25.0 (11)	0.0 (0)	25.0 (11)
X6	3.9 (5)	0.0 (0)	4.6 (5)	7.1 (3)	0.0 (0)	8.6 (3)	2.3 (1)	0.0 (0)	2.3 (1)
Total	(127)	(18)	(109)	(42)	(7)	(35)	(44)	(0)	(44)

	Auyana			Awa		
	All	Female	Male	All	Female	Male
Y4	0.0 (0)	0.0 (0)	0.0 (0)	0.0 (0)	0.0 (0)	0.0 (0)
Y5	0.0 (0)	0.0 (0)	0.0 (0)	0.0 (0)	0.0 (0)	0.0 (0)
+3	0.0 (0)	0.0 (0)	0.0 (0)	7.7 (2)	0.0 (0)	11.8 (2)
+4	40.0 (6)	100.0 (2)	30.8 (4)	23.1 (6)	33.3 (3)	17.6 (3)
+5	20.0 (3)	0.0 (0)	23.1 (3)	23.1 (6)	22.2 (2)	23.5 (4)
+6	0.0 (0)	0.0 (0)	0.0 (0)	7.7 (2)	0.0 (0)	11.8 (2)
X4	6.7 (1)	0.0 (0)	7.7 (1)	11.5 (3)	11.1 (1)	11.8 (2)
X5	33.3 (5)	0.0 (0)	38.5 (5)	23.1 (6)	33.3 (3)	17.6 (3)
X6	0.0 (0)	0.0 (0)	0.0 (0)	3.8 (1)	0.0 (0)	5.9 (1)
Total	(15)	(2)	(13)	(26)	(9)	(17)

Note: The figures in parentheses refer to the number of individuals studied.

TABLE 62

Cusp Numbers and Groove Patterns of the Mandibular Left Third Molar: Frequency (Percent) Array for Isolates

	Sasaura						Baieanabuta						Ilakia					
	All		Female		Male		All		Female		Male		All		Female		Male	
Y4	0.0	(0)	0.0	(0)	0.0	(0)	0.0	(0)	0.0	(0)	0.0	(0)	0.0	(0)	0.0	(0)	0.0	(0)
Y5	5.9	(1)	0.0	(0)	6.3	(1)	4.8	(1)	0.0	(0)	4.8	(1)	0.0	(0)	0.0	(0)	0.0	(0)
+3	0.0	(0)	0.0	(0)	0.0	(0)	4.8	(1)	0.0	(0)	4.8	(1)	0.0	(0)	0.0	(0)	0.0	(0)
+4	41.2	(7)	100.0	(1)	37.5	(6)	4.8	(1)	0.0	(0)	4.8	(1)	26.7	(4)	28.6	(2)	25.0	(2)
+5	5.9	(1)	0.0	(0)	6.3	(1)	57.1	(12)	0.0	(0)	57.1	(12)	20.0	(3)	14.3	(1)	25.0	(2)
+6	5.9	(1)	0.0	(0)	6.3	(1)	0.0	(0)	0.0	(0)	0.0	(0)	0.0	(0)	0.0	(0)	0.0	(0)
X4	11.8	(2)	0.0	(0)	12.5	(2)	0.0	(0)	0.0	(0)	0.0	(0)	6.7	(1)	14.3	(1)	0.0	(0)
X5	17.6	(3)	0.0	(0)	18.8	(3)	28.6	(6)	0.0	(0)	28.6	(6)	40.0	(6)	42.9	(3)	37.5	(3)
X6	11.8	(2)	0.0	(0)	12.5	(2)	0.0	(0)	0.0	(0)	0.0	(0)	6.7	(1)	0.0	(0)	12.5	(1)
Total		(17)		(1)		(16)		(21)		(0)		(21)		(15)		(7)		(8)

Note: The figures in parentheses refer to the number of individuals studied.

TABLE 63

CHI-SQUARE TESTS FOR COMPARISON OF FREQUENCY DISTRIBUTIONS:
CUSP NUMBERS AND GROOVE PATTERNS OF THE MANDIBULAR
MOLARS FOR PAIRED GROUPS

	Groups	χ^2	Degrees of Freedom	Probability
Right mandibular second molar	*Language groups*			
	Gadsup-Awa			
	Females	4.1708	4	N.S.
	Males	9.8551	4	.044
	All	5.6537	5	N.S.
	Isolates			
	Sasaura-Ilakia			
	Females	1.4652	1	N.S.
	Males	14.5596	4	.006
	All	5.7810	4	N.S.
	Sasaura-Baieanabuta			
	Females	0.0000	1	N.S.
	Males	8.0076	3	.046
	All	8.5981	3	N.S.
Left mandibular second molar	*Language groups:* None			
	Isolates			
	Sasaura-Ilakia			
	Females	5.4000	2	N.S.
	Males	8.0769	3	.046
	All	3.0636	3	N.S.
Left mandibular third molar	*Language groups:* None			
	Isolates			
	Sasaura-Baieanabuta			
	Females	0.0000	0	N.S.
	Males	19.5607	7	.007
	All	20.6151	7	.004

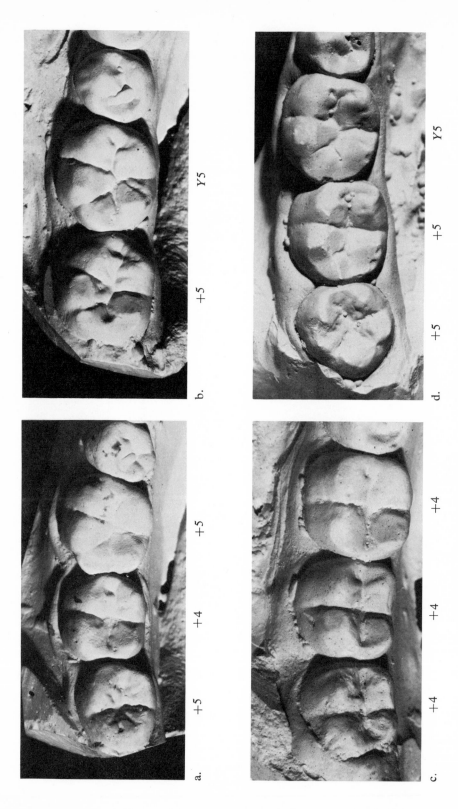

a.   +5   +4   +5   +5

b.   +5   +5   Y5

c.   +4   +4   +4

d.   +5   +5   Y5

Plate 14. Examples of cusp numbers and groove patterns of the mandibular molars in the Eastern Highland natives

a.   3 cusps   3 cusps

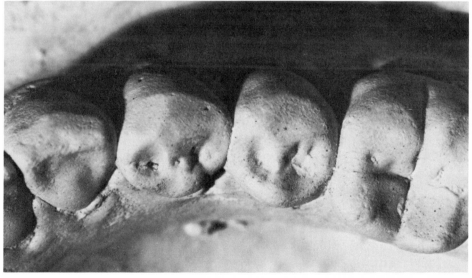

b.   2 cusps   2 cusps

Plate 15. Examples of cusp numbers of the mandibular premolars in the Eastern Highlands natives

The +5 arrangement of cusps and grooves was observed in 33 percent of the mandibular third molars evaluated. Other observations were: +4 (24 percent), $X5$ (22 percent), $X4$ (7 percent), +3 (4 percent), $X6$ (4 percent), $Y5$ (3 percent), +6 (2 percent), and $Y4$ (1 percent).

Chi-square tests revealed significant differences between the Sasaura and Baieanabuta isolates for the mandibular left third molar.

6. *Cusp Numbers of Mandibular Premolars* (Tables 64-68; Plate 15)

The mandibular first premolar was observed to be bicuspal in 55 percent of the teeth, with the tricuspal form present in 41 percent of the teeth examined. Teeth with 4 cusps (4 percent) and 5 cusps were also observed but the latter occurred only once.

Chi-square tests presented significant differences when comparing the right first premolar cuspal frequencies between Gadsup and Awa and Tairora and Awa. The left first premolar was significantly different for the Tairora and Awa.

The second premolar was present in the tricuspal form 75 percent of the time. Three other cuspal types were present: 4 cusps (13 percent), 2 cusps (11 percent), and 5 cusps (1 percent).

7. *Supernumerary Cusps* (Tables 69, 70; Plate 16)

The protostylid type of paramolar cusp of mandibular molars accounted for 42 percent (23 individuals) of the supernumerary cusps examined. The paramolar cusp of the maxillary molars (40 percent, 22 individuals) and the occlusal cusps (18 percent, 10 individuals) accounted for the remaining supernumerary cusps observed.

Chi-square tests presented statistically significant differences for Tairora and Auyana, and Tairora and Awa.

8. *Supernumerary Teeth* (Table 71; Plate 17)

Supernumerary teeth were found to be present in 8 of the 218 sets of casts studied, which is approximately 4 percent of the natives. Chi-square tests were not performed on these data.

DISCUSSION

1. *Shovel-Shape of the Maxillary Incisors*

The shovel-shape appearance of the lingual surface of maxillary incisors was reported upon by Hrdlička in 1920 in an extensive survey

TABLE 64

CUSP NUMBERS OF THE MANDIBULAR RIGHT FIRST PREMOLAR: FREQUENCY (PERCENT) ARRAY FOR LANGUAGE GROUPS

	Total			Gadsup			Tairora		
	All	Female	Male	All	Female	Male	All	Female	Male
2 cusps	54.7 (117)	68.4 (26)	51.7 (91)	52.9 (37)	70.0 (7)	50.0 (30)	44.3 (31)	0.0 (0)	45.6 (31)
3 cusps	41.1 (88)	31.6 (12)	43.2 (76)	45.7 (32)	30.0 (3)	48.3 (29)	47.1 (33)	100.0 (2)	45.6 (31)
4 cusps	3.7 (8)	0.0 (0)	4.5 (8)	1.4 (1)	0.0 (0)	1.7 (1)	7.1 (5)	0.0 (0)	7.4 (5)
5 cusps	0.5 (1)	0.0 (0)	0.6 (1)	0.0 (0)	0.0 (0)	0.0 (0)	1.4 (1)	0.0 (0)	1.5 (1)
Total	(214)	(38)	(176)	(70)	(10)	(60)	(70)	(2)	(68)

	Auyana			Awa		
	All	Female	Male	All	Female	Male
2 cusps	54.5 (12)	75.0 (3)	50.0 (9)	71.2 (37)	72.7 (16)	70.0 (21)
3 cusps	45.5 (10)	25.0 (1)	50.0 (9)	25.0 (13)	27.3 (6)	23.3 (7)
4 cusps	0.0 (0)	0.0 (0)	0.0 (0)	3.8 (2)	0.0 (0)	6.7 (2)
5 cusps	0.0 (0)	0.0 (0)	0.0 (0)	0.0 (0)	0.0 (0)	0.0 (0)
Total	(22)	(4)	(18)	(52)	(22)	(30)

Note: The figures in parentheses refer to the number of individuals studied.

TABLE 65
Cusp Numbers of the Mandibular Left First Premolar: Frequency (Percent) Array for Language Groups

	Total			Gadsup			Tairora		
	All	Female	Male	All	Female	Male	All	Female	Male
2 cusps	55.1 (118)	65.8 (25)	52.8 (93)	55.7 (39)	60.0 (6)	55.0 (33)	41.4 (29)	0.0 (0)	42.6 (29)
3 cusps	41.1 (88)	31.6 (12)	43.2 (76)	42.9 (30)	30.0 (3)	45.0 (27)	50.0 (35)	100.0 (2)	48.5 (33)
4 cusps	3.3 (7)	2.6 (1)	3.4 (6)	1.4 (1)	10.0 (1)	0.0 (0)	7.1 (5)	0.0 (0)	7.4 (5)
5 cusps	0.5 (1)	0.0 (0)	0.6 (1)	0.0 (0)	0.0 (0)	0.0 (0)	1.4 (1)	0.0 (0)	1.5 (1)
Total	(214)	(38)	(176)	(70)	(10)	(60)	(70)	(2)	(68)

	Auyana			Awa		
	All	Female	Male	All	Female	Male
2 cusps	59.1 (13)	75.0 (3)	55.6 (10)	71.2 (37)	72.7 (16)	70.0 (21)
3 cusps	40.9 (9)	25.0 (1)	44.4 (8)	26.9 (14)	27.3 (6)	26.7 (8)
4 cusps	0.0 (0)	0.0 (0)	0.0 (0)	1.9 (1)	0.0 (0)	3.3 (1)
5 cusps	0.0 (0)	0.0 (0)	0.0 (0)	0.0 (0)	0.0 (0)	0.0 (0)
Total	(22)	(4)	(18)	(52)	(22)	(30)

Note: The figures in parentheses refer to the number of individuals studied.

TABLE 66

CHI-SQUARE TESTS FOR COMPARISON OF FREQUENCY DISTRIBUTIONS:
CUSP NUMBERS OF THE MANDIBULAR FIRST PREMOLARS FOR PAIRED LANGUAGE GROUPS

	Groups	χ^2	Degrees of Freedom	Probability
Right mandibular first premolar	Gadsup-Awa			
	Females	0.0253	1	N.S.
	Males	6.0368	2	.050
	All	5.8267	2	N.S.
	Tairora-Awa			
	Females	4.3636	1	.036
	Males	5.4517	3	N.S.
	All	9.0521	3	.029
Left mandibular first premolar	Tairora-Awa			
	Females	4.3636	1	.036
	Males	6.4214	3	N.S.
	All	11.2250	3	.012

of the incidence of the trait for various racial groups. The Mongols, Eskimos, and American Indians exhibited almost 100 percent incidence of the trait. Typical shovel-shaped incisors were also noted for the American Negroes (12 percent), and American whites (8 percent). In modern populations, pronounced shovel-shaped incisors indicate a definite Mongoloid origin. Hrdlička's results have been substantiated by other investigators (Goldstein 1948; Pedersen 1949; Dahlberg 1945, 1949; Tratman 1950; and Moorrees 1957).

Pronounced shovel-shaped incisors are not common in the dentition of the Eastern Highlands natives, occurring in only 6 percent of the samples. This conforms somewhat to the percentage given for the American whites and Negroes (Hrdlicka 1920). Campbell (1925) stated that the shovel-shaped maxillary incisor was by no means a frequent characteristic of the Australian aboriginal incisor. It did occur, although rarely, in the pronounced form. In comparison with data that Riesenfeld (1956) presented, a marked similarity was noted for the low incidence of shovel-shape found in the Negroid areas of Ralum and New Guinea. This trend implies that the genetic influence of the Mongoloid race is slight in this area. The lateral incisor presents some form of the shovel-shape trait more often than the central. This supports what Moorrees (1957) observed.

Differences are noted between the various language groups and suspected isolates of the Eastern Highlands. Interpopulation differ-

TABLE 67

CUSP NUMBERS OF THE MANDIBULAR RIGHT SECOND PREMOLAR:
FREQUENCY (PERCENT) ARRAY FOR LANGUAGE GROUPS

	Total			Gadsup			Tairora		
	All	Female	Male	All	Female	Male	All	Female	Male
2 cusps	10.3 (22)	10.5 (4)	10.3 (18)	8.6 (6)	10.0 (1)	8.3 (5)	8.6 (6)	0.0 (0)	8.8 (6)
3 cusps	76.1 (162)	76.3 (29)	76.0 (133)	80.0 (56)	70.0 (7)	81.7 (49)	70.0 (49)	100.0 (2)	69.1 (47)
4 cusps	12.7 (27)	13.2 (5)	12.6 (22)	10.0 (7)	20.0 (2)	8.3 (5)	20.0 (14)	0.0 (0)	20.6 (14)
5 cusps	0.9 (2)	0.0 (0)	1.1 (2)	1.4 (1)	0.0 (0)	1.7 (1)	1.4 (1)	0.0 (0)	1.5 (1)
Total	(213)	(38)	(175)	(70)	(10)	(60)	(70)	(2)	(68)

	Auyana			Awa		
	All	Female	Male	All	Female	Male
2 cusps	22.7 (5)	25.0 (1)	22.2 (4)	9.8 (5)	9.1 (2)	10.3 (3)
3 cusps	68.2 (15)	75.0 (3)	66.7 (12)	82.4 (42)	77.3 (17)	86.2 (25)
4 cusps	9.1 (2)	0.0 (0)	11.1 (2)	7.8 (4)	13.6 (3)	3.4 (1)
5 cusps	0.0 (0)	0.0 (0)	0.0 (0)	0.0 (0)	0.0 (0)	0.0 (0)
Total	(22)	(4)	(18)	(51)	(22)	(29)

Note: The figures in parentheses refer to the number of individuals studied.

TABLE 68

CUSP NUMBERS OF THE MANDIBULAR LEFT SECOND PREMOLAR: FREQUENCY (PERCENT) ARRAY FOR LANGUAGE GROUPS

	Total			Gadsup			Tairora		
	All	Female	Male	All	Female	Male	All	Female	Male
2 cusps	11.3 (24)	15.8 (6)	10.3 (18)	8.6 (6)	10.0 (1)	8.3 (5)	11.4 (8)	0.0 (0)	11.8 (8)
3 cusps	74.6 (159)	68.4 (26)	76.0 (133)	77.1 (54)	70.0 (7)	78.3 (47)	70.0 (49)	50.0 (1)	70.6 (48)
4 cusps	12.7 (27)	15.8 (6)	12.0 (21)	12.9 (9)	20.0 (2)	11.7 (7)	15.7 (11)	50.0 (1)	14.7 (10)
5 cusps	1.4 (3)	0.0 (0)	1.7 (3)	1.4 (1)	0.0 (0)	1.7 (1)	2.9 (2)	0.0 (0)	2.9 (2)
Total	(213)	(38)	(175)	(70)	(10)	(60)	(70)	(2)	(68)

	Auyana			Awa		
	All	Female	Male	All	Female	Male
2 cusps	22.7 (5)	50.0 (2)	16.7 (3)	9.8 (5)	13.6 (3)	6.9 (2)
3 cusps	68.2 (15)	50.0 (2)	72.2 (13)	80.4 (41)	72.7 (16)	86.2 (25)
4 cusps	9.1 (2)	0.0 (0)	11.1 (2)	9.8 (5)	13.6 (3)	6.9 (2)
5 cusps	0.0 (0)	0.0 (0)	0.0 (0)	0.0 (0)	0.0 (0)	0.0 (0)
Total	(22)	(4)	(18)	(51)	(22)	(29)

Note: The figures in parentheses refer to the number of individuals studied.

TABLE 69

SUPERNUMERARY CUSPS:
FREQUENCY (PERCENT) ARRAY FOR LANGUAGE GROUPS

	Total			Gadsup			Tairora		
	All	Female	Male	All	Female	Male	All	Female	Male
Protostylid	41.8 (23)	40.0 (2)	42.0 (21)	33.3 (6)	33.3 (1)	33.3 (5)	58.8 (10)	0.0 (0)	58.8 (10)
Paramolar cusps	40.0 (22)	40.0 (2)	40.0 (20)	44.4 (8)	33.3 (1)	46.7 (7)	11.8 (2)	0.0 (0)	11.8 (2)
Occlusal cusps	18.2 (10)	20.0 (1)	18.0 (9)	22.2 (4)	33.3 (1)	20.0 (3)	29.4 (5)	0.0 (0)	29.4 (5)
Total	(55)	(5)	(50)	(18)	(3)	(15)	(17)	(0)	(17)

	Auyana			Awa		
	All	Female	Male	All	Female	Male
Protostylid	28.6 (2)	0.0 (0)	28.6 (2)	38.5 (5)	50.0 (1)	36.4 (4)
Paramolar cusps	71.4 (5)	0.0 (0)	71.4 (5)	53.8 (7)	50.0 (1)	54.5 (6)
Occlusal cusps	0.0 (0)	0.0 (0)	0.0 (0)	7.7 (1)	0.0 (0)	9.1 (1)
Total	(7)	(0)	(7)	(13)	(2)	(11)

Note: The figures in parentheses refer to the number of individuals studied.

TABLE 70

CHI-SQUARE TESTS FOR COMPARISON OF FREQUENCY DISTRIBUTIONS:
SUPERNUMERARY CUSPS FOR PAIRED LANGUAGE GROUPS

Groups	χ^2	Degrees of Freedom	Probability
Tairora-Auyana			
Females	0.0000	2	N.S.
Males	9.0180	2	.011
All	9.0180	2	.011
Tairora-Awa			
Females	0.0000	2	N.S.
Males	6.2389	2	.045
All	6.6968	2	.037

TABLE 71

SUPERNUMERARY TEETH: FREQUENCY ARRAY FOR LANGUAGE GROUPS

	Total	Gadsup	Tairora	Auyana	Awa
Female	2	0	0	0	2
Male	6	0	5	1	0

ences have been noted in other studies. Hrdlička (1920) was able to show that differences were present between tribes of the American Indians. Differences also were observed between two Bantu groups (Carbonell 1963).

Language group comparison shows that there is an increase of the trace shovel trait as we proceed south from the Gadsup area. Auyana is an exception to this trend; it shows a greater percentage of the absent shovel for the central incisor than the Gadsup. However, the lateral incisor of the Auyana shows an increased percentage for the shovel-shape trait.

There were significant differences for both maxillary incisors between Awa and Gadsup; differences also were significant for the lateral incisors between Awa and Tairora. Isolate differences between Sasaura and Ilakia for the lateral incisor are also present.

The comparison of data regarding the shovel-shape trait is always difficult because of the subjective method for evaluating the trait. Moorrees (1951) advised caution when using data for groups with low incidence of the trait for population comparisons. This fact does not imply that evaluating the trait for the Eastern Highlands native is unnecessary. Riesenfeld (1956) stated that one of the significant problems in the study of the native peoples of the Pacific is the question of

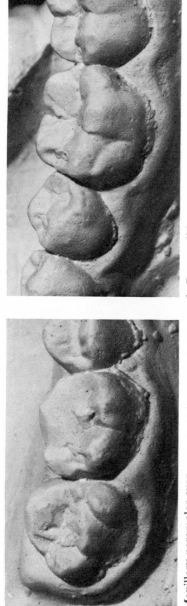

a. Maxillary paramolar cusp

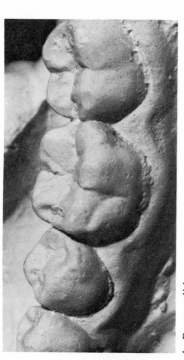

b. Protostylid

c. Occlusal cusp

Plate 16. Examples of supernumerary cusps in the Eastern Highlands natives

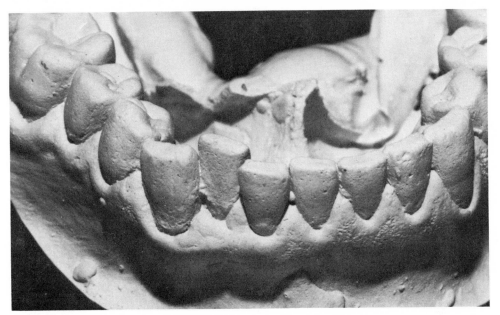

a. Supernumerary incisor

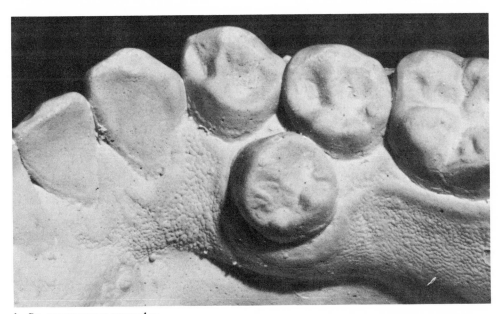

b. Supernumerary premolar

Plate 17. Examples of supernumerary teeth in the Eastern Highlands natives

Mongoloid influence in that area. The present study implies that this influence is quite limited in the Eastern Highlands native. While knowledge of the degree to which the trait is present is important, the value of comparing the incidence of occurrence with other racial groups is questioned.

2. *Variations of the Crown of the Maxillary Lateral Incisor*

The lateral incisor is the most variable human tooth with the exception of the third molars (Dahlberg 1945). Campbell (1925) asserted that the diminutive or peg-shaped lateral incisor was rare for the Australian aboriginal. Sinclair (1947) reported that the anomalous lateral incisor occurred in approximately 3 percent of the New Guinea natives he studied. Riesenfeld (1956) found variations in the lateral incisor for 5 percent of the individuals he investigated. Dahlberg (1949) found that 8 percent of the lateral incisors for 238 Pima Indians were anomalous or missing.

The Eastern Highlands native has the peg-shaped or missing lateral incisor approximately 4 percent of the time. This compares closely to the work of Sinclair (1947) and Riesenfeld (1956). A lateral incisor with lingual cusps is much more common, occurring in 18 percent of the casts studied. Pedersen (1949) stated that lingual cusps did occur rarely on the lateral incisors of the East Greenland Eskimo but gave no percentages for comparison. This variation of the lateral incisor is included as an anomaly for language group and isolate comparison.

The Gadsup has anomalous lateral incisors only 14 percent of the time, whereas this figure increases to 33 percent and 39 percent for the Auyana and Awa, respectively. The lateral incisor with lingual cusps accounts for most of the variation observed in the Awa. The differences are statistically significant between Gadsup and Auyana, and Gadsup and Awa. The isolates representing these language groups also present significant differences. The Baieanabuta isolate presents an anomalous incisor (41 percent). The Ilakia isolate shows an anomalous lateral more often than the Sasaura isolate.

The trend showing increased variation for the lateral incisors is especially evident for the Awa. The Gadsup language group and Baieanabuta isolate show variation to a lesser degree.

3. *Carabelli's Anomaly of the Maxillary First Molars*

Carabelli's anomaly is present in its larger form in a high percentage of Melanesian people (Dahlberg 1963). Campbell (1925) found the anomalous cusp occurring on the Australian aboriginal molar in 33 percent of the teeth he studied. A pronounced cusp was rarely seen. Shaw (Pedersen 1949) observed this trait rarely in the Bantu data. The Eskimo possesses a low frequency of the Carabelli anomaly as demonstrated by Pedersen (1949), Dahlberg (1949), and Moorrees (1957). The cusp possesses little value for differentiation of Mongoloid subraces because of its low incidence. A higher incidence of the anomaly was found for American whites (41 percent) (Dahlberg 1945).

Kraus (1951) believes that with accurate descriptions of the variations of this anomaly, and a working knowledge of the mechanism of inheritance, this trait could become a criterion of the first order for racial differentiation.

Carabelli's anomaly is present in its pronounced forms in 19 percent of the casts studied from the Eastern Highlands area. This compares to what Dahlberg (1963) has stated for the Melanesian, although he listed no percentages. Some form of the trait is present in 73 percent of the cases, with the groove being the most common expression (41 percent). No trend is demonstrable among the various language groups studied. Significant differences do not exist for the language groups or isolates.

It is quite possible that a pedigree study among these people would yield more valuable information. This would allow a better understanding of the effects of hybridization for the distribution of the Carabelli phenotype (Kraus 1959).

4. *Cusp Numbers of the Maxillary Molars*

The number of cusps of the maxillary molars is changing from a quadricuspal to a tricuspal pattern. The distolingual cusp is being eliminated (Moorrees 1957).

Moorrees (1957) reporting on the Aleut dentition found that the frequency for four cusps was 100 percent for the first molars, 69 percent for the second molars, and 31 percent for the third molars. Campbell (1925) reported that the Australian aboriginal had quadricuspal first and second molars 100 percent of the time. The third molar had four cusps 77 percent of the time. Dahlberg (1949) used a comparable system to grade molar cusps. He stated that all racial groups had a high percentage of four well-developed cusps for the first molars but that in the second molar there commonly was a reduction to 4 − and 3 gradations. The 3 and 3 + classifications, along with other irregular forms, are often noted for the third molars. Dahlberg (1945) compared the maxillary molars of three racial groups. The frequency percentage of the quadricuspal second molars was 87 for the Melanesians, 58 for the American whites, and 31 for the Eskimo.

The Eastern Highlands native compares closely with the Melanesian group, in this case having a quadricuspal second molar in 87 percent of the casts studied. The frequency percentage of the quadricuspal third molar was 58 for the Melanesians, 45 for the American whites, and 18 for the Eskimos. In this comparison, the Eastern Highlands native conforms more closely to the American white, showing a third molar with four cusps 46 percent of the time. The remaining 54 percent of the third molars are tricuspal, which compares very closely to the percentage (53.8 percent) that Goldstein (1948) found for a group of Texas Indians. Pedersen (1949) found the third molars of the East Greenland Eskimo were commonly tricuspal (61.4 percent).

Language group comparisons for the right maxillary second molar reveal significant differences between Gadsup and Awa, and Tairora and Awa. Gadsup has $4-$ and $3+$ for the right second molars, whereas Awa shows 4, $4-$, $3+$, and 3, displaying more variation. Awa presents the same variations that Tairora does but the distribution of these patterns is significantly different. The left second molar shows that a significant difference occurs between Gadsup and Awa similar to that for the right second molar.

Isolate comparison for the right second molar reveals that the Sasaura and Ilakia isolates differ for the males.

These data on the cusp numbers of the maxillary molars show that the pattern is quadricuspal for the first molar (100 percent) and the second molar (87 percent). The third molar shows a definite shift to a tricuspal form 54 percent of the time.

5. *Cusp Numbers and Groove Patterns of the Mandibular Molars*

Gregory (1916) discovered that man, the great apes, and Dryopithecinae have a basically similar arrangement of cusps and grooves for the mandibular molars. This pattern was designated $Y5$ (Moorrees 1957). The first molar, being the most conservative of the three molars, retains the $Y5$ while the second molar most frequently is modified to a $+4$ pattern. The third molar is modified to a pattern between these two types (Dahlberg 1945). Hellman (1928) has shown that the European whites show modifications of the Dryopithecoid $Y5$ pattern more than West African Negroes and Mongoloids.

White males present an incidence of 87 percent for the Y5 pattern of the mandibular first molars, showing some modification for this trait. Mongol males are similar to the Chinese, Eskimos, and American Indian, showing a 100 percent occurrence of the Y5 pattern. Negroes have the Y5 pattern 99 percent of the time (Hellman 1928). The Eastern Highlands male shows a modified arrangement of cusps and grooves with the Dryopithecoid pattern (Y5) occurring only 57 percent of the time. The shift to a +5 stage is noted 26 percent of the time.

Language group and isolate comparisons do not show any significant differences for the patterns observed for the mandibular first molars. Females display a lower percentage for the Y5 (45 percent) with a shift toward the +4 (17 percent) and +5 (22 percent) stages.

The mandibular second molars show changes in form with a +4 cusp and groove pattern resulting 94 percent of the time for the white male, 81 percent for the Mongol male, and 63 percent for the Negro male (Hellman 1928). The Eastern Highlands male presents a +4 stage for the second molar 70 percent of the time which is similar to the Negro percentage. A sex difference is present with the females showing the +4 (82 percent) more commonly than the males (70 percent). This sex difference is also noted for Awa, the +4 being observed in 85 percent of the females and 57 percent of the males. Moorrees (1957) noted sex differences, showing the male retaining the Y5 more than the females.

Differences are present between Gadsup and Awa males in a comparison of the right mandibular second molar. The Sasaura and Baieanabuta, and Sasaura and Ilakia isolates also present significant differences for this tooth. The latter isolates show significant differences for the mandibular left second molars also.

Many differences in occlusal surface patterns occur for the third molar. The white male shows advanced stages (+4, 62 percent and +5, 34 percent) just as for the other mandibular molars. The Mongol retains the Dryopithecoid cusp number but shifts to the + groove pattern (+5, 77 percent). This group has the advanced stage (+4) in 23 percent of the subjects. The Negro male presents the Dryopithecoid Y5 pattern more than the other racial groups (20 percent) and shows the advanced stage (+4) to only a limited extent (17 percent) (Hellman 1928). The Eastern Highlands male presents more variations in occlusal surface patterns for the third molars than for the other molars. The Dryopithecoid Y groove pattern is present in only 4 percent of the males; however, the Dryopithecoid number of cusps (5) is present in 62 percent of these male subjects. The *X* groove pattern described by Jorgensen (1955) is noted in a large percentage (34 percent) of the males and females. The females show the +4 variation for the third molars in 51 percent of the casts studied.

Significant differences between the Sasaura and Baieanabuta isolates are present for the left mandibular third molar. Many third molars were missing, making the reliability of this difference questionable.

A genetic study would help explain the mode of inheritance and the amount of change for the different combinations of groove patterns and cusp numbers. However, racial comparisons of the prevalence of these traits help determine the rate at which these changes are occurring.

6. *Cusp Numbers of the Mandibular Premolars*

The mandibular premolars are known to have two or three cusps in man and the anthropoids. The three-cusped premolar is considered to be a specialized form that has arisen to compensate for the reduced size of the lingual cusp of the first premolar (Moorrees 1957).

Pedersen (1949) described the number of cusps for the premolars of the East Greenland Eskimo; he found that the first premolar showed two cusps in 100 percent of his samples. The second premolar showed two cusps (63.8 percent), more often than the three-cusped type (36.2 percent). Ludwig (1957) found that the second premolar was bicuspal for the Caucasoid 60.1 percent of the time. The Mongoloid showed the bicuspal type of second premolar 91 percent of the time. This is higher than what Moorrees (1957) found for the two-cusped second premolar of the Aleut (78.6 percent). The Negro presented the lowest percentage of bicuspal second premolars (52.8 percent) (Ludwig 1957).

The Eastern Highlands native shows a bicuspal mandibular first premolar 55 percent of the time. The three-cusped first premolar is the second most prevalent type observed (41 percent). These data differ from that which Pedersen (1949) found for the East Greenland Eskimo. Awa presents a two-cusped right first premolar significantly more often than Gadsup. Both first premolars show this difference when comparing Tairora and Awa.

The second mandibular premolar shows a high percentage (75 percent) of the tricuspal pattern. This is higher than Moorrees (1957) found for the Aleut (21.4 percent). Pedersen (1949) observed tricuspal second premolars for the East Greenland Eskimo in 36.2 percent of his sample. Ludwig (1957) reported that the Negroid second premolar was three-cusped 41.7 percent of the time. This compares more closely to the Eastern Highlands native than any other racial group studied. The 5.5 percent of four-cusped second premolars that Ludwig observed for Negroes also compares favorably with the 12.7 percent that the Eastern Highlands native shows for the four-cusped second premolar.

Comparative data concerning the mandibular premolars for various racial types are lacking. This makes it difficult to evaluate the observations for the premolars of the Eastern Highlands native.

7. *Supernumerary Cusps*

Supernumerary cusps are often observed on the molars and premolars. Three types of supernumerary cusps were evaluated for the Eastern Highlands native.

The protostylid type of paramolar cusp on the mesiobuccal surface of mandibular molars has been described in detail by Dahlberg (1949). It is of evolutionary significance because it has been found in early fossil forms of man but rarely in most modern men (Dahlberg 1950). Dahlberg found this cusp was present in 31 percent of the permanent first mandibular molars in eighty casts of the Pima Indian. Pedersen (1949) stated that the paramolar cusp is as common for the East Greenland Eskimo as for any other race and is more common than that reported for whites (2 percent). However, Moorrees (1957) found no paramolar cusps on the Aleut molars or premolars that he studied. The Eastern Highlands native shows a high percentage (11 percent) for the protostylid. Although this is lower than what Dahlberg (1950) reported for the Pima Indian, it is a definite trait in the dentition of the Eastern Highlands native.

The paramolar cusp on the mesiobuccal surface of maxillary molars is almost as common as the protostylid in the Eastern Highlands native; 10 percent of the casts show this supernumerary cusp. Fabian (Pedersen 1949) found that this type of supernumerary cusp was often present in the Melanesian but gave no percentages for comparison.

Another type of supernumerary cusp was reported upon by Moorrees (1957). He observed the cusp on the occlusal surface of a mandibular second premolar for one Aleut male. Kato (Moorrees 1957) found the occlusal cusp on the premolars of Japanese people approximately 1 percent of the time. This cusp was noted in 4 percent of the Eastern Highlands natives studied.

Language group comparisons show that the occurrence of the three supernumerary cusp types is significantly different for the Tairora and Auyana, and Tairora and Awa males. Reliability of this comparison is questionable. However, data for supernumerary cusps show that these morphological traits are common in the dentition of the Eastern Highlands native. Past racial studies do not contribute enough information to allow comparisons for this trait.

8. *Supernumerary Teeth*

Investigations comparing the incidence of supernumerary teeth in different racial groups as well as tribes are limited by several factors. Without x-rays it is not possible to detect unerupted supernumerary teeth. Limited occurrence reduced reliability of these comparisons ·even further.

Past studies indicate that the incidence of hyperodontia or supernumerary teeth is variable even in populations that are of similar racial origin (Moorrees 1957). Pedersen (1949) found supernumerary teeth in the East Greenland Eskimo to be less than 2 percent but his sample size was quite small. Moorrees (1957) reported no supernumerary teeth for the Aleutian Eskimos he studied. Shaw (Pedersen 1949) found supernumerary teeth occurring in 2.7 percent of the South African Bantus he studied. The Australian aboriginal showed supernumerary teeth in 1.8 percent of the people and skulls studied (Campbell 1925). Sinclair (1947), in a report on dental conditions in Papua, New Guinea, stated that supernumerary teeth occurred in approximately 2 percent of the natives studied.

The Eastern Highlands natives show a 3.6 percent incidence for supernumerary teeth. This is not significantly different from the percentages presented in previous studies. Tairora shows five natives with supernumerary teeth whereas Gadsup, which is of comparable size, has no incidence of this morphologic abnormality. This variation is not included in the language group and isolate comparisons.

SUMMARY AND CONCLUSIONS

The purpose of this investigation was to describe, and evaluate morphologically, selected traits of the dentition of the natives of the Eastern Highlands of New Guinea. Dental casts were evaluated for

TABLE 72

SUMMARY OF CHI-SQUARE TESTS WITH SIGNIFICANT DIFFERENCES FOR PAIRED LANGUAGE GROUPS

Groups	Shovel-Shape of the Maxillary Incisors		Variations of the Maxillary Lateral Incisor Crown	Cusp Numbers of the Maxillary Molars		Cusps and Grooves of the Right Second Mandibular Molars	Cusp Numbers of the Mandibular Premolars		Super-numerary Cusps
	Central	Lateral		Right second	Left second		Right first	Left first	
Gadsup-Tairora									
Gadsup-Awa	Females All	Females Males All	Males All	Females Males All	Males	Males	Males		
Gadsup-Auyana			Males All						
Tairora-Awa		Males All		Females Males			Females All	Females All	Males All
Tairora-Auyana									Males All
Awa-Auyana									

TABLE 73

Isolates	Shovel-Shape of the Maxillary Lateral Incisors	Variations of the Maxillary Lateral Incisor Crown	Cusp Numbers of the Right Second Maxillary Molars	Cusps and Grooves of the Mandibular Molars		
				Right second	Left second	Left third
Sasaura-Baieanabuta				Males		Males All
Sasaura-Ilakia	Females Males All	Males	Males	Males	Males	
Baieanabuta-Ilakia		Males All				

morphologic patterns and the observations recorded for the four language groups and the three largest isolates. These data were compared to data obtained for other racial studies. Chi-square tests were used to compare the frequency distributions of traits for the language groups and isolates. The summarized results are as follows:

1. The shovel-shape trait of the maxillary incisors is observed in the natives of the Eastern Highlands in a small percentage of the casts studied. Pronounced forms occur with very low incidence. This supports the assumption that the genetic influence of the Mongoloid race is slight. Tribal comparisons show that the Awa have more pronounced forms of this trait than the Gadsup and Tairora. The Ilakia isolate of the Awa presents more pronounced forms of the shovel-shape trait for lateral incisors than does the Sasaura isolate of the Gadsup.

2. Variations of the crown of the maxillary incisors occur to a lesser degree than has been found in the American Indian (Dahlberg 1949). However, it is present to a degree similar to that seen in other peoples of this area (Sinclair 1947; Riesenfeld 1956). Auyana and Awa present anomalous lateral incisors in a significantly higher percentage of casts than does Gadsup. Isolate comparisons reflect these language group differences, showing that the Ilakia lateral incisor is more variable than that observed for Baieanabuta or Sasaura.

3. Carabelli's anomaly is present in a high percentage of the casts, the groove being the most common expression. The occurrence of Carabelli's anomaly compares favorably with observations of the Melanesians (Dahlberg 1963); however, it differs from that reported for Mongoloid subraces (Pedersen 1949; Moorrees, 1957).

4. The number of cusps observed for the maxillary molars is generally four. This is similar to what Campbell reported for the Australian aboriginal (1925). The maxillary second molar, quadricuspal for the most part, shows variation in comparisons among the language groups and isolates. Of these, Awa differs significantly from Gadsup and Tairora. Differences between isolates are present for Sasaura and Ilakia. The third molar is tricuspal in most of the casts evaluated.

5. The mandibular first molar shows a lower percentage of the Dryopithecoid $Y5$ pattern than do all other racial groups that have been studied. The second molar has shifted largely to a $+4$ pattern. This is similar to observations for the West African Negro (Hellman 1928). Females present a higher incidence of the $+4$ pattern than the males. The third molar presents many variations of the occlusal surface. The Dryopithecoid number of cusps (5) is present to a much larger degree than for the second molar; however, the groove pattern has shifted to a $+$ or an X in most of the casts studied. Language group comparisons show that Gadsup and Awa have significantly different morphologic patterns for the second molars. These differences are also seen in the Sasaura and Ilakia isolates. Differences exist between Sasaura and Baieanabuta for the mandibular second and third molars.

6. The mandibular first premolars possess significantly different numbers of cusps when comparing the Awa to the Gadsup and Tairora. The bicuspal first premolar is present most often in the Awa. The mandibular second premolar is tricuspal in most of the casts studied, its frequency paralleling the Negroid second premolar more closely than any other racial group (Ludwig 1957). This racial similarity was also reflected for the quadriscupal type of second premolar.

7. Supernumerary cusps are common morphologic traits in the dentition of the natives of the Eastern Highlands. The protostylid and maxillary paramolar cusps are the most common of these. The occlusal cusp, which was rarely observed in other racial studies, is found in several of the casts. Though handicapped by small sample size, significant differences are shown between the Tairora and the Awa and Auyana.

8. Supernumerary teeth present a low incidence just as in other racial groups. The distribution of supernumerary teeth is unusual in that the largest sample, the Gadsup, shows no supernumerary teeth whereas Tairora presents several examples.

The following conclusions were drawn:

1. The dental morphology of the Eastern Highlands native is suggestive of the Negroid pattern, although this pattern has not been defined specifically. It is similar to the West African Negro, the Melanesian, and the Australian aboriginal dentitions. The Mongoloid influence on the dentition of these people appears to be slight.

2. The greatest variation in the morphology of the dentition is found between the Eastern Highlands groups that are separated by the greatest distances. Groups that are located in closer proximity show fewer differences in the morphologic patterns under investigation.

3. Although the morphology of teeth is for the most part genetically determined, the differences cannot be explained on this basis alone. Very little credit has been given to environmental influence on dental characters (Witkop 1961). In view of the assumption that these natives are only a few thousand years removed from a common genetic source, the variability observed indicates that environment may be of importance in dental morphology.

4. The following morphologic dental traits are characteristic for the natives of the Eastern Highlands: (A) a low incidence of shovel-shaped maxillary incisors; (B) a high incidence of Carabelli's anomaly; (C) a high incidence of quadricuspal maxillary first and second molars with a much lower incidence of quadricuspal third molars; (D) a low incidence of the ancestral Dryopithecoid pattern ($Y5$) for cusps and grooves of the mandibular molars; (E) a high incidence of tricuspal mandibular premolars; (F) a high incidence of supernumerary cusps.

5. Sex differences exist for some of the morphologic dental traits studied; however, the differences are not significant when evaluated with the chi-square test.

6. The bilateral expression of the dental traits studied was not completely symmetrical; however, no significant differences were noted.

7. It will be difficult to establish the value of the dentition as a criterion of race until further attempts are made in classifying various racial groups, such as has been done for the Mongoloid.

Appendix IV: An Odontometric and Observational Assessment of the Dentition

RUSSELL CONDA BOYD II, D.D.S.

INTRODUCTION

Measurements of the dentition have long provided data for anthropologic study.[1] It is unfortunate, however, that the methods and measurements utilized by each worker have been as legion as the investigations, so that valid odontometric comparisons of populations are difficult to draw. Assessments of the dentition with respect to racial typing have been largely confined to groups with Mongoloid ancestry, with the result that Dahlberg speaks of two main divisions of dentitions: Mongoloid and non-Mongoloid. The need is self-evident for additional studies on Negro and white populations to establish the master patterns for their respective dentitions, if indeed they exist.

The particular inferences concerning racial background in the studies to date have dealt primarily with tooth morphology rather than tooth size. There is increasing evidence, however, that tooth size is, to a very great extent, genetically controlled (Garn 1965). This being true, it would seem that dental measurement, as well as dental

1. This study is based upon a thesis submitted in partial fulfillment of the requirements for the degree of Master of Science in dentistry, University of Washington, 1966. For such guidance and assistance in their respective fields, I am deeply indebted to the following individuals: Dr. R. A. Littlewood for making the casts available and for his continued information concerning the people and territory of New Guinea; Dr. Richard Kronmal for his patient efforts in making the computer a useful tool and his knowledgeable statistical assistance; Dr. B. C. Moffett for his astute literary assistance and his always available guidance.

Most particularly I would like to say thank you to my wife, Joan, for her patience and understanding during the time I was working on this paper.

morphology, can provide presumptive indications of genetic differences and similarities between groups of man.

While standardization of measure would enhance the value of odontometry in population studies, there are limitations of which the investigator must be aware. As Selmer-Olson points out (1949), "The size of the teeth have a limited value as a racial characteristic. The reason for this is primarily that variation within the different collections is great, seen in comparison with the difference one finds between them." With this in mind then, it becomes apparent that we must be particularly cognizant of the number of observations in attempting to show significant differences between groups.

The intragroup variation seen on any one measurement forces us to seek a technic for combining variables to allow greater group discrimination. Such a technic is the multivariate analysis. Comparisons of single variables between groups may, for example, show no significant difference, but a particular combination of these variables within a group may clearly discriminate that group from the rest. Bronowski and Long (1952) state that "the methods of modern statistics are not alien to anthropology, but are capable of assessing a fossil or a limb as a unit, and not as a haphazard jumble of piecemeal measurements." In the present study the adaptability of this statistical method to dental anthropology is explored.

Selmer-Olson in his monograph on the Norwegian Lapp (1949) reviews some twenty-five studies of dental measure. He effectively criticizes each as to sample, size, technic variations, and statistical treatment of the data. Only those of comparative interest to the present study are mentioned.

D. T. Campbell (1925) offered data on 630 skulls, chiefly from Southern Australia. While his tooth size data were restricted to the anterior teeth, his palatal measurements are complete. Moorrees (1957) compared the dentition of two groups of natives in the Aleutian Islands. The study is of particular interest here because of the comparison of the two "breeding isolates" present in the sample. Selmer-Olson (1949) himself provides material on the Norwegian Lapps, another "in-bred" population.

Special mention should be made of the work of the Department of Dental Science, University of Adelaide, South Australia. Barrett, Brown, and co-workers have produced a series of articles dealing with various aspects of the dental structures of a single tribe of Australian aboriginals. These studies are very complete and comprehensive and because of geographic implications, offer interesting comparative data to those of the present study, which deals with the dentition of a group of natives of the Eastern Highlands of New Guinea. These people have been divided into four language groups. Within each of these there are clusters of hamlets which according to Littlewood represent "breeding isolates." By definition, there is less than a 50 percent gene exchange per generation between any of these isolates. Thus we have subpopulations which at one time were of common stock, who have had a chance to develop independent of one another for possibly 1,000 or more years (McKaughan 1964, 1972).

Comparisons of tooth size between these groups then should serve to give us some indication of the genetic manifestations of their separation. In addition the description of the dentition of the population as a unit should prove useful in determining the origin of these people. If related stocks of contemporary man do show similarity in their dental characteristics, and this would be expected in the light of genetic evidence, these characteristics must be identified and their discriminating value quantified.

MATERIALS AND METHODS

The sample consists of dental casts of 218 natives of the Eastern Highlands of New Guinea. These casts were produced in the field from impressions of irreversible hydrocolloid (alginate) made during R. A. Littlewood's thirteen months of investigation. The distribution of the sample as to sex, language group, and isolate can be seen in Table 74. The casts were measured and assessed at random with no knowledge of tribal or isolate grouping to prevent unconscious bias. With two exceptions, all measurements were made using a sliding caliper with a vernier scale, the points of which had been sharpened to improve accuracy. These measurements were made to the nearest 0.1 millimeter. The two measurements of arch length were made from an overlying transparent millimeter grid, and were read to the nearest 0.5 millimeter.

1. *Tooth Measure*

Mesiodistal crown diameter: the greatest mesiodistal dimension of the tooth crown measured parallel to the occlusal and labial or buccal surface. This measurement was chosen because it was felt to be less influenced by interproximal attrition, which was considerable.

Labiolingual crown diameter: the greatest distance between the

TABLE 74

SAMPLE DISTRIBUTION AS TO LANGUAGE GROUP, ISOLATE, AND SEX

Language Group	Isolate	Males	Females	Isolate Total	Language Group Total
Gadsup		64	10		74
	Sasaura	37	3	40	
	Akuna	18	2	20	
	Ontenu	9	5	14	
Tairora		68	2		70
	Baieanabuta	25	6	31	
	Abiera	12	2	14	
	Babaraai	13	. . .	13	
	Batainabura	12	. . .	12	
Auyana		18	4		22
	Central Auyana	14	4	18	
	Kawaina	4	. .	4	
Awa		30	22		52
	Tauna	17	5	22	
	Ilakia	13	17	30	
Total number of subjects					218

labial and lingual surfaces of the tooth crown in a plane perpendicular to that in which the mesiodistal diameter was measured.

2. *Arch Measure* (Bjork 1962; Plate 18a)

Interincisor width (I): the width of the dental arch measured between the points of contact between the lateral incisor and the canine on each side. In the event of spacing, the mesial prominence of the canine was chosen. If the canine was obviously malposed, the distal prominence of the lateral was utilized.

Interpremolar width (P): the width between the points of contact betweeen the second premolar and the first molar on each side, in the continuation of the central sulci.

Intermolar width (M): the width between the contact points between the second and third molars on each side in the prolongation of the central sulci. When the third molar was absent, the distal prominence of the second molar was used.

Arch length (L): measured in the midsagittal plane from the contact point of the central incisors to the midpoint of a line joining the distal surfaces of the second molars.

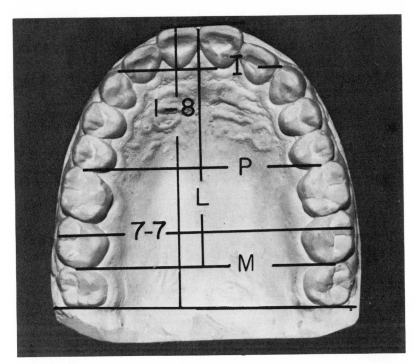

a

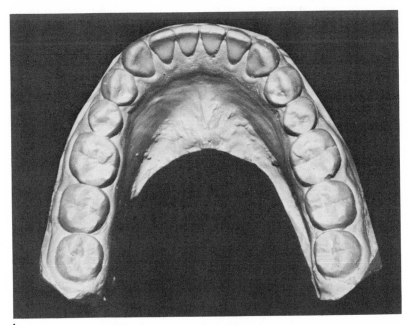

b

Plate 18. a: Measurements of width and length of maxillary arch. I = inter-incisor width; 1—8 = anthropometric arch length; P = interpremolar width; L = arch length; 7—7 = anthropometric arch width; M = intermolar width. b: Typical mandibular arch form

3. *Anthropometric Arch Measure* (Plate 18a)

Arch width (7-7): the greatest distance between the buccal surfaces of the second molars.

Arch length (1-8): the distance between a tangent to the labial surfaces of the central incisors and a plane tangent to the distal surfaces of the third molars perpendicular to the occlusal plane.

4. *Overbite and Overjet*

Overbite was measured by making a light mark with a sharpened pencil on the labial surface of the lower central incisor at the level of the incisal edge of the maxillary central incisor when the models were in occlusion. The distance from this mark to the incisal edge of the lower incisor was then recorded as overbite.

Overjet was measured from the labial surface of the lower central incisor to the juncture of the labial surface and incisal edge of the maxillary central incisor when the models were in occlusion.

In addition to the comparative metric data, both tribal and isolate, certain features of the dentition of this sample are described herein. The statistical interpretation of these additional data is not sophisticated and they are presented solely as items of interest to those involved in other such studies.

5. *Nonmetric Determinations*

Incisor relation: recorded as psaliodont, scissors bite; labiodont, end to end; or anterior crossbite (Plate 19).

Spacing, crowding: spacing recorded as present or absent in each or both arches. Crowding recorded as absent, slight if less than 5 mm. arch length deficiency overall, or marked if greater than 5 mm. arch length existed.

Attrition: recorded after Broca (1879). Grade 1: facets seen, only enamel worn; Grade 2: dentin exposed, "cupping" at cusp tips; Grade 3: cuspal integrity worn away; Grade 4: wear to cemento-enamel junction.

Arch form (Plate 20) recorded as (A) hyperbolic, when the arms of the arch are widely divergent posteriorly; (B) parabolic, when they diverge somewhat less so; (C) hypsiloid, when the arms of the arch are exactly parallel; and (D) elliptical, when the arms of the arch converge posteriorly, whatever the degree of convergence may be. This variable was recorded for the maxilla only. Virtually all of the mandibular arches were parabolic in form.

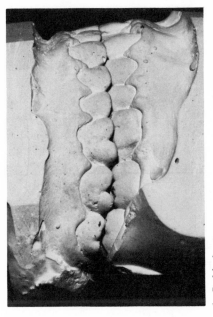

a. Psaliodont

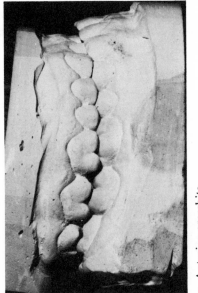

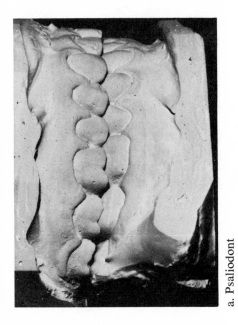

b. Labiodont

c. Anterior crossbite

Plate 19. Examples of three types of incisor occlusion

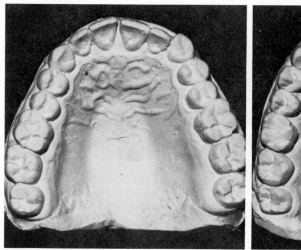

a. Hyperbolic

b. Parabolic

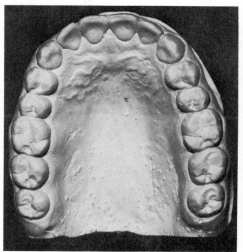

c. Hypsiloid

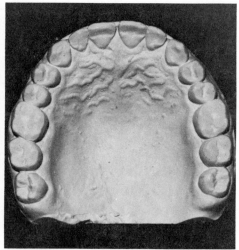

d. Ellipsoid

Plate 20. Examples of maxillary arch form

Molar relation was recorded as being Angle's Class I, II, or III. The data were initially recorded on key-sort cards, but transferred to eighty-column, twelve-row IBM cards before tabulation began. The IBM 7040-7094 direct couple computer system of the University of Washington Computer Facility was used to process the data. The computer programs utilized included the Massey XTAB A-2 as modified by Dr. Richard Kronmal and Dr. Stephen R. Yarnall, which gave case lists, means, standard deviations, and standard errors for groups and selected subgroups; the BMD 07D, which for selected strata of any variable, gave histograms, means, standard deviations, ranges, and F tests for all other variables; and the BMD 07M, which offered a stepwise discriminant analysis using selected variables. The BMD 07D was run with both language groups and isolates as the base variable. The BMD 07M was asked to distinguish language groups from the group as a whole, each language group from every other, and the isolates within each language from one another. Another program, the BMD 05M Discriminant Analysis for several groups, was run on the same groups as the 07M to assess the value of the stepwise approach offered by the latter.

A brief discussion of the adaptation of the discriminant analysis to these data might prove helpful to future users of this technic. The most difficult problem to overcome was that of missing data. A missing variable on a particular case cannot be compensated for and necessitates elimination of either the case or the variable. The first procedure was to screen the data to determine which variables had the fewest missing values. The number of variables allowable was determined by the formula:

$$\frac{(Number\ of\ Variables)^2 - Number\ of\ Variables}{2} < Number\ of\ Cases$$

so that the number of variables examined did not exceed the number of cases. In addition, the number of variables cannot exceed the number of cases in any one group. Twelve variables were selected as having the best combination of few missing values and high *F* ratio. These are shown in Table 75. Other variables which fulfilled the criteria, such as attrition and incisor occlusion, were omitted in a desire to discriminate on measurements only.

Even with this method of selection, 31 cases of the original 180 males had to be eliminated because of missing values, that is, unmeasurable teeth, whether missing, carious, or distorted on the model. The distribution by tribe and isolate of these cases is shown in Table 76. It is apparent that we could not use all twelve variables on all combinations of language groups. When comparing Awa with Auyana, for example, there were 37 cases so that it was necessary to further reduce the number of variables for those discriminations. In this situation there is a distinct advantage to a stepwise discrimination in that all variables can be read in, but, by specifying the number of steps at the maximum level allowed by the sample size, only that number of the most discriminating variables will be analyzed.

TABLE 75

VARIABLES USED IN MULTIVARIATE ANALYSIS

Variable Number		Measurement
1.	10	Arch form, maxilla
2.	16	Interincisor width
3.	17	Interpremolar width
4.	19	Arch length (Bjork)
5.	58*	Maxillary first premolars
6.	59*	Maxillary second premolars
7.	60*	Mandibular first premolars
8.	61*	Mandibular second premolars
9.	62*	Maxillary first molars: mesiodistal
10.	63*	Maxillary first molars: buccolingual
11.	64*	Mandibular first molar: mesiodistal
12.	65*	Mandibular first molar: buccolingual

*These variables were created by adding the mean measures for right and left sides.

TABLE 76

SAMPLE DISTRIBUTION FOR MULTIVARIATE ANALYSIS: ALL MALES

Language Group	Isolate	Isolate Total	Language Group Total
Gadsup			56
	Sasaura	33	
	Akuna	16	
	Ontenu	7	
Tairora			56
	Baieanabuta	24	
	Abiera	10	
	Babaraai	11	
	Batainabura	11	
Auyana			16
	Central Auyana	12	
	Kawaina	4	
Awa			21
	Tauna	13	
	Ilakia	8	
Total number of subjects			149

RESULTS AND DISCUSSION

1. *Incisor Relation*

Table 77 shows the mean overbite and overjet for each grade of attrition in the three categories of incisor occlusion. Even those individuals with considerable wear did not show a significant decrease in overbite and overjet. In addition, 25 of the 51 cases of labiodont and 12 of the 26 cases of anterior crossbite occlusions showed Grade 1 wear. The 12.4 percent of individuals with anterior crossbite was felt to be higher than one would expect.

TABLE 77

RELATIONSHIP OF ATTRITION TO INCISOR OCCLUSION

	Grade of Attrition											
	1			2			3			4		
	N	Overbite	Overjet	N	Overbite	Overjet	N	Overbite	Overjet	N	Overbite	Overjet
Psalio-dont	98	2.38	1.98	29	2.28	2.15	5	2.32	2.65	0	...	...
Labio-dont	25	0	0	17	0	0	9	0	0	0	...	...
Anterior crossbite	12	−2.53	−2.15	9	−2.55	−1.88	5	−1.78	−1.52	0	...	...

Note: All overbite and overjet measurements are expressed in millimeters.

Primitive populations have been characterized as having "end-to-end" anterior occlusions, produced rather mysteriously by excessive wear. Several authors have alluded to the wear of posterior cusps as necessary before the mandible can drift forward into an end-to-end relationship. Moorrees (1957) referred directly to this occurrence, and stated flatly that without wear, end-to-end occlusion did not develop. Campbell (1925) implied that there is no actual shift, because he observed that the molars stayed in their same relative positions as the edge-to-edge occlusion developed. Beyron (1964), working on the Australian aboriginal, graphs overbite and overjet with age and finds a decrease in overbite, but not in overjet as the sample ages. To expand on this premise, if wear were the key to the development of an end-to-end relationship, the overbite and overjet means should be in inverse proportion to the degree of wear. This was not the case in the present sample. In addition, some explanation must be sought for the almost 50 percent of the end-to-end and anterior crossbite occlusions which did not have excessive wear.

The considerable incidence of anterior crossbite is another interesting finding. The fact that the majority of these cases have Class I molar relationships rules out the consideration of mandibular shifting as the sole cause. It appears instead that at least part of the answer to both labiodont and anterior crossbite situations lies in arch form. The anterior segments of the maxillary arches in this sample, and indeed in all samples in which end-to-end occlusion is a characteristic, are quite broad and flat. The corresponding anterior segments of the mandibular arches are more curved, resulting in a relative forward placement of the mandibular incisors. Undoubtedly, both wear and arch form contribute to the incidence of other than psaliodont occlusions in primitive peoples.

2. *Molar Relation*

It must be mentioned at the outset that all assessments of occlusion were made by manipulating the casts by hand into what was felt to be centric relation. In the majority of cases the wear patterns are such that there is no question of where the individual functioned. These observations then were obtained from casts in functional centric occlusion. To what extent this differs from anatomic centric in each individual cannot be evaluated.

Two hundred two individuals or 93.52 percent of the sample were judged to have Class I molar relationship. Class II molars were recorded for eight casts or 3.7 percent and Class III molars for six casts or 2.78 percent. Of the eight Class II cases, five were assessed as Class II subdivision. Whether these are the result of true Class II tendencies or of occlusal prematurities with accompanying mandibular shift is not known.

The predominant incidence of Class I found in this sample is in agreement with other studies of nonwhite populations. Moorrees reported 86.8 percent Class I among the Aleuts (1957). Sinclair et al. (1947) found a variation in three villages of Papuan, New Guinea, natives of from 88 percent to 100 percent Class I molars. Moorrees, however, found no Class II relationships among the Aleuts, whereas Sinclair et al. found 2 percent, 0, and 11 percent in their three-village study. The incidence of Class III molars is considerably lower than that reported for the Aleuts (11 percent), but comparable to the Papuans' 1 percent. This low incidence of Class III molars is interesting in light of the frequency of anterior crossbite noted previously.

3. *Crowding and Spacing*

Table 78 presents the incidence of crowding and spacing in the sample. There are 75 cases with some degree of mandibular crowding and 57 cases with maxillary crowding. Only 9 cases were recorded as having marked crowding, 7 mandibular and 2 maxillary. Spacing was recorded in 62 cases. Of these, 31 include both arches, 22 involve the maxillary arch only, and 9 involve the mandibular arch alone. This variable was not quantified.

TABLE 78

FREQUENCY (PERCENT) OF CROWDING AND SPACING AMONG LANGUAGE GROUPS

		Gadsup	Tairora	Auyana	Awa	Total
Maxilla	Spacing	18.9 (14)	32.9 (23)	45.5 (10)	17.3 (9)	25.7 (56)
	Slight crowding	24.3 (18)	25.7 (18)	22.7 (5)	28.8 (15)	25.7 (56)
	Marked crowding	1.3 (1)	1.4 (1)	0	0	0.9 (2)
Mandible	Spacing	20.3 (15)	22.9 (16)	31.8 (7)	11.5 (6)	20.2 (44)
	Slight crowding	23.0 (17)	34.3 (24)	27.8 (6)	40.4 (21)	31.2 (68)
	Marked crowding	2.7 (2)	1.4 (1)	0	7.7 (4)	3.2 (7)

Note: The figures in parentheses refer to the number of individuals studied.

The distribution of crowding and spacing is relatively uniform, except for a significantly greater degree of mandibular crowding in the Awa. However, this significance is not distinguishable at the isolate level.

In an attempt to relate crowding to tooth size, the mean mesiodistal tooth measure from second molar to second molar was computed in each arch for those groups of cases having space, absence of crowding, slight crowding, or marked crowding. These figures are presented in Table 79. The progressive increase in tooth size as crowding becomes more severe is apparent. That tooth size plays a part in crowding-spacing cannot be questioned; however, the significance of its role is not as clear cut. The space to which these teeth are assigned is equally as important as tooth size. The Awa, for example, had the highest incidence of slight mandibular crowding (40.4 percent), even

TABLE 79

TOOTH SIZE RELATIONSHIP TO CROWDING AND SPACING

		Degree of Crowding			
		Spacing	Absent	Slight	Marked
Maxilla	Mean Mesiodistal Tooth Material 7-7	120.623 (56)	120.473 (104)	121.950 (56)	122.200 (2)
Mandible	Mean Mesiodistal Tooth Material 7-7	111.740 (44)	113.447 (99)	115.024 (68)	118.740 (7)

Note: The figures in parentheses refer to the number of individuals studied.

though this group was found to have generally smaller teeth. This can be explained only by the fact that the arch length available in the Awa dentition was reduced even more than the tooth size.

Moorrees and Reed (1954) devised a very complex statistical approach making use of an analysis of variance to study the problem of crowding and spacing. They concluded that 99.3 percent of the variations noted in crowded and spaced cases was due to a lack of association between tooth size and arch size, and only 0.7 percent due to variations of one or the other. Thus we see that crowding and spacing must be analyzed for each individual case, and that to generalize is meaningless.

4. *Attrition*

The degree of attrition seen in the sample is considerable by contemporary standards. There is evidence of at least faceting of enamel on every cast. Table 80 shows the distribution of attrition with age and indicates, as would be expected, that there is a direct relationship between the two. The role of wear in the development of a labiodont occlusion has already been discussed. The variation in wear between groups is significant at both language group and isolate levels. The Awa, particularly the Ilakia isolate, exhibit the greatest incidence of wear; however, the degree of significance is not clear as these groups also presented a higher average age.

The interproximal wear of the older individuals in the sample is also readily apparent. That this might affect the tooth size figures is a very real possibility; therefore, the greatest mesiodistal width, rather than the diameter from contact to contact, was assessed. As has been found in other studies, Beyron (1964), Campbell (1925), Moorrees

TABLE 80

Frequency (Percent) of Various Degrees of Attrition at Different Age Levels

	Grade of Attrition				
	1	2	3	4	Total
Ages 10 to 24	94.3 (66)	5.7 (4)	0	0	32.1 (70)
Ages 25 to 35	60.6 (63)	34.6 (36)	4.8 (5)	0	47.7 (104)
Ages 36 to 55	18.2 (8)	45.5 (20)	36.4 (16)	0	20.2 (44)
Total	62.8 (137)	27.5 (60)	9.6 (21)	. . .	100 (218)

Note: The figures in parentheses refer to the number of individuals studied. Chi-square significant at $P = 0.001$ level.

(1957), Begg (1965), and Sinclair et al. (1947), the interproximal wear, although considerable, is not accompanied by any spacing. Apparently, the tendency to maintain contact, the so-called mesial component of force, is strong enough to keep pace with the wear.

The pattern of occlusal wear in those individuals having Grade 2 wear and above was usually helicoidal (Plate 21), as reported first by Campbell (1925) in the Australian aborigines. This distinct rolling of the mandibular occlusal surfaces to the lingual as they progress from the anterior to the posterior, and the reverse in the maxilla, is attributable to variation in width between maxillary and mandibular arches in the molar regions. The characteristic arch form is such that in the region of the first molars the maxillary arch is wider than mandibular, but in progressing distally, the relationship changes, so that in the third molar region, the mandibular width is greater than the maxillary. This, then, results in different patterns of wear on first molars than those on third molars and produces the helicoidal roll.

5. *Arch Form*

The distribution of arch forms throughout the tribes is shown in Table 81. The parabolic form accounted for 63.3 percent of the overall sample, the ellipsoid 22.95 percent, the hypsiloid 10.55 percent, and the hyperbolic 3.21 percent. The chi-square test for significance of overall language group distribution was negative; however, the incidence of the parabolic form in the Gadsup was 15 percent greater than in any other language group. This was reflected in the individual comparisons of language groups, with the variation between Gadsup and Tairora and between Gadsup and Awa being significant at the 5 percent level.

As has been mentioned previously, the palatal arch form in this population tends to be broad and shallow. The maxillary arcade shape

TABLE 81

LANGUAGE GROUP DISTRIBUTION AND PERCENT ARRAY OF MAXILLARY ARCH FORMS

	Hyperbolic	Parabolic	Hypsiloid	Ellipsoid
Gadsup	2.7 (2)	74.3 (55)	6.8 (5)	16.2 (12)
Tairora	2.9 (2)	58.6 (41)	10.0 (7)	28.6 (20)
Auyana	4.6 (1)	54.6 (12)	13.6 (3)	27.3 (6)
Awa	3.9 (2)	57.7 (30)	15.4 (8)	23.1 (12)
Total	3.2 (7)	63.3 (138)	10.6 (23)	22.9 (50)

Note: The figures in parentheses refer to the number of individuals studied.

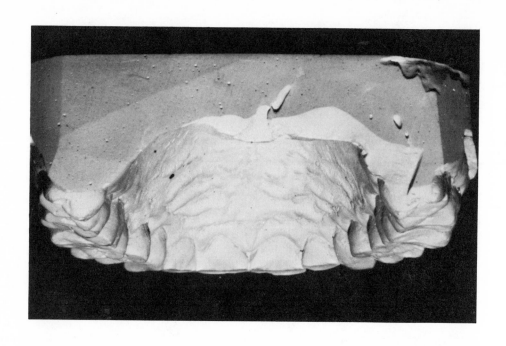

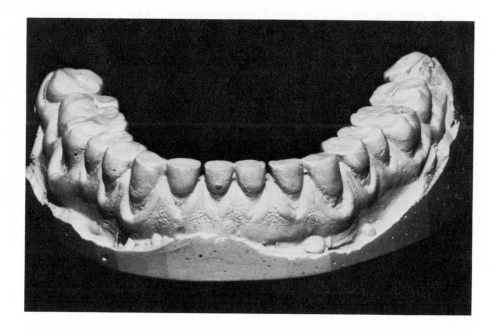

Plate 21. Example of helicoidal pattern of posterior wear

is characterized by a wide, flat incisor region, straight, slightly diverging buccal segments, with a definite "toeing in" of the third molars. The significance of this form on incisor occlusion and wear patterns has been previously discussed in those sections of the results.

The predominance of the parabolic form in these natives is in contrast to that of the Australian aborigine. Campbell (1925) reports that group as usually having the hypsiloid or U-shaped arch. Moorrees (1957) on the other hand reports a 77 percent incidence of parabolic maxillary arcade shape in the Aleuts.

The variation noted in arch form even within the isolates poses interesting questions. In groups developing in separate genetic atmospheres, one might expect to find different predominant forms as characteristic of that group. Sinclair et al. (1947) raise the question of whether such variation within groups, as we see here, might not be indicative of considerable racial admixture. To theorize racial background with such an admittedly subjective classification as a basis, however, is highly presumptive.

6. *Arch Dimensions*

Measurements of dental arch dimension are summarized in Tables 82 and 83 for the language groups and Table 84 for the isolates. Significant language group differences are illustrated in Figure 16.

The mean values of all arch measures except arch length, are significantly larger in males than females at the $p = 0.01$ level. The arch length means show the males larger at the $p = 0.05$ level of significance.

Arch width variation in tribal comparison is confined to the incisor region. Significance was noted between Tairora and Awa and between Auyana and Awa at $P = 0.01$, and between Gadsup and Auyana at $P = 0.05$. There are no significant differences in either premolar or molar width.

Arch length differences were noted between Gadsup and Awa and between Tairora and Awa at $P = 0.01$, and between Auyana and Awa at $P = 0.05$. For the anthropometric arch length measure, all three of the above differences are significant at $P = 0.01$.

Thus between Gadsup and Tairora and between Gadsup and Auyana we have one significant arch dimension variable. Between Gadsup and Awa there are two such significances. The greatest arch size variation apparently lies between Tairora and Awa and between Auyana and Awa, the comparisons of which yield three significantly different measurements.

TABLE 82

DENTAL ARCH DIMENSIONS
(after Bjork)

	Interincisor Width			Interpremolar Width			Intermolar Width			Arch Length		
	N	$\bar{x}$	S.D.	N	$\bar{x}$	S.D.	N	$\bar{x}$	S.D.	N	$\bar{x}$	S.D.
	Males											
Gadsup	63	32.04	1.88	63	50.06	2.60	62	58.32	2.83	60	48.46	2.48
Tairora	65	32.57	2.12	68	50.40	2.99	63	58.08	2.99	61	48.00	2.87
Auyana	17	33.42	2.23	17	50.69	2.58	18	58.50	4.37	18	47.47	3.10
Awa	25	31.22	1.62	29	49.24	2.45	26	57.35	3.75	26	45.31	3.12
Total males	170	32.26	2.05	177	50.11	2.74	169	58.10	3.22	165	47.69	2.98
	Females											
Gadsup	10	30.45	1.79	10	46.76	2.93	9	56.22	4.53	9	46.50	4.07
Tairora	2	32.10	1.84	2	47.10	2.83	2	54.05	0.21	2	51.50	4.24
Auyana	3	29.80	2.21	4	46.05	1.19	4	54.40	1.39	4	44.50	3.37
Awa	21	31.03	1.47	21	47.47	1.69	20	54.19	2.15	18	46.22	2.58
Total females	36	30.83	1.64	37	47.10	2.07	35	54.73	2.90	33	46.41	3.38
Grand total	206	32.01	2.05	214	49.59	2.87	204	57.52	3.40	189	47.47	3.08

Note: Means and standard deviations are expressed in millimeters. N refers to the number of casts studied.

A scan of the male language group means for all six arch variables makes apparent one consistency. For all measures used, the Awa group has the smallest means. The variation among the other three groups is not patterned.

Variation between the isolates is considerable, but is difficult to evaluate without comparison of each group to every other group for each variable. This was felt to be unnecessary effort in light of the small size of some of the samples. However, comparisons of isolates to the others within their language group were done. In the Gadsup, the Sasaura and Akuna isolates are comparable in their mean arch dimensions. The Ontenu isolate is considerably smaller in all measures, particularly those of arch length, than the above isolates. The differences are not statistically significant, however.

Within the Tairora, there is little variation in isolate means. The variation that exists does not follow a consistent pattern.

For the isolates of Awa greater differences are demonstrable. The Tauna isolate presents the smallest means of any group for arch width variables. In incisor width and anthropometric arch width Tauna is significantly smaller than the Ilakia isolate at $P = 0.05$. The Ilakia

TABLE 83

ANTHROPOMETRIC DENTAL ARCH DIMENSIONS

	Width			Length		
	N	$\bar{x}$	S.D.	N	$\bar{x}$	S.D.
	Males					
Gadsup	61	67.79	2.95	39	58.10	2.70
Tairora	63	67.89	3.09	50	57.48	3.17
Auyana	17	68.10	4.40	16	57.56	3.45
Awa	23	66.56	3.90	18	54.21	3.48
Total males	164	67.69	3.32	123	57.21	3.33
	Females					
Gadsup	9	63.73	1.94	6	54.33	4.26
Tairora	2	63.85	0.21	0	-	-
Auyana	4	62.87	1.65	1	53.00	0
Awa	21	63.36	2.31	6	54.83	2.77
Total females	36	63.43	2.05	13	54.46	3.32
Grand total	200	66.92	3.53	136	56.95	3.41

Note: Means and standard deviations are expressed in millimeters. N refers to the number of casts studied.

measurements are comparable to those of isolates in other language group for arch width, but are significantly smaller in arch length. In arch width, then, the Tauna isolate is particularly small, whereas in arch length, both Awa isolates are noticeably smaller.

Comparisons with other populations are difficult because of variation in measurement technics. Table 85 presents those data which can be compared. The arch width in the present sample is apparently greater than that of the Australian aborigine in each of the three dimensions measured. In arch length, however, the situation is reversed and the Australians seem larger. This, of course, indicates a difference in basic arch shape or form.

These findings compare favorably with those of Simpson (1947) who reported in the Papuan natives arch widths greater than those found in Campbell's Australian study. Simpson did not report arch lengths.

Moorrees' data on the Aleuts were pooled as to sex. Similar means for the present sample indicate considerably larger measurements for both arch width and arch length than those of the Aleuts.

TABLE 84

Dental Arch Dimensions for Isolates: Males

	Sasaura	Akuna	Ontenu	Baieanabuta	Abiera	Babaraai	Batainabura	Auyana	Tauna	Ilakia
Interincisor width	32.2	32.2	31.1	32.1	33.3	33.1	32.4	33.7	30.6	32.1
Interpremolar width	49.9	50.7	49.2	50.0	50.2	51.2	50.5	51.1	48.7	49.9
Intermolar width	58.5	58.2	57.7	57.4	58.4	58.2	59.3	58.6	56.5	58.4
Arch length	48.7	48.5	47.2	47.4	49.5	47.0	49.1	47.9	46.1	44.4
Anthropometric arch width	67.7	68.2	67.2	67.2	68.0	68.1	69.3	68.9	65.2	68.6
Anthropometric arch length	58.4	58.8	55.8	57.0	59.3	56.5	58.5	57.9	54.6	54.0

Note: Dimensions are expressed in millimeters.

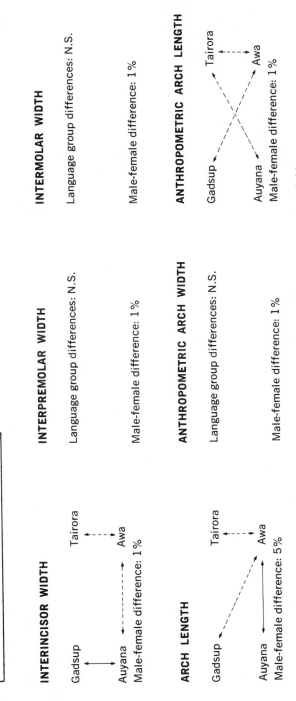

Figure 16. Significant language group and sex differences in arch variables

TABLE 85

DENTAL ARCH DIMENSIONS OF DIFFERENT POPULATIONS: MALES

	Inter-incisor Width	Inter-premolar Width	Intermolar Width	Arch Length	Anthropo-metric Arch Width
Eastern Highlands	32.26	50.11	58.09	47.68	67.69
Australians (Barrett 1965)	. . .	. . .	. . .	49.94	66.74
Australians (Beyron 1964)	31.55	46.70	56.67	49.60	. . .
Swedes (Seipel)	28.52	44.97	54.74	46.62	. . .

Note: Dimensions are expressed in millimeters.

7. *Tooth Size*

Tables 86-87 present the means of the mesiodistal diameters of the individual teeth, both overall and by sex and language group. The isolate figures are seen in Tables 88-90. Comparisons of language groups for each variable are presented in Figures 17 and 18.

As in the arch variables, there was a very apparent sex difference in tooth size. A total of eleven significant differences were encountered of the eighteen comparisons made (including buccolingual diameter of maxillary and mandibular first molars), all indicating the male teeth as larger. The highest F values, that is, greatest differences, were noted for the canines and first molars. The mandibular canines showed the most sex difference, followed in order by the buccolingual diameter of maxillary first molars, maxillary canines, mesiodistal of mandibular first molars, mesiodistal of maxillary first molars, and buccolingual of mandibular first molars. This agrees in part with the findings of Morrees in the Aleut (1957). He found, too, that the greatest sex difference was reflected in the canine teeth, particularly the mandibular. He did not find, however, the involvement of the first molar seen here. Garn (1965) also has alluded to the greater degree of sexual dimorphism apparent in the canines.

The sex differentiation in the Awa did not follow this pattern. In fact, the Awa females had larger mesiodistal measurements for some teeth than the males. A summary of these means is presented in Table 91. It is apparent that for incisors, maxillary and mandibular, and for premolars, maxillary and mandibular, the females have larger teeth. For canines and molars, generally the males exhibit larger means. This pattern of sexual difference is not evident for the other three tribes. However, since nearly 58 percent of the total female sample are Awa, it explains why even more overall sample sex differentiation is not apparent.

TABLE 86

MESIODISTAL CROWN DIAMETERS OF MAXILLARY TEETH

	Language	Males			Females			All		
Tooth	Group	N	$\bar{x}$	S.D.	N	$\bar{x}$	S.D.	N	$\bar{x}$	S.D.
I_1	Gadsup	125	9.35	0.55	20	9.03	0.49	145	9.30	0.55
	Tairora	125	9.36	0.62	4	8.93	0	129	9.35	0.61
	Auyana	32	9.31	0.69	8	8.91	0.93	40	9.23	0.74
	Awa	54	9.14	0.57	30	9.26	0.54	84	9.18	0.56
	Total	336	9.32	0.60	62	9.12	0.57	398	9.28	0.59
I_2	Gadsup	124	7.61	0.60	20	7.25	0.73	144	7.56	0.63
	Tairora	126	7.58	0.58	4	7.50	0.57	130	7.58	0.58
	Auyana	34	7.53	0.77	7	6.88	0.68	41	7.41	0.77
	Awa	50	7.33	0.54	35	7.49	0.51	85	7.39	0.53
	Total	334	7.55	0.61	66	7.35	0.61	400	7.52	0.61
C	Gadsup	128	8.26	0.42	19	7.83	0.39	147	8.20	0.44
	Tairora	133	8.27	0.52	4	8.27	0.11	137	8.27	0.48
	Auyana	34	8.27	0.47	8	7.69	0.43	42	8.16	0.51
	Awa	57	8.18	0.45	42	8.02	0.47	99	8.11	0.46
	Total	352	8.25	0.45	72	7.95	0.45	425	8.20	0.47
PM_1	Gadsup	127	7.49	0.40	20	7.22	0.49	147	7.45	0.42
	Tairora	133	7.61	0.51	4	7.50	0.35	137	7.60	0.50
	Auyana	35	7.38	0.43	8	6.76	0.75	43	7.27	0.55
	Awa,	58	7.27	0.46	43	7.42	0.49	101	7.35	0.48
	Total	353	7.49	0.47	75	7.33	0.55	428	7.46	0.49
PM_2	Gadsup	124	6.95	0.48	20	6.82	0.52	144	6.93	0.48
	Tairora	136	6.97	0.42	4	7.35	0.14	140	6.98	0.42
	Auyana	36	6.67	0.33	8	6.21	0.45	44	6.60	0.38
	Awa	60	6.65	0.47	43	6.89	0.55	103	6.75	0.51
	Total	356	6.88	0.46	75	6.83	0.56	431	6.87	0.48
M_1	Gadsup	124	11.10	0.49	20	10.50	0.55	144	11.02	0.54
	Tairora	131	11.08	0.56	4	10.55	0.28	135	11.07	0.56
	Auyana	36	10.95	0.56	8	10.25	0.56	44	10.82	0.62
	Awa	54	10.90	0.54	41	10.90	0.71	95	10.90	0.62
	Total	345	11.05	0.54	73	10.70	0.67	418	10.99	0.58
M_2	Gadsup	121	10.19	0.64	17	9.96	0.53	138	10.16	0.63
	Tairora	127	10.19	0.71	4	10.32	0.18	131	10.20	0.70
	Auyana	35	10.10	0.64	8	9.70	0.84	43	10.03	0.68
	Awa	49	10.04	0.63	39	9.91	0.69	88	9.99	0.65
	Total	333	10.16	0.66	68	9.92	0.64	400	10.12	0.66
M_3	Gadsup	78	9.34	0.91	9	8.71	0.81	88	9.26	0.92
	Tairora	94	8.96	0.84	0	. . .	. . .	94	8.96	0.84
	Auyana	29	9.29	0.53	3	0.10	0.67	32	9.26	0.55
	Awa	34	8.87	0.76	10	9.03	0.83	44	8.90	0.76
	Total	235	9.11	0.85	22	8.87	0.80	258	9.09	0.84
M_1*	Gadsup	122	12.33	0.49	20	11.58	0.63	142	12.23	0.58
	Tairora	131	12.40	0.63	4	11.95	0.07	135	12.38	0.63
	Auyana	36	12.26	0.58	8	11.65	0.39	44	12.14	0.59
	Awa	55	12.16	0.49	41	11.88	0.65	96	12.04	0.57
	Total	344	12.32	0.56	73	11.78	0.60	417	12.23	0.60

Note: Means and standard deviations are expressed in millimeters. N refers to the number of teeth studied.

*Buccolingual diameter.

TABLE 87

MESIODISTAL CROWN DIAMETERS OF MANDIBULAR TEETH

Tooth	Language Group	Males			Females			All		
		N	$\bar{x}$	S.D.	N	$\bar{x}$	S.D.	N	$\bar{x}$	S.D.
I_1	Gadsup	123	5.52	0.32	20	5.44	0.22	143	5.51	0.30
	Tairora	128	5.65	0.38	4	5.62	0.25	132	5.65	0.37
	Auyana	36	5.66	0.37	7	5.31	0.66	43	5.61	0.44
	Awa	53	5.57	0.39	32	5.73	0.45	85	5.63	0.41
	Total	340	5.59	0.36	63	5.59	0.43	403	5.59	0.37
I_2	Gadsup	120	6.40	0.38	20	6.25	0.27	140	6.38	0.37
	Tairora	128	6.46	0.42	4	6.27	0.11	133	6.45	0.41
	Auyana	35	6.49	0.40	8	6.09	0.40	43	6.41	0.42
	Awa	53	6.41	0.38	36	6.48	0.42	89	6.44	0.39
	Total	336	6.43	0.40	68	6.36	0.39	405	6.42	0.39
C	Gadsup	128	7.39	0.34	20	6.89	0.39	148	7.32	0.38
	Tairora	128	7.48	0.41	4	6.90	0.28	132	7.46	0.42
	Auyana	35	7.38	0.41	8	6.80	0.33	43	7.29	0.45
	Awa	59	7.31	0.37	44	7.02	0.32	103	7.19	0.37
	Total	350	7.41	0.38	76	6.96	0.34	426	7.33	0.41
PM_1	Gadsup	127	7.60	0.46	20	7.30	0.47	147	7.56	0.48
	Tairora	131	7.65	0.56	4	7.27	0.74	135	7.64	0.57
	Auyana	36	7.56	0.40	8	6.94	0.55	44	7.45	0.49
	Awa	57	7.30	0.58	43	7.48	0.66	100	7.37	0.62
	Total	351	7.57	0.53	75	7.36	0.60	426	7.53	0.55
PM_2	Gadsup	127	7.50	0.51	20	7.25	0.54	147	7.47	0.50
	Tairora	133	7.51	0.49	4	7.70	0.07	137	7.52	0.49
	Auyana	36	7.29	0.43	8	6.87	0.35	44	7.21	0.44
	Awa	59	7.19	0.41	43	7.47	0.65	102	7.30	0.56
	Total	355	7.43	0.50	75	7.36	0.60	430	7.42	0.52
M_1	Gadsup	125	11.82	0.57	20	11.33	0.57	145	11.75	0.59
	Tairora	130	11.88	0.62	3	11.63	0.42	133	11.87	0.61
	Auyana	36	11.81	0.61	8	10.82	0.74	44	11.63	0.73
	Awa	54	11.66	0.63	41	11.55	0.62	95	11.61	0.62
	Total	345	11.82	0.60	72	11.41	0.64	417	11.75	0.63
M_2	Gadsup	122	11.18	0.53	20	10.69	0.79	142	11.11	0.59
	Tairora	129	11.09	0.69	4	11.10	0.42	133	11.09	0.69
	Auyana	35	11.20	0.61	7	10.24	0.68	42	11.04	0.71
	Awa	48	10.86	0.72	39	10.68	0.86	87	10.78	0.79
	Total	334	11.10	0.64	70	10.66	0.81	404	11.02	0.69
M_3	Gadsup	72	10.87	0.97	14	9.83	0.96	86	10.70	1.04
	Tairora	83	10.59	0.93	ⁱ0	-	-	83	10.59	0.93
	Auyana	24	10.38	0.88	4	9.47	0.18	28	10.25	0.91
	Awa	40	10.34	1.11	20	10.30	0.77	60	10.32	1.00
	Total	219	10.61	0.99	38	10.04	0.83	257	10.53	0.99
M_1*	Gadsup	125	11.24	0.49	20	10.76	0.36	145	11.18	0.50
	Tairora	127	11.38	0.52	3	11.33	0.07	130	11.38	0.51
	Auyana	36	11.12	0.49	8	10.45	0.49	44	10.99	0.55
	Awa	53	11.12	0.46	39	11.26	0.54	92	11.13	0.49
	Total	341	11.26	0.51	70	10.97	0.53	411	11.21	0.52

Note: Means and standard deviations are expressed in millimeters. N refers to the number of teeth studied.

*Buccolingual diameter.

TABLE 88

TOOTH SIZE MEASUREMENTS FOR ISOLATES WITHIN GADSUP: MALES

Tooth	Sasaura			Akuna			Ontenu		
	N	$\bar{x}$	S.D.	N	$\bar{x}$	S.D.	N	$\bar{x}$	S.D.
Maxilla									
I_1	72	9.33	0.54	35	9.54	0.55	18	9.03	0.41
I_2	70	7.66	0.60	36	7.69	0.64	18	7.27	0.46
C	74	8.26	0.46	36	8.26	0.36	18	8.25	0.41
PM_1	73	7.52	0.38	36	7.54	0.39	18	7.24	0.39
PM_2	70	6.95	0.46	36	7.07	0.51	18	6.76	0.43
M_1	72	11.08	0.44	34	11.22	0.44	18	10.95	0.72
M_2	71	10.18	0.51	35	10.30	0.83	15	10.00	0.66
M_3	39	9.36	1.00	29	9.64	0.71	10	8.37	0.37
M_1*	71	12.29	0.51	33	12.44	0.42	18	12.29	0.52
Mandible									
I_1	72	5.56	0.33	33	5.50	0.27	18	5.42	0.34
I_2	69	6.40	0.38	33	6.48	0.38	18	6.28	0.38
C	74	7.40	0.34	36	7.42	0.28	18	7.30	0.46
PM_1	73	7.62	0.48	36	7.69	0.45	18	7.37	0.41
PM_2	73	7.53	0.52	36	7.62	0.46	18	7.14	0.44
M_1	71	11.76	0.54	36	11.87	0.66	18	11.77	0.79
M_2	70	11.17	0.54	36	11.20	0.51	16	10.93	0.52
M_3	36	10.71	0.89	27	11.29	0.65	9	10.22	1.37
M_1*	71	11.20	0.52	36	11.28	0.42	18	11.33	0.53

Note: Means and standard deviations are expressed in millimeters. N refers to the number of teeth studied.
*Buccolingual diameter.

Tooth size comparisons between the language groups yielded the following results. The Gadsup-Tairora and Gadsup-Auyana comparisons show two variables (teeth) each with significant differences at $P = 0.05$. The Tairora-Auyana comparison yields three significant differences, all concentrated in the maxillary premolar area. In assessing these results it is well to remember that when using a $P = 0.05$ level of significance, one variable in twenty may be significant by chance alone. The Auyana-Awa comparison produces only one variable with $P = 0.05$ significance.

The greatest differences in tooth size were apparent between Tairora and Awa with ten variables, and between Gadsup and Awa with twelve variables significantly different at $P = 0.05$. These differences were for the most part found in the premolar teeth. All eight premolar teeth were significantly different in both comparisons.

On the basis of these figures then, the greatest language group difference in tooth size is found between Gadsup and Awa. There is al-

Appendix IV: An Assessment of the Dentition

TABLE 89

TOOTH SIZE MEASUREMENTS FOR ISOLATES WITHIN TAIRORA: MALES

Tooth	Baieanabuta			Abiera			Babaraai			Batainabura		
	N	$\bar{x}$	S.D.	N	$\bar{x}$	S.D.	N	$\bar{x}$	S.D.	N	$\bar{x}$	S.D.
Maxilla												
I_1	56	9.37	0.56	21	9.48	0.72	24	9.31	0.52	24	9.31	0.81
I_2	57	7.53	0.52	22	7.88	0.64	25	7.46	0.47	22	7.55	0.74
C	61	8.12	0.46	23	8.62	0.41	25	8.46	0.23	24	8.12	0.60
PM_1	61	7.64	0.52	22	7.54	0.36	26	7.55	0.44	24	7.67	0.68
PM_2	62	6.95	0.44	24	7.04	0.44	26	6.99	0.29	24	6.94	0.49
M_1	58	11.02	0.51	24	11.29	0.55	26	10.96	0.44	23	11.16	0.79
M_2	58	10.02	0.68	24	10.46	0.76	23	10.21	0.48	22	10.37	0.85
M_3	48	8.97	0.63	11	9.67	0.98	15	8.57	1.02	20	8.83	0.80
$M_1{}^*$	58	12.34	0.54	24	12.77	0.52	26	12.08	0.64	23	12.53	0.78
Mandible												
I_1	58	5.74	0.39	20	5.65	0.33	26	5.48	0.24	24	5.60	0.45
I_2	59	6.52	0.47	19	6.54	0.41	26	6.32	0.23	24	6.37	0.44
C	59	7.49	0.45	19	7.54	0.38	26	7.53	0.23	24	7.37	0.52
PM_1	58	7.67	0.64	23	7.69	0.52	26	7.59	0.42	24	7.68	0.61
PM_2	60	7.49	0.45	23	7.62	0.67	26	7.53	0.32	24	7.46	0.59
M_1	57	11.88	0.61	23	12.17	0.56	26	11.66	0.41	24	11.83	0.80
M_2	58	11.04	0.69	21	11.33	0.74	26	10.96	0.43	24	11.13	0.89
M_3	39	10.55	0.92	8	10.91	1.23	17	10.66	0.80	19	10.47	1.03
$M_1{}^*$	55	11.27	0.53	23	11.73	0.39	26	11.30	0.48	23	11.39	0.61

Note: Means and standard deviations are expressed in millimeters. N refers to the number of teeth studied.

*Buccolingual diameter.

most as great a difference demonstrable between Tairora and Awa. The remaining language group comparison show little difference in tooth size that could not be due to chance. These results are comparable to those of Barksdale (Appendix III) who draws similar conclusions as to language group relationships.

The statistical significance of isolate variation within single language groups is tempered by sample size. For the Gadsup isolates, for example, examination of the mean figures of tooth size, Table 88, reveals that in fifteen of the eighteen tooth size variables, the Ontenu isolate had means smaller than either Sasaura or Akuna. The fact that there were only nine males studies in the Ontenu isolate severely restricts the statistical interpretation of the data. There were, however, four variables with a level of significance of $P = 0.05$ in the Gadsup isolate comparison.

This apparent variation of the Ontenu isolate from the pattern established by the two larger Gadsup isolates is interesting in view of the

TABLE 90

Tooth Size Measurements for Isolates within Awa: Males

Tooth	Tauna			Ilakia		
	N	$\bar{x}$	S.D.	N	$\bar{x}$	S.D.
Maxilla						
I_1	29	9.06	0.47	25	9.22	0.67
I_2	28	7.19	0.54	22	7.48	0.69
C	32	8.18	0.51	25	8.17	0.39
PM_1	34	7.21	0.46	24	7.35	0.48
PM_2	34	6.61	0.46	26	7.70	0.49
M_1	31	10.78	0.47	23	11.06	0.62
M_2	29	9.86	0.55	20	10.31	0.65
M_3	14	8.83	0.50	20	8.90	0.92
$M_1{}^*$	32	12.00	0.40	23	12.38	0.53
Mandible						
I_1	31	5.46	0.34	22	5.74	0.39
I_2	31	6.35	0.33	22	6.49	0.44
C	33	7.25	0.34	26	7.39	0.40
PM_1	32	7.23	0.45	25	7.38	0.73
PM_2	33	7.04	0.35	26	7.38	0.50
M_1	30	11.53	0.64	24	11.81	0.59
M_2	25	10.61	0.62	23	11.13	0.76
M_3	18	10.32	1.25	22	10.35	1.03
$M_1{}^*$	30	10.98	0.49	23	11.30	0.37

Note: Means and standard deviations are expressed in millimeters. N refers to the number of teeth studied.
* Buccolingual diameter.

geographical situation found. As can be seen from Map 3 the Ontenu isolate is set apart from the remainder of the Gadsup family and indeed is granted language group status of its own by Wurm (1964). McKaughan (1964, 1972), however, feels that Ontenu and Gadsup belong together on the basis of his language studies. Language notwithstanding, the Ontenu are measurably smaller in dentition and dental area than the other isolates within the Gadsup.

No such demonstrable variation exists within the Tairora. The four isolates within this group, while showing some differences in mean values for tooth-size variables, do not exhibit any pattern to this variation. There is only one instance of significance noted of the thirty-six comparisons drawn.

Variation between Tauna and Ilakia isolates of the Awa is quite noticeable for tooth size variables, as was noted in the comparison of arch measure. Five significant differences were demonstrated in this comparison with the means for the Ilakia isolate being larger in each

MAXILLARY CENTRAL INCISOR

Language group differences: N.S.

Gadsup — Tairora
Auyana — Awa

Male-female difference: N.S.

MAXILLARY 1ST PREMOLAR

Gadsup — Tairora
Auyana — Awa

Male-female difference: 5%

MAXILLARY 2ND MOLAR

Language group differences: N.S.

Gadsup — Tairora
Auyana — Awa

Male-female difference: 1%

MAXILLARY LATERAL INCISOR

Language group differences: N.S.

Gadsup — Tairora
Auyana — Awa

Male-female difference: N.S.

MAXILLARY 2ND PREMOLAR

Gadsup — Tairora
Auyana — Awa

Male-female difference: N.S.

MAXILLARY 3RD MOLAR

Language group differences: N.S.

Gadsup — Tairora
Auyana — Awa

Male-female difference: N.S.

MAXILLARY CANINE

Language group differences: N.S.

Male-female difference: 1%

MAXILLARY 1ST MOLAR

Language group differences: N.S.

Male-female difference: 1%

MAXILLARY 1ST MOLAR (BUCCOLINGUAL)

Language group differences: N.S.

Male-female difference: 1%

Legend:
--- Significant difference at 1% level
— Significant difference at 5% level

Figure 17. Significant language group and sex differences in maxillary tooth size

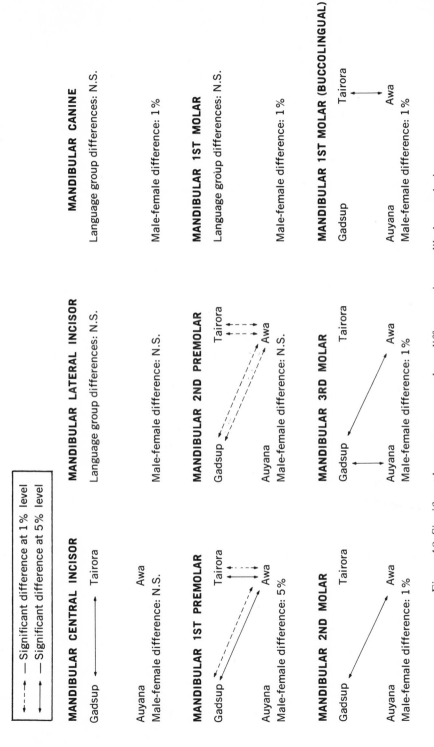

Figure 18. Significant language group and sex differences in mandibular tooth size

TABLE 91

DIMENSIONAL COMPARISON OF AWA MALES AND FEMALES

Variable	Males	Females
Arch measurement		
Interincisor width	31.22*	31.03
Interpremolar width	49.24*	47.47
Intermolar width	57.34*	54.10
Arch length	45.31	46.22*
Anthropometric arch width	66.56*	63.36
Anthropometric arch length	54.20	54.83*
Maxilla		
I_1	9.13	9.26*
I_2	9.32	9.50*
C	8.17*	8.02
PM_1	7.26	7.46*
PM_2	6.66	6.90*
M_1	10.90	10.90
M_2	10.04*	9.92
M_3	8.86	9.02*
M_1†	12.16*	11.87
Mandible		
I_1	5.58	5.72*
I_2	6.41	6.48*
C	7.31*	7.02
PM_1	7.30	7.48*
PM_2	7.18	7.46*
M_1	11.66*	11.56
M_2	10.86*	10.68
M_3	10.34*	10.30
M_1†	11.12	11.16*

* Indicates larger measure.
† Buccolingual diameter.

instance. Thirty-four of the thirty-six tooth size measures showed the Tauna isolate smaller, although often by only a small amount.

When the isolates were analyzed together, without regard to language group, a total of twelve significant differences in means were revealed. However, the isolates which represented the largest and smallest figures, hence the significant difference, for a particular variable, were not consistent for the twelve variables, so that the interpretation of this finding is unrevealing.

Thus generally we see the Awa as smaller in tooth dimension than the other three. The males of the tribe in particular have smaller teeth, for premolars and incisors smaller even than their female counterparts. Why this phenomenon exists in the Awa is not clear. It would appear that environmental factors, such as nutrition, would effect the dentition without regard for sex. The interesting work of Garn et al. (1965) on the possible sex linkage of tooth-size inheritance might be applicable. At the present level of knowledge in the field, however, we will have to accept the data as an interesting finding and not attempt interpretation.

The reduction in size of the Awa dentition is manifest in a progressively greater degree of difference between them and the Auyana, Tairora, and Gadsup. Thus those tribes most separated geographically appear to have the most distinct differences in tooth size.

Comparison of the mean mesiodistal measures of the teeth in the present sample with those of other populations indicates that these people have quite large teeth. In fact, the only studies presenting consistently larger teeth are those on the Australian aborigine, and the difference here is not great. The Aleuts do apparently have larger third molars and mandibular second molars. The present sample is very close in molar size to that of the New Britain Melanesians (Stein and Epstein 1934). Table 92 shows the data for several populations, including the present one. Unfortunately, there is a paucity of studies dealing with Negroid peoples, so that other comparisons within that race are not possible. Data on American Negroes, for example, would

TABLE 92

EXAMPLES OF MEAN TOOTH SIZE IN VARIOUS POPULATIONS: MALES

Tooth	Eastern Highlands New Guinea	Australian Aboriginals	Aleuts	Swedes	American Whites	New Britain Melanesians
Maxilla						
I_1	9.32	9.35	8.45	8.84	8.78	. . .
I_2	7.55	7.65	7.29	6.81	6.64	. . .
C	8.25	8.31	8.03	8.10	7.95	. . .
PM_1	7.49	7.69	7.15	7.18	7.01	. . .
PM_2	6.88	7.19	6.65	6.97	6.82	. . .
M_1	11.05	11.34	10.37	10.69	10.81	11.1
M_2	10.16	10.70	10.00	10.47	10.35	10.1
M_3	9.11	9.87	9.16	9.48	. . .	9.2
Mandible						
I_1	5.59	5.87	5.23	5.51	5.42	. . .
I_2	6.43	6.60	6.09	6.13	5.95	. . .
C	7.41	7.49	7.20	7.12	6.96	. . .
PM_1	7.57	7.49	7.01	7.27	7.07	. . .
PM^2	7.43	7.56	7.17	7.41	7.29	. . .
M_1	11.82	12.04	11.56	11.24	11.18	11.3
M_2	11.10	11.45	11.19	11.15	10.76	11.2
M_3	10.61	11.61	11.13	11.32	. . .	11.5

be of great interest in evaluating studies such as this. At present, however, we will be content with reporting that in terms of mesiodistal tooth diameter, the present sample ranks second to the Australian aborigine in all teeth except third molars and mandibular second molars.

A presentation of findings of the discriminant analysis portion of the study must be prefaced by the reminder that not all of the variables measured were used in the analysis. Any variation in the incisor region, for example, was lost to analysis because of the comparatively large number of missing values in the sample for these variables.

The initial results will concern the discrimination of the four language groups from the entire available sample of 149 males. The percentage of correct placement of individuals into their respective groups was felt to be a satisfactory method of evaluating the results, although it admittedly has some shortcomings in that it does not examine the classification functions for each case. One can glean some information by examining the probabilities by which each case is correctly or incorrectly classified. The BMD 05M also has as output, the generalized Mahalanobis D-square value, which can be used as a chi-square test that the mean values are the same for all groups for all variables. Similar information is presented by the F matrix, output of the BMD 07M. This matrix presents the F value of each tribe with each other tribe for the variables entered in the analysis to that point. Thus we have a "running comparison" of tribal difference as we introduce new variables. The percentage correct predictions and Mahalanobis D-square results are presented in Tables 93 and 94. The correct classification of only 43 percent in the Gadsup and Tairora appears disappointing initially; however, when one realizes that by flipping a coin, only 25 percent would fall into the correct group, it becomes apparent that at least some discriminating factors are present. Apparently the Awa dentition is the most distinct for the variables used, indicated by a correct prediction rate of 66.7 percent. These findings agree with those obtained by comparison of F values in the previous portion of the study.

This relationship is further corroborated by examination of the output of the BMD 07M, or stepwise discriminant analysis.

Of the twelve variables the first to be entered by the program was arch length. The F matrix established for means of this variable indicates little difference between means of Gadsup, Tairora, and Auyana. This measure of the Awa, however, is significantly different

TABLE 93

RESULTS OF DISCRIMINANT ANALYSIS: LANGUAGE GROUPS

Group	Percentage Correctly Classified	Malahanobis D-Square Value	Degrees of Freedom	Level of Significance
Gadsup	42.86			
Tairora	42.86			
Auyana	56.25			
Awa	66.67	67.35	36	$P = 0.001$
Gadsup	64.29			
Tairora	67.86	19.36	12	N.S.
Gadsup	75.00			
Auyana	93.75	29.53	12	$P = 0.005$
Gadsup	73.21			
Awa	71.43	33.69	12	$P = 0.001$
Tairora	76.79			
Auyana	81.25	29.40	12	$P = 0.005$
Tairora	75.00			
Awa	76.19	19.28	12	N.S.
Auyana	81.25			
Awa	80.95	27.07	9	$P = 0.01$

TABLE 94

RESULTS OF DISCRIMINANT ANALYSIS: ISOLATES

Isolate	Percentage Correctly Classified	Mahalanobis D-Square Value	Degrees of Freedom	Level of Significance
Gadsup				
Sasaura	39.10			
Akuna	62.50			
Ontenu	85.71	17.93	14	N.S.
Tairora				
Baieanabuta	70.00			
Abiera	45.83			
Babaraai	72.72			
Batainabura	54.54	47.93	30	$P = 0.05$
Awa				
Tauna	76.92			
Ilakia	75.00	11.88	6	N.S.

Note: Auyana data are presented with language group.

from that of Gadsup, Tairora, and Auyana in decreasing order of significance. The addition of a second variable, however, that of interincisor width, alters the design of the F matrix, so that while Gadsup and Awa still show the greatest difference, the Gadsup-Auyana, Tairora-Awa, and Auyana-Awa differences are of very much the same magnitude. At the completion of the third step, with the maxillary second premolar diameter entered as the new variable, the F matrix is again altered, this time indicating the greatest difference between Gadsup and Auyana. So it is with each succeeding step, that instead of strengthening the relationship indicated by the first variable, each new variable has its own relationship of tribal mean values, which in combination with that of the preceding variables produces an entirely new spectrum. This blending of variable relationships, while complicating interpretation of data at any point along the way, gives us, at the completion of the final step, the degree of significance of group differences with all these factors having been considered.

For the tribal analysis the final F matrix indicates Gadsup and Awa significantly different at $P = 0.01$, Gadsup-Auyana significantly different at $P = 0.05$, and the Tairora-Auyana difference just at the $P = 0.05$ level. The remainder of the combinations are not significantly different.

In another approach to group discrimination, the language groups were matched individually and the programs asked to discriminate between them. These results, percentage of correct prediction and Mahalanobis D-square values, are found in Table 93. Because of the nature of the statistical approach, it was felt that the Mahalanobis D-square value could be used to compare the results of one run against another.

Those values for the various comparisons, all with twelve degrees of freedom, are Gadsup-Tairora, 19.36 (not significant); Gadsup-Auyana, 29.53 ($P = 0.005$), and Gadsup-Awa 33.69 ($P = 0.001$). Thus we see once again the same language group relationship as in the other analyses. Interestingly enough, when we examine the percentage of correct predictions we see that the greatest success was registered for the Auyana. Mean values notwithstanding, there was apparently something quite descriptive about the set of values for the individuals in this group.

As we can see, there is apparently some difference in the dentitions of all groups. The lowest percentages of successful discrimination were for the Gadsup-Tairora run, and even here the 50 percent success that is explainable by chance is exceeded by a sizeable margin.

The analyses attempting to discriminate isolates within a language group substantiate the earlier results of the comparisons of means. In Gadsup the Ontenu members were correctly classified 6 of 7 times, the Sasaura only 10 of 33, and the Akuna 10 of 16. It is obvious then that of these individuals, the Ontenu were the most easily distinguishable even though the sample size prevented assessment of statistical significance.

In Tairora, the greatest variation was shown between Babaraai and Baieanabuta and between Abiera and Baieanabuta on the basis of the *F* matrix, and the greatest percentages of successful prediction are for Baieanabuta and Babaraai. In the Awa isolates, again we are hampered by sample size in determining significance, but the analysis correctly classifies 12 of 13 Tauna and 7 of 8 Ilakia individuals. Somewhere in their measurements there is a distinctive difference.

The initial twelve variables used as the discriminating set include both arch dimensions and tooth dimensions. It was felt that restricting the analysis to tooth size variables would also prove interesting. The eight variables used are those dealing with tooth size listed in Table 75. The results are essentially the same as in the previous analysis as to language group relationship. The *F* matrix shows less significance but identical interrelationships of language group means. The group classification was not as accurate for these variables; however, the Awa percentage was still highest and Gadsup and Tairora lowest and identical. The format of the *F* matrix after inclusion of the initial variable was identical in language group relationships to that obtained in the twelve variable analyses.

Thus we see that the most discriminating variables of both arch size and tooth size vary in direct relationship to the geographic arrangement of the groups involved. That is, those groups most separated geographically have the greatest difference in mean values. As the geographic separation becomes reduced, so does the difference in mean value of these measurements. This linear relationship does not hold true for each succeeding individual variable, but as their interrelationship with other variables are considered by each step in the analysis, the overall discrimination of cases into the proper group improves. This then leads us to believe that the addition of other related variables, for example, tooth morphology, to our tooth size data would be of value in future group discriminations on a dental basis.

Why the aforementioned language group relationships of tooth size exist is open to debate. Gadsup has been longest subject to the influence of modern civilization, with Awa only recently contacted. The improved nutrition and medical care thus offered are environmental factors which cannot be discounted. The Awa natives are smaller in overall body size than those of the other language groups, the terrain in which they live is different, their diet is apparently based on a different staple—all factors, which in addition to or by influence of hereditary factors, might help explain the apparent differences noted. The likelihood of some genetic drift in samples of this size is of course quite strong. Assuming common origin, it is less difficult to explain consistent differences in tooth and arch size of tribes on the basis of these factors. A thousand years is rather little time to expect pure genetic selection to have altered so many traits.

SUMMARY

A sample of 218 sets of dental casts representing 180 males and 38 female natives of the Eastern Highlands of New Guinea was measured and assessed. Those variables recorded included mesiodistal diameter of all teeth, maxillary arch dimensions in six different measurements, overbite and overjet, maxillary arch form, spacing and crowding, attrition, and molar relation. The data was processed by IBM 7040-7094 direct couple computer system. The sample was divided among four language groups, and the language groups further segregated into breeding isolates made up of one or more villages. The premise that these people were of common origin is accepted, and differences in their dentition would reflect their approximately one thousand years of separation.

There is, in addition, a definite need for dental studies of populations of non-Mongoloid ancestry. If we are to be able to trace groups racially, we must increase our sophistication to something more than Mongoloid and non-Mongoloid separation.

The edge-to-edge anterior bite often stated as characteristic of primitive populations was noted in this sample. The incidence of anterior crossbite was greater than anticipated. The overbite-overjet measurements were not remarkable. However, the fact that they did not decrease in those cases with more pronounced attrition was interesting. This finding, as well as the fact that approximately 50 percent of those casts with labiodont and anterior crossbite occlusion had minimal wear, indicates that perhaps wear is not the sole key to the attainment of end-to-end occlusion as has been proposed.

The distribution of the various categories of incisor occlusion throughout the language groups was uniform. The predominant incidence of Class I molar relationship is apparently a characteristic of more homogenous populations. The 93 percent found here is comparable with studies on the Australian aborigine and the Aleut.

Crowding and spacing of teeth were evident in the sample, although marked examples of either were rare. Surprisingly, the group with the smallest teeth, the Awa, showed the greatest tendency to crowd. Their general body size and, more applicable, arch size were also noticeably smaller. However, in the overall sample, the absolute tooth size of those individuals with crowding was greater than for those with spacing.

Attrition, both occlusal and interproximal, was typically found in the dentition of these people. As expected, the degree of attrition became greater with age. The distribution of attrition among the language groups was difficult to assess because of age variations between language groups.

The arch form was reported as predominantly parabolic. A considerable tendency for the maxillary third molars to be "toed in," even to the point of being in crossbite, was noted. The characteristic broad, flat palate was generally present, with particular width between the cuspids.

The males of the sample had significantly larger arches than the females in all measures. The tribal variation noted was most pronounced between Tairora and Awa and between Auyana and Awa, with interincisor width and the two measures of arch length reflecting the variation. Among the males for all arch measurements studied, the Awa had the smallest dimensions recorded.

Within Gadsup the Ontenu isolate is noticeably smaller in arch size than either Sasaura or Akuna. Variation is demonstrable too between Tauna and Ilakia isolates of Awa with Tauna being smaller in arch width and Ilakia smaller in arch length, though the difference is not great.

The tooth size comparisons between language groups indicate the greatest variation between Gadsup and Awa. The Tairora and Awa measurements are also quite dissimilar with less difference noted between Awa and Auyana. The remaining combinations of language group comparisons show little difference in tooth size means.

The sex difference noted for the overall sample indicates that the males tend to have larger teeth, with the greatest difference in canines and first molars. For the Awa, however, the females had generally larger incisors and premolars than the males. The isolate comparisons within Gadsup again indicate that Ontenu, as distinctive from Sasaura or Akuna, is smaller in tooth size measurements. Some variation, too, exists between Tauna and Ilakia isolates with Ilakia having consistently larger tooth size means, though not significantly so.

The results of a discriminant analysis, run with both tooth size and arch size variables and separately with only tooth size variables, closely approximate the aforementioned findings. The same basic pattern of language group and isolate relationships is apparent.

Indications are, as expected, that the more variables entered for analysis, the more accurate the discrimination of individuals into proper groups. This would suggest that when attempting discrimination of groups on the basis of dentition, one should include all applicable variables that can be obtained. The inclusion of such factors as tooth morphology with tooth size might be of value.

CONCLUSIONS

1. Significant language group differences in the size of the dentition and dental arches are demonstrable, presumably reflecting their separation of at least one thousand years.

2. Tooth size and arch size variations, paralleling the geographic separation, are possibly a result of genetic drift and environmental influences rather than pure genetic selection.

3. The tooth size of Eastern Highlands peoples more closely approximates that of the Australian aborigine and New Britain Melanesian than any other populations noted in the literature.

4. The value of multivariate analysis in studies of dentition would apparently be enhanced if a wider spectrum of variables were used as discriminators.

5. The labiodont occlusion characteristic of so-called primitive populations occurs frequently as a result of arch form, independent of the presence of attrition.

6. The Class II malocclusion (Angle) is seldom found among natives of the Australian Territory of New Guinea.

Bibliography

Ashton, E. H., M. J. R. Healy, and S. Lipton
  1957 "The Descriptive Use of Discriminant Functions in Physical Anthropology." *Proceedings of the Royal Society of London,* series B, 146:552-72.
Barnicot, N. A.
  1952 "Albinism in South-western Nigeria." *Annals of Eugenics* 17:211-32.
Barrett, M. J., T. Brown, G. Arato, and I. Ozols
  1964 "Dental Observations on Australian Aborigines: Buccolingual Crown Diameters of Permanent Teeth." *Australian Dental Journal* 9:280.
Barrett, M. J., T. Brown, and M. R. Macdonald
  1963 "Dental Observations on Australian Aborigines: Mesiodistal Crown Diameters of Permanent Teeth." *Australian Dental Journal* 8:150-55.
  1965 "Size of Dental Arches in a Tribe of Central Australian Aborigines." *Journal of Dental Research* 44:912-20.
Baumgarten, A., E. Giles, and C. C. Curtain
  1968 "The Distribution of Haptoglobin and Transferrin Types in Northwest New Guinea." *American Journal of Physical Anthropology,* n.s. 29:29-38.
Begg, P. R.
  1965 *Orthodontic Theory and Technique.* Philadelphia and London: W. B. Saunders Co.
Beyron, Henry
  1964 "Occlusal Relations and Mastication in Australian Aborigines." *Acta Odontologica Scandinavia* 22:597-678.

Birdsell, J. B.
   1950 "Some Implications of the Genetical Concept of Race in Terms of Spatial Analysis." *Cold Spring Harbor Symposia on Quantitative Biology* 15:259-314.
Boas, Franz
   1912 *Changes in Bodily Form of Descendants of Immigrants.* (Final report.) New York: Columbia University Press.
Broca, P.
   1879 "Instructions relatives a l'étude anthropologique du système dentaire." *Bulletin, Société d'Anthropologie de Paris* 2:128-65.
Bronowski, J., and W. M. Long
   1951 "Statistical Methods in Anthropology." *Nature* 168:794.
   1952 "Statistics of Discrimination in Anthropology." *American Journal of Physical Anthropology,* n.s. 10:385-94.
Brookfield, H.C.
   1964 "The Ecology of Highland Settlement: Some Suggestions." *American Anthropologist* (special publication, *New Guinea: The Central Highlands*) 66 (part 2): 20-38.
Brookfield, H. C., and J. P. White
   1968 "Revolution or Evolution in the Prehistory of the New Guinea Highlands." *Ethnology* 7:43-52.
Campbell, T. D.
   1925 *Dentition and Palate of the Australian Aboriginal.* University of Adelaide, Keith Sheridan Foundation. Adelaide: Hassell Press.
Carbonell, Virginia M.
   1963 "Variations in the Frequency of Shovel-Shape Incisors in Different Populations." Pp. 211-33 in D. R. Brothwell (ed.), *Dental Anthropology,* vol. 5. New York: Pergamon Press.
Coon, Carleton S.
   1939 *The Races of Europe.* New York: Macmillan Co.
Crow, J. F.
   1954 "Breeding Structure of Populations, II: Effective Population Number." Pp. 543-56 in O. Kempthorne (ed.), *Statistics and Mathematics in Biology.* New York: Hofner.
Curtain, C., D. C. Gajdusek, C. Kidson, J. G. Gorman, L. Champness, and R. Rodrigue
   1965 "Haptoglobin and Transferrins in Melanesia: Relation to Hemoglobin, Serum Haptoglobin and Serum Iron Levels in Population Groups in Papua–New Guinea." *American Journal of Physical Anthropology,* n.s. 23:363-80.
Dahlberg, A. A.
   1945 "The Changing Dentition of Man." *Journal of the American Dental Association* 32:676-90.

1949 "The Dentition of the American Indian." Pp. 138-75 in *Papers on the Physical Anthropology of the American Indian.* New York: Viking Fund.

1950 "The Evolutionary Significance of the Protostylid." *American Journal of Physical Anthropology* 8:15-25.

1957 Materials for the establishment of standards for classification of tooth characters, attributes, and techniques in morphological studies of the dentition.

1963 "Analysis of American Indian Dentition." Pp. 149-77 in D. R. Brothwell (ed.), *Dental Anthropology,* vol. 5. New York: Pergamon Press.

1965 "Geographic Distribution and Origin of Dentitions." *International Dental Journal* 15:348-55.

Dixon, W. J.

1965 Biomedical Computer Programs. Health sciences computing facility, Department of Preventive Medicine and Public Health, School of Medicine, University of California, Los Angeles.

Dunn, L. C.

1947 "The Effects of Isolates of the Frequency of a Rare Human Gene." *Proceedings of the National Academy of Sciences* 33:359-63.

Dunn, Olive Jean

1964 *Basic Statistics: A Primer for the Biomedical Sciences.* New York: John Wiley and Sons.

Gajdusek, D. C., and V. Zigas

1961 "Studies on *Kuru,* I: The Ethnologic Setting of *Kuru.*" *American Journal of Tropical Medicine and Hygiene* 10:80-91.

Gajdusek, D. C., V. Zigas, and J. Baker

1961 "Studies on *Kuru,* III: Patterns of *Kuru* Incidence: Demographic and Geographic Epidemiological Analysis." *American Journal of Tropical Medicine and Hygiene* 10:599-627.

Garn, S. M.

1959 *The Dentition of the Growing Child.* Cambridge, Mass. Harvard University Press.

1961 "The Genetics of Normal Human Growth." Part 2 of L. Gedda (ed.), *Genetica Medica.* Rome: Grigorio Mendel Institute.

1965 "Genetic, Nutritional, and Maturational Correlates of Dental Development." *Journal of Dental Research* 44 (suppl. to no. 1): 228-41.

Garn, S. M., A. B. Lewis, R. S. Kerewsky, and K. Jegart

1965 "Sex Differences in Intraindividual Tooth-Size Communalities." *Journal of Dental Research* 44:476-79.

Giles, E., E. Ogan, R. J. Walsh, and M. A. Bradley

1966 "Blood Group Genetics of Natives of the Morobe District and Bougainville, Territory of New Guinea." *Archeology and Physical Anthropology in Oceania* 1:135-54.

Giles, E., R. J. Walsh, and M. A. Bradley
1966 "Micro-evolution in New Guinea: The Role of Genetic Drift." *Annals of the New York Academy of Sciences* 134:665.

Goldstein, M. S.
1948 "Dentition of Indian Crania from Texas." *American Journal of Physical Anthropology*, n.s. 6:63-84.

Goose, D. H.
1963 "Dental Measurement: An Assessment of Its Value in Anthropological Studies." Pp. 125-48 in D. R. Brothwell (ed.), *Dental Anthropology*. New York: Pergamon Press.

Gregory, W. K.
1916 "Studies on the Evolution of the Primates." *American Museum of Natural History Bulletin* 35 (no. 19): 239-356.

Greulich, W. W.
1958 "Growth of Children of the Same Race under Different Environmental Conditions." *Science* 127:515-16.

Harrison, G. A., J. S. Weiner, J. M. Tanner, and N. A. Barnicot
1964 *Human Biology*. London and New York: Oxford University Press.

Hellman, Milo
1928 "Racial Characters in Human Dentition." *Proceedings of the American Philosophical Society* 67:157-74.

Hiernaux, Jean
1956 "Analyse de la variation des caracteres physique humains en une région de l'Afrique centrale: Ruanda-Urundi et Kivu." *Annales du musée Royal du Congo Belge, Science de l' Homme, Anthropologie,* Vol. 3. Tervuren.

1963 "Heredity and Environment: Their Influence on Human Morphology. A Comparison of Two Independent Lines of Study." *American Journal of Physical Anthropology,* n.s. 21:575-90.

Hooton, E. A.
1946 *Up from the Ape*. New York: Macmillan Co.

Howells, W. W.
1953 "Correlations of Brothers in Factor Scores." *American Journal of Physical Anthropology,* n.s. 11:121-40.

1966a "Variability in Family Lines vs. Population Variability." *Annals of the New York Academy of Sciences* 134:624-31.

1966b "Population Distances: Biological, Linguistic, Geographical and Environmental." *Current Anthropology* 7:531-40.

Hrdlička, Aleš
1920 "Shovel-shaped Teeth." *American Journal of Physical Anthropology* 3:429-65.

Huizinga, J.
1962 "From *DD* to *D²* and Back: The Qualitative Expression of Resemblance." *Koninklijk Nederlandsch Akademie van Wetenschappen,* series C, 65 (no. 4): 380-91.

Ivanovsky, A.
1923 "Physical Modification of the Populations of Russia under Famine." *American Journal of Physical Anthropology* 6:331-53.

Jolicoeur, P.
1959 "Multivariate Geographical Variation in the Wolf Canis lupis L." *Evolution* 13:283-99.

Jorgensen, K. D.
1955 "The Dryopithecus Pattern in Recent Danes and Dutchmen." *Journal of Dental Research* 34:195-208.

Karve, I., and K. C. Malhotra
1968 "A Biological Comparison of Eight Endogamous Groups of the Same Caste." *Current Anthropology* 9:109-24.

Kimura, M., and G. H. Weiss
1964 "The Stepping Stone Model of Population Structure and the Decrease of Genetic Correlation with Distance." *Proceedings of the National Academy of Sciences* 33:359-63.

Kraus, B. S.
1951 "Carabelli's Anomaly of the Maxillary Molar Teeth." *American Journal of Human Genetics* 3:348-55.
1959 "Occurrence of the Carabelli Trait in Southwest Ethnic Groups." *American Journal of Physical Anthropology,* n.s. 17 (no.2): 117-24.

Kraus, B. S., and M. S. Furr
1953 "Lower First Premolars, I: A Definition and Classification of Discrete Morphologic Traits." *Journal of Dental Research* 32:554-64.

Lasker, G. W.
1946 "Migration and Physical Differentiation." *American Journal of Physical Anthropology,* n.s. 4:273-300.

Li, C. C.
1955 *Population Genetics.* Chicago: University of Chicago Press.

Littlewood, R. A.
1962 "An Analysis of Inbreeding and Effective Breeding Size in the Tasmanian Hybrid Population of Bass Strait." Doctoral dissertation. University of California, Los Angeles.
1966 "Isolate Patterns in the Eastern Highlands of New Guinea." *Journal of the Polynesian Society* 75:95-106.

Livingstone, F. B.
1963 "Blood Groups and Ancestry: A Test case from the New Guinea Highlands." *Current Anthropology* 4:541-42.

Ludwig, Fred J.
  1957 "The Mandibular Second Premolar: Morphologic Variation and Inheritance." *Journal of Dental Research* 36:263-73.
Lundstrom, Anders
  1952 "On the Correlation between Tooth Size and the Irregularities of the Teeth (Crowding-Spacing)." *Archives of Orthodontics* 1:19-33.
MacIntosh, N. W. G., R. J. Walsh, and O. Kooptzoff
  1958 "The Blood Groups of the Native Inhabitants of the Western Highlands of New Guinea." *Oceania* 27:143-57.
McKaughan, H.
  1964 "A Study of Divergence in Four New Guinea Languages." *American Anthropologist* (special publication, *New Guinea: The Central Highlands*) 66:98-121.
  1972 *The Languages of the Eastern Family of the East New Guinea Highland Stock*. Anthropological Studies in the Eastern Highlands of New Guinea, edited by J. B. Watson, vol. 1. Seattle: University of Washington Press.
Majumdar, D. N., P. C. Mahalanobis, and C. R. Rao
  1949 "Anthropometric Survey of the United Province, 1941: A Statistical Study." *Sankhya,* vol. 9, nos. 2-3.
Majumdar, D. N., and C. R. Rao
  1958 *Race Elements in Bengal*. Calcutta: Asia Publishing House.
Martin, R.
  1928 *Lehrbuch der Anthropologie*. 2nd ed. Jena: Fischer.
Massey, F. J., R. A. Kronmal, and S. R. Yarnall
  1966 Computer programs for biomedical data processing.
Meggitt, M. F.
  1958 "The Enga of the New Guinea Highlands." *Oceania* 27:143-57.
  1962 "Growth and Decline of Agnatic Descent Groups among the Mae Enga." *Ethnology* 1:158-65.
Moorrees, C. F. A.
  1951 "The Dentition as a Criterion of Race with Special Reference to the Aleut." *Journal of Dental Research* 30:815-21.
  1957 *The Aleut Dentition*. Cambridge, Mass.: Harvard University Press.
Moorrees, C. F. A., and R. Reed
  1954 "Biometrics of Crowding and Spacing of Teeth in the Mandible." *American Journal of the Physical Anthropology,* n.s. 12:77-88.
Morton, N. E.
  1968 "Problems and Methods in the Genetics of Primitive Groups." *American Journal of Physical Anthropology,* n.s. 28:191-202.
Neel, J. V., and W. J. Schull
  1954 *Human Heredity*. Chicago: University of Chicago Press.

Newman, H. H., F. N. Freeman, and K. H. Holzinger
   1937 *Twins: A Study of Heredity and Environment*. Chicago: University of Chicago Press.
Nijenhuis, L. E.
   1961 *Blood Groups Frequencies in the Netherlands, Curaçao, Surinam and New Guinea: A Study in Population Genetics*. Amsterdam: Drukkerij "Aemstelstad."
Osborne, R. H., and F. V. De George
   1959 *Genetic Basic of Morphological Variation*. Cambridge, Mass.: Harvard University Press.
Pataki, K. J.
   1965 "Shifting Population and Environment among the Auyana: Some Considerations on Phenomena and Schema." M.A. dissertation. University of Washington.
Pearson, E. S., and H. O. Hartley
   1954 *Biometrika Tables for Statisticians*. Vol. I. New York: Cambridge University Press.
Pedersen, P. O.
   1949 "The East Greenland Eskimo Dentition." *Meddelelser Om Gronland* 142:1-244.
Pollitzer, W. S.
   1958 "The Negroes of Charleston (S.C.): A Study of Hemoglobin Types, Serology, and Morphology." *American Journal of Physical Anthropology*, n.s. 16:235-40.
Race, R. R., and Ruth Sanger
   1962 *Blood Groups in Man*. 4th ed. Oxford: Blackwell Scientific Publications.
Riesenfeld, Alphonse
   1956 "Shovel-shaped Incisors and a Few Other Dental Features among the Native Peoples of the Pacific." *American Journal of Physical Anthropology*, n.s. 14:505-21.
Rountree, P. M., and P. K. Littlewood
   1964 "The Nasal Flora of the Auyana People in the Eastern Highlands of New Guinea." *Medical Journal of Australia* 2 (no. 9): 336-37.
Sanghvi, L. D.
   1953 "Comparison of Genetical and Morphological Methods for a Study of Biological Differences." *American Journal of Physical Anthropology*, n.s. 11:385-404.
Selmer-Olson, R.
   1949 *An Odontometrical Study on the Norwegian Lapps*. Skrifter utgitt av det Norske Videnskaps-Akademi Oslo, I. Matematisk-Naturvidenskapelig Klasse, no. 3.

Shapiro, H. L., and F. Hulse
1940 *Migration and Environment*. New York: Oxford University Press.
Simmons, R. T., J. J. Graydon, L. L. Baker, and D. C. Gajdusek
1961 "Studies on *Kuru*, V: A Blood Group Genetical Survey of the *Kuru* Region and Other Parts of Papua New Guinea." *American Journal of Tropical Medicine and Hygiene* 10:639-64.
Simmons, R. T., N. B. Tindale, and J. B. Birdsell
1962 "A Blood Group Genetical Survey in Australian Aborigines of Bentinck, Mornington and Forsyth Islands, Gulf of Carpentaria." *American Journal of Physical Anthropology*, n.s. 20:303-20.
Sinclair, B. Y., D. A. Cameron, and N. E. Goldsworthy
1947 *Report of the New Guinea Nutrition Survey Expedition: Observations on Dental Conditions among Native Peoples in Papua, New Guinea*. Sydney: Pettifer.
Stein, M. R., and J. L. Epstein
1934 "The Molar Teeth of the New Britain Melanesians." *Journal of the American Dental Association* 21:1409-13.
Swindler, D. R.
1962 *A Racial Study of the West Nakanai*. New Britain Studies. Philadelphia: University Museum, University of Pennsylvania.
Tratman, E. K.
1950 "A Comparison of the Teeth of People of Indo-European Racial Stock with Mongoloid Racial Stock." *Dental Record* 90:31-53, 63-88.
Vandenberg, S. G.
1962 "How Stable Are Heritability Estimates? A Comparison of Heritability Estimates from Six Anthropometric Studies." *American Journal of Physical Anthropology*, n.s. 20:331-38.
Watson, J. B.
1963 "A Micro-evolution Study in New Guinea." *Journal of the Polynesian Society* 72 (no. 3): 188-92.
1964 "A Previously Unreported Root Crop from the New Guinea Highlands." *Ethnology* 3:1-5.
1965a "From Hunting to Horticulture in the New Guinea Highalnds." *Ethnology* 4:295-309.
1965b "The Significance of Recent Ecological Change in the Central Highlands of New Guinea." *Journal of the Polynesian Society* 74:438-50.
1965c "Loose Structure Loosely Construed: Groupless Groupings in Gadsup?" *Oceania* 35:267-71.
1967 "Tairora: The Politics of Despotism in a Small Society." *Anthropological Forum* 2:53-104.

Watson, J. B., V. Zigas, O. Kooptzoff, and R. J. Walsh
  1961 "The Blood Groups of Natives in Kainantu, New Guinea." *Human Biology* 33:25-41.
Witkop, Carl J.
  1961 *Genetics and Dental Health*. New York: McGraw-Hill Book Co.
Wright, Sewall
  1931 "Evolution in Mendelian Population." *Genetics* 16:97-159.
  1943 "Isolation by Distance." *Genetics* 28:114-38.
  1951 "The Genetical Structure of Populations." *Annals of Eugenics* 15: 323-54.
Wurm, S. A.
  1961 Language of the Eastern, Western and Southern Highlands, Territory of Papua and New Guinea. Map. Canberra: Australian National University.
  1964 "Australian New Guinea Languages and the Distribution of Their Typological Features." *American Anthropologist* 66 (no. 4): 77-97.

Index